CORPORATE AMERICA AND
ENVIRONMENTAL POLICY

# CORPORATE AMERICA AND

# ENVIRONMENTAL POLICY

How Often Does Business Get Its Way?

## Sheldon Kamieniecki

Stanford Law and Politics
An Imprint of Stanford University Press
*Stanford, California 2006*

Stanford University Press
Stanford, California
© 2006 by the Board of Trustees of the Leland
Stanford Junior University. All rights reserved.

Printed in the United States of America on acid-free, archival-quality
paper.

Library of Congress Cataloging-in-Publication Data
Kamieniecki, Sheldon.
   Corporate America and environmental policy : how often does
business get its way? / Sheldon Kamieniecki.
      p.   cm.
   Includes bibliographical references and index.
   ISBN 0-8047-4815-2 (cloth : alk. paper)—ISBN 0-8047-4832-2
(pbk. : alk. paper)
   1. Corporate power—United States.   2. Environmental policy—
United States.   3. Industrial management—Environmental aspects—
United States.   4. Business and politics—United States.   5. Cor-
porations—Political aspects—United States.   6. Big business—
United States.   I. Title.
   HD2795.K25   2006
   333.70973—dc22                                    2005033152

Original Printing 2006

Last figure below indicates year of this printing:
15   14   13   12   11   10   09   08   07   06

Typeset by G & S Book Services in 10/13.5 Sabon

Special discounts for bulk quantities of Stanford Law and Politics
are available to corporations, professional associations, and other
organizations. For details and discount information, contact the
special sales department of Stanford University Press.
Tel: (650) 736 –1783; fax: (650) 736 –1784.

*To Cindy Pamela Gadye, MD*

# Contents

# Preface

The findings reported in this study directly challenge prevailing assumptions both in- and outside the scholarly community about the regularity of business involvement in agenda building and policymaking as well as the ability of business to influence government decisions concerning pollution control and natural resource management. This outcome was unexpected. When I first began working on this book more than three years ago, I anticipated finding that American corporations are regularly involved in environmental agenda building and policymaking and that they exert a great deal of influence over government decision making. Like many, I accepted the conventional wisdom that business frequently opposes proposals that will improve environmental quality in order to protect its profits. After all, reports in the media nearly always place the blame for the defeat of environmental initiatives on the undue influence of business. As an environmentalist myself, I have been quite disappointed in the lack of progress the United States has made, especially recently, in the areas of pollution control and natural resource conservation. Most policy analysts attribute this lack of progress to the ability of corporate America to block or dilute critical federal legislation and to the inability of environmental groups to compete in the policymaking process. Thus, when I told my colleagues and students that I was writing a book analyzing the extent to which business influences environmental policy, nearly all of them responded: "Why bother? We already know that corporations usually get their way in debates over environmental issues."

Of course, good social scientists are supposed to remain objective and not allow their biases and prior expectations to influence their theory and methodology. In order to accumulate knowledge, we must make a strong effort to remain neutral in the way we carry out our research. Once the data are collected, we are obligated to share the findings—regardless what they say—with the scholarly community. I was determined to adhere to these principles and conduct a fair and balanced assessment of the role of business interests in environmental and natural resource policymaking.

As the data show, business interests do not participate in environmental policy debates at a high rate, and when they do, they have mixed success in influencing policy outcomes. These results generally hold when one examines agenda building in Congress, agency rulemaking, and, to some extent, the courts. Analyses of salient conflicts involving pollution control and natural resources also tend to bear this out. Business interests, instead, appear to select strategically the controversies in which they become involved and how much money they spend on lobbying activities of various kinds. A major conclusion of my work is that agenda building within the environmental policy domain is a highly complex process and cannot be explained by a single theory. This and other surprising related findings are the subject of this book.

Many people provided important assistance throughout my research. Fred Gordon, a graduate student research assistant, collected and coded all the congressional bills related to environmental and natural resource issues considered between 1970 and 2000. He worked many long hours hunting down possible data sources and making certain that the information was accurately coded and entered. Denise McCain-Tharnstrom, also a graduate student research assistant, was instrumental in obtaining data on cases involving environmental issues in the federal courts of appeals. In addition, she collected information on some of the case studies. Both Fred and Denise read draft chapters and provided me with valuable comments. Those in government, business, and the environmental community who agreed to speak to me (often in confidence) concerning the case studies and other issues related to this research provided vital information and valuable insights.

I am grateful to those who helped me collect and interpret the data for my analysis of the influence of business interests over the contents of proposed rules by the United States Environmental Protection Agency (EPA), Fish and Wildlife Service (FWS), and Forest Service. Allison Rogers and Lou Taylor at EPA headquarters in Washington DC helped me obtain most of the public comments on the EPA rules examined in this study. I also want to thank Jody Sutton, Patte Widdifield, and especially Gabrielle Renshaw of the Content Analysis Team, Service Center, in Salt Lake City, Utah, for providing me with the data and information on the public comments concerning the proposed rules by the FWS and the Forest Service that are analyzed in this book. Given the enormous number of public comments on these rules, I could not have conducted this portion of the analysis without their assistance. Grants from the James H. Zumberge Faculty Research and Innovation Fund at the University of Southern California (USC) and from the John Randolph and Dora Haynes Foundation funded the research reported in this study.

Several colleagues played a major role in helping me shape the research questions, select the data sources and case studies, and interpret the findings. I benefited from a conference call arranged by Daniel Mazmanian in August 2002 about my work. He, Monty Hempel, Michael Kraft, and Daniel Press participated. It was Dan Press who argued for the importance of studying whether business usually gets what it wants in environmental policy. In addition, Mike Kraft provided excellent advice and guidance in the final selection of the case studies examined in this volume, and Dan Mazmanian read early drafts of my beginning chapters and provided many useful suggestions. Ann Crigler pointed me toward important work in the political science and communications literature on issue framing. Finally, I want to thank all the faculty and students I interacted with while I was a visiting professor at the Donald Bren School of Environmental Science and Management, University of California, Santa Barbara, during the 2001–2002 academic year. They provided me with constructive feedback on various aspects of my research.

I am indebted to several individuals for reading the entire manuscript or certain key chapters in their areas. Frank Baumgartner, Jeffrey Berry, Helen Ingram, Mike Kraft, and Evan Ringquist read the entire manuscript and offered enormously helpful recommendations for improving the work. Mark Smith was particularly generous with his time, fielding questions about specific details regarding the methodology he used in his outstanding and provocative book, *American Business and Political Power*. He also was kind enough to take time out from his own book project and read and comment on Chapters 1, 3, 4, and 8. Marissa Martino Golden provided good suggestions on collecting and analyzing data on rulemaking from the EPA, FWS, and Forest Service. Robert O'Brien provided excellent advice and guidance on methodology and data analysis. Cheryl Stewart, a USC graduate student, read drafts of the first three chapters and contributed several valuable ideas. Finally, I appreciate the effort of Amanda Moran at Stanford University Press to ensure that the review process went smoothly. The peer reviews solicited by the Press contained many good ideas for improving the manuscript. In the end, of course, I assume full responsibility for any errors in my work.

In addition, I want to thank all of the students who have enrolled in my undergraduate course and graduate seminar on environmental policy over the years. Their interpretation of the literature and their views about the policymaking process helped shape my own thinking and approach to the subject matter examined in this volume. I hope that they and others enjoy reading my book as much as I enjoyed writing it.

Finally, I want to thank my wife, Cindy Pamela Gadye, MD, to whom this book is dedicated, for her continuous encouragement throughout the research and writing phases of the study. She was kind enough to sacrifice many weekends and some nights so that I could finish the book. I do not think I could have completed this book without her consistent and strong support. I am deeply indebted to her.

Sheldon Kamieniecki
Pasadena, California

# Abbreviations

| | |
|---|---|
| APA | Administrative Procedure Act |
| API | American Petroleum Institute |
| BLM | Bureau of Land Management, U.S. |
| BMP | best management practices |
| BP | British Petroleum |
| CAC | Clean Air Coalition |
| CAET | Content Analysis Enterprise Team, U.S. Forest Service |
| CARB | California Air Resources Board |
| CERCLA | Comprehensive Environmental Response, Compensation, and Liability Act (Superfund) of 1980 |
| CESQGs | conditionally exempt small-quantity generator (wastes) |
| CFCs | chlorofluorocarbons |
| CMA | Chemical Manufacturers' Association |
| COP | Conference of the Parties |
| $CO_2$ | carbon dioxide |
| C&SF | Central and South Florida |
| CSI | Common Sense Initiative |
| DfE | Design for the Environment |
| DOE | Department of Energy, U.S. |
| DPS | distinct population segments |
| EAA | Everglades Agricultural Area |
| EDocket | Environmental Protection Agency Docket, U.S. |

| EIS | environmental impact statement |
| EPA | Environmental Protection Agency, U.S. |
| ESA | Endangered Species Act of 1973 |
| EU | European Union |
| FCCC | Framework Convention on Climate Change |
| FREE | Foundation for Research on Economics and the Environment |
| FWS | Fish and Wildlife Service, U.S. |
| GAO | Government Accounting Office, U.S. |
| GCC | Global Climate Coalition |
| GDP | gross domestic product |
| GE | General Electric Company |
| GHG | greenhouse gas |
| HCA | habitat conservation area |
| HUD | Department of Housing and Urban Development, U.S. |
| ICE | Information Council on the Environment |
| ICSU | International Council of Scientific Unions |
| IJC | International Joint Commission |
| IPCC | Intergovernmental Panel on Climate Change |
| LEV | low-emission vehicle |
| MBA | Master of Business Administration |
| MCL | maximum contaminant level |
| MSATs | mobile source air toxics |
| NAPAP | National Acid Precipitation Program |
| NAS | National Academy of Sciences |
| NASA | National Aeronautics and Space Administration |
| NEPA | National Environmental Policy Act of 1969 |
| NFMA | National Forest Management Act of 1976 |
| NHTSA | National Highway Traffic Safety Administration |
| NMA | National Mining Association |
| NOAA | National Oceanic and Atmospheric Administration |
| NOPR | Notice of Proposed Rulemaking |
| $NO_x$ | nitrogen oxides |
| NRDC | Natural Resources Defense Council |
| OMB | Office of Management and Budget, U.S. |
| OTC | Ozone Transport Coalition |
| PAC | political action committee |

| | |
|---|---|
| PCBs | polychlorinated biphenyls |
| PIPA | Program on International Policy Attitudes |
| ppb | parts per billion |
| ppm | parts per million |
| P2 | pollution prevention |
| RCRA | Resource Conservation and Recovery Act of 1976 |
| RECLAIM | Regional Clean Air Incentives Market |
| RNC | Republican National Committee |
| SCLDF | Sierra Club Legal Defense Fund |
| SFWMD | South Florida Water Management District |
| SLAPPs | strategic lawsuits against public participation |
| $SO_2$ | sulfur dioxide |
| STA | Stormwater Treatment Area |
| SUV | sports utility vehicle |
| UMW | United Mine Workers |
| UNEP | United Nations Environmental Programme |
| WCA | Western Conservation Area |
| WHO | World Health Organization |
| WMO | World Meteorological Organization |
| ZEV | zero-emission vehicle |

CORPORATE AMERICA AND
ENVIRONMENTAL POLICY

# 1   Business and American Democracy

The remedy for ignorance is investigation.
*William H. Riker,* The Strategy of Rhetoric

The largest and most wide-ranging corporate scandals in American history marked the end of the twentieth century. Following the post-economic boom of the 1990s, once profitable and highly respected companies such as Enron Corporation, Worldcom Incorporated, ImClone Systems Incorporated, Adelphia Communications Corporation, Commercial Financial Services, and Tyco International were found to have engaged in illegal accounting practices and fraudulent stock trading. Arthur Anderson, one of the nation's most revered accounting firms, looked the other way as Enron financial executives "cooked their books." The $7 trillion U.S. mutual fund industry was also under siege, with dozens of fund companies (including some of the biggest firms, such as Putnam Investment Management and Janus Capital Group) accused of illegal late trading of mutual fund shares and other wrongdoing. At the same time brokerage giant Morgan Stanley agreed to pay $50 million to settle charges by the Securities and Exchange Commission (SEC) that it had received substantial hidden fees from fourteen of the country's largest mutual fund companies in return for promoting their funds to investors over those offered by dozens of competitors. For the first time Americans watched televised images of impeccably groomed corporate executives led away in handcuffs by law enforcement officials. Chairman of the New York Stock Exchange Richard Grasso was forced to resign for accepting an enormous compensation package worth almost $188 million. Andrew Fastow, the former finance chief who built Enron's complicated web of off-the-books partnerships to hide debt and boost profit, pleaded guilty to fraud-related charges in 2004. Apparently, no one was spared. Even Martha Stewart, America's lifestyles icon who always projected an air of grace, humility, and sophistication, was convicted of securities fraud, obstruction of justice, and making false statements for illegally selling $228,000 of ImClone stock. Undoubtedly, the incident tarnished her wholesome image and, for many, underscored the lengths some business leaders are willing to go to protect their wealth. Enron, Global Crossing, Worldcom, and other companies filed for bankruptcy, stranding employees and investors with worthless stock while company executives like Kenneth Lay and Bernard Ebbers reaped huge financial rewards. A survey by *CFO* magazine found that about one in six chief financial officers felt pressured by chief executives to misrepresent corporate financial results, and 5 percent (the actual figure is probably higher) admitted they had violated accounting rules in the last five years (*Los Angeles Times* 2002b).[1]

The high incidence of illegal activities by leaders of some of America's largest corporations comes at a time when businesses are trying hard to earn the public's trust and confidence on a variety of fronts, including in the areas of environmental protection and natural resource policy. Companies have long complained that environmental regulations are too burdensome and costly and that they should be given much more flexibility in attaining pollution control standards. Firms are asking the government to end direct command-and-control regulation and trust them to select the most cost-effective methods and equipment to abate pollution and manage natural resources (Anderson and Leal 2001). Business leaders believe this can be accomplished by instituting market-based mechanisms and voluntary action programs, among other things (Anderson and Leal 2001; Marcus, Geffen, and Sexton 2002; OECD 2003). Many now support efforts to improve environmental quality and are willing to change certain practices in order to achieve that end. Environmentalists, of course, have frequently complained that corporations are not sincere, only care about profits, and will not cease polluting or wasting natural resources unless forced to do so by government. No doubt, public confidence in American business has significantly eroded as a result of the unparalleled charges leveled against once prominent companies and their executives and of the flood of media coverage that has accompanied legal action. The corporate scandals at the turn of the twentieth century may have important implications for the debate over the true commitment of industry to improve environmental quality and natural resource conservation, though this is not a focus of this research. At the very least, given the serious nature of these scandals, this is certainly an appropriate time to examine the extent of corporate influence over environmental policymaking.

This book adds to the environmental politics and policy literature by conducting a comprehensive investigation of business influence in agenda building and environmental policymaking in the United States over time. In addition to determining how much business interests influence environmental and natural resource policy, the book tests possible explanations for their level of success in shaping the government's agenda and policy. This introductory chapter lays the groundwork for the investigation by providing a general discussion of democratic theory in relationship to business and interest groups. It also explores the disagreements that exist between corporate leaders and environmentalists over the contribution of industry to improved environmental quality and natural resource protection. The study draws on the theoretical literature on issue definition and framing and agenda-building processes, and offers a general conceptual framework for analyzing the influence of corporate America over environmental policymaking. Theories that specifically address the internal operation and characteristics of companies are also discussed, though they are not a major focus of this book. The research then explores how much firms have influenced Congress, the EPA and certain natural resource agencies, and the courts on environmental and natural issues since 1970, when the environmental movement began. No other study has examined the ability of business to influence environmental policy in all three branches of government and in such detail. The results of this research provide a compelling rationale for exploring agenda building in specific cases involving environmental and natural resource issues. Accordingly, the book presents an analysis of six cases in which private firms were involved in disputes concerning pollution control and natural resource management.

More specifically, the study addresses the following three research questions: How much do certain sectors of industry (for example, agriculture, chemical, mining, logging, energy production, and so on) and business as a whole affect environmental policy? Related to this, what determines business success or failure in the environmental policy arena? Lastly, is the amount of influence business has proportionate to other interests in society appropriate in view of the competitive needs and well-being of a large, complex, and democratic society? The findings of the analysis involving the first two questions are used as a basis for tackling the third question at the end of the book.

Therefore, the central question of the book is, how often does business get its way on environmental issues? Do corporations, given the immense wealth and resources they command, exert an unequal and unfair influence over American government whereby they are able to compel elected representatives and agency officials to reject or compromise substantially appropriate and necessary environmental rules and regulations?[2] A related concern, often ignored in the interest group literature, is the frequency with which firms are able to prevent environmental and natural resource policy proposals from even reaching the government agenda. Although recent research suggests that firms do not possess the amount of influence necessary to shape or block public policymaking on a consistent basis more generally (see, for example, Berry 1999; M. Smith 2000), few studies have critically analyzed their ability to affect agenda setting specifically within the environmental policy sphere. This investigation addresses this issue by empirically assessing the ability of companies to affect legislative, administrative, and judicial decision making and mold the government's environmental and natural resource policy agenda since the beginning of the environmental movement.

### The Role of Interest Groups in a Democracy

As students of American politics are aware, James Madison attempted to address the thorny issue of the "mischiefs of faction" within the context of the new U.S. Constitution in *Federalist Paper Number Ten*. A major concern among leaders and citizens at the time was whether the proposed government under the new Constitution would prevent a faction, large or small, from taking control of the country. Madison wrote that factions would naturally arise because of the freedoms granted citizens under the Constitution to associate and form groups. He knew that rational individuals would recognize the advantage of acting in numbers rather than alone. In Madison's view, factions would be a natural product and price of liberty. Government must control them, but it cannot suppress them. According to him, factions would be limited in their power under the new Constitution because the national government would be divided into three separate branches with important checks and balances on one another. "Ambition must be made to counteract ambition," he said. He also explained that elected representatives would have the intelligence and the wisdom to serve the larger interests of the nation and would help control efforts at tyranny from any source. In addition, citizens would have guaranteed civil rights and civil liberties to protect them from the "mischiefs of faction."

The potential danger of excluding certain segments of the population from the political process was a major concern of the founding fathers as well. Although Madison believed the causes of factions were rooted in human diversity, he thought inequality in the possession of economic resources was at the heart of the problem:

> But the most common and durable source of factions has been the various and unequal distribution of property. Those who hold and those who are without property have ever formed distinct interests in society. Those who are creditors and those who are debtors fall under like discrimination. A landed interest, a manufacturing interest, a mercantile interest, a monied interest, with many lesser interests, grow up of necessity in civilized nations, and divide them into different classes, actuated by different sentiments and views. (*Federalist Paper Number 10*)

Madison argued that all individuals and groups, from the poor to the affluent, would be equally protected by the Constitution.

Even though Madison wrote his essay more than two hundred years ago, many of the issues he addressed remain relevant to American politics. At least since the early 1960s, presidents and members of Congress from both parties have complained vociferously about the undue influence of interest groups in Washington DC, primarily because of the rapid growth in the number, size, and resources of these groups. The general public, too, has grown increasingly skeptical of the role of interest groups in the political system. Today, interest groups are blamed for legislative gridlock on vital issues such as health care reform, education reform, energy policy, and environmental policy as well as for the increased politicization of the judicial-nominating and -approval process.

In particular, the size and wealth of business lobbying organizations have grown dramatically since World War Two, prompting some observers to argue that they are now too powerful and are undermining democracy and threatening the well-being of society (for example, Korten 1995). The weakening of the political parties, the rising costs of media advertising and election campaigns, and the increasing contributions by Political Action Committees (PACs) to candidates and parties have led to calls for reform in the way American elections are financed. Business interests, among others, are key targets of critics who demand the enactment of meaningful campaign finance reform at the federal level. The campaign finance reform legislation enacted in 2002 bans "soft money," among other things, and is a significant attempt to level the playing field. Loopholes in the act exist, however, and it will be necessary to adopt additional regulations in the future in order to correct inequities in the financing of campaigns. Thus, despite Madison's assurances, the question of how we allow business and other interest groups to form and participate but control their influence remains a dilemma in modern times.

### Democratic Concepts and Theory

Much has been written about the required conditions for a successful democracy, and there is widespread agreement that the presence of a multiparty system, competitive elites, the secret ballot, free and open elections held at regular intervals, majority rule, and guaranteed civil rights and civil liberties are important. Public participation in political and governmental affairs is also a critical ingredient in the functioning of a democratic society.[3] Opportunities for citizen involvement normally include attending public hearings and meetings, writing elected officials, joining interest groups, and voting in elections. At the same time, elected representatives are expected to make decisions that reflect the public will and are held accountable for their actions (Jones and Baumgartner 2004). They must allow citizens open access to the decision-making process and demonstrate that they are responsive to the needs and demands of the broad public.

Although classical democratic theorists anticipated that citizens would have considerable knowledge about political issues and government policy, possess a strong motivation for involvement in political life, and exhibit a high level of participation in public affairs, most of the expectations concerning the requirements for effective democracy have been tempered by the results of empirical research conducted during the last fifty years (see, for example, Campbell et al. 1960; Verba and Nie 1972; Milbrath and Goel 1977; Wolfinger and Rosenstone 1980; Burnham 1987; Carmines and Stimson 1989; Teixeira 1992; Wattenberg 1998; Putnam 2000; Abramson, Aldrich, and Rohde 2003). In general, Americans tend to have relatively low interest and knowledge about the issues and candidates of the day, often hold inconsistent views on the issues, and vote with great irregularity. Since the 1960s, for instance, voter turnout has generally hovered at or below the 50 percent mark in presidential elections. In spite of these deficiencies, American democracy has been fairly stable and has flourished, primarily because the various channels of communication between the people and government have remained open, thereby allowing citizens to voice their approval or disapproval and take effective action at certain points in time (for example, the civil rights movement, the protest against the Vietnam War, the women's and environmental movements, and the patriotic fervor following the attack on the World Trade Center). Thus, there are a variety of ways (for example, by joining interest groups and through the media and now the Internet) for Americans to communicate their views and beliefs about salient issues without becoming actively involved in politics on a continuous basis. At the very least, citizens continue to hold cherished democratic values and do not wish to change radically the present political system.

There is disagreement over how much public participation is required to sustain a democratic society (Hahn and Kamieniecki 1987). Those who contend that democracy is best served by a high rate of involvement correctly point out that a democratic society, unlike a traditional oligarchy, depends on the consent of its citizens (for example, Pateman 1970; Verba and Nie 1972; Milbrath and Goel 1977; Hahn and Kamieniecki 1987; Putnam 2000). Consent cannot be taken for granted where a large segment of the public is apathetic, uninterested, and unaware. Consensus, in fact, actually may be weak in such a state (Lipset 1981; Hahn and Kamieniecki 1987). Moreover, low rates of turnout almost always indicate that the socially and economically disadvantaged are underrepresented in government (Key 1958; Verba and Nie 1972; Milbrath and Goel 1977). Elected leaders are usually less receptive to unorganized, lower-status citizens than to the more privileged, involved, and organized strata, which includes business interests (Verba and Nie 1972).[4] Low levels of public participation and the underrepresentation of the disadvantaged segments of the public may also indicate a lack of effective citizenship and of support for the political system, which eventually can threaten the stability of democracy (Hahn and Kamieniecki 1987). At the same time, some question whether high involvement is really beneficial and suggest that low levels of participation mean that most citizens are basically satisfied with current conditions (Lipset 1981). Such a position, however, perpetuates the belief that low levels of citizen participation are acceptable, if not desirable. Citizen participation is regarded as essential to the functioning of a democracy; indeed, it is at the heart of democratic theory.

Although the sharp rise in the number and diversity of interest groups is seen by some as a healthy trend and a way to offset declining levels of public participation and the continued weakening of the political parties, the question remains exactly whose interests are being served and with what effect (Jones and Baumgartner 2004). Despite the substantial increase in the size and number of environmental organizations since the 1960s, the emergence of the environmental justice movement in the 1990s suggests there is a deep concern among many over the disproportionate exposure to pollution by poor and minority groups in urban centers throughout the nation (see, for instance, Mohai and Bryant 1992; Kamieniecki and Steckenrider 1997; Ringquist 1997, 2003; Foreman 1998; Schlosberg 1999). Yet, only recently have large mainstream environmental groups begun to pay attention to environmental justice issues. And even if one believes that the influence of business interests has waned in recent years due to the rise of competing citizen groups, as many have argued (for example, Berry 1999), business still appears to exert a great deal of power in the halls of government, *especially* in the environmental policy arena. The crucial question is, to what degree does the campaign and lobbying activities of business result in denying segments of the public and future generations of Americans the opportunity to enjoy the benefits of high environmental quality and the country's natural resources?

Even though business is not always a model citizen, it nevertheless must be allowed to collaborate and participate fully in democratic society. A number of liberals and environmentalists have called for severe restrictions on business activity, a significant restructuring of capitalism, and a redistribution of wealth in America. A series of U.S. Supreme Court decisions in the 1870s and 1880s (generally involving granaries and railway corporations), however, established a doctrine of corporate personhood, thereby providing business with important rights and liberties to participate freely in politics and policymaking. In the *In re Sinking Funds* cases, 99 U.S. 718 (1878), the Court found that the Fifth Amendment due process clause prohibited the United States and the states from depriving *persons or corporations* of property without due process of law. Another important case, *Santa Clara County v. Southern Pacific Railway Corporation* 118 U.S. 394 (1886) further established that corporations are persons under the Fourteenth Amendment by ruling that the Fourteenth Amendment's equal protection clause applies to corporations. More recently, the Court has ruled that denying corporations the ability to contribute money to political campaigns infringes on their freedom of speech and is unconstitutional. At the same time, of course, it is illegal for corporations to wiretap, harass, and physically threaten members of opposition groups as a way to quiet their protests.

### Corporate America and Environmental Policy: Opposing Views

The influence of business over environmental policy is often used as an example of the substantial and unfair leverage certain interest groups have over government actions, especially when compared to the level of influence of average citizens (Korten 1995; Ehrlich and Ehrlich 1996; Dryzek 1997; Gonzalez 1997; Suzuki and McConnell 1997; De-Shalit 2000; Press and Mazmanian 2003; Brown 2001; Glazer and Rothenberg 2001; Kettl 2002). Many believe that the power business wields in American politics threatens democracy and, among other things, undermines the nation's efforts to control pollution and conserve natural resources (Milbrath 1989; Cahn 1995; Korten 1995; Ehrlich and Ehrlich 1996; Dryzek 1997; Suzuki and McConnell 1997; Brown 2001; Gonzalez 2001; Devra Davis 2002; Press and Mazmanian 2003). Environmentalists assert that "big business" has continuously been an impediment to the formulation and implementation of clean air and water quality standards. Ranchers and land developers, they argue, have successfully fought endangered species protection; oil, coal, and natural gas companies have opposed strict energy-conservation measures and have lobbied against the adoption of renewable sources of energy; mining companies have thwarted the revision of mining laws and regulations; and chemical companies have fought legislation intended to control pesticides, promote the safe disposal of hazardous waste, and abate old, abandoned toxic waste sites.

Corporate leaders and conservative analysts strongly disagree with this assessment (for example, Simon 1981, 1999; Easterbrook 1995; Wildavsky 1995; Lomborg 2001; P. Moore 2002). They feel that environmentalists are exaggerating problems and are predicting dire consequences in order to alarm Americans unnecessarily, raise money for their cause, and shape public policy. In addition, they maintain that many present laws, regulations, and government programs are too expensive to comply with, will result in only modest—if any—improvements in environmental quality, and, therefore, are unnecessary. In their view, corporations have a great deal at stake financially (as do their shareholders), and they have every right to express their positions and lobby government to protect their interests. After all, this is what democracy is all about.

Environmentalists counter these arguments in several ways. They point out that the true costs of pollution (for example, to public health and property) are excluded in cost / benefit and economic-based assessments as well as in the actual cost of manufacturing processes and goods. When these factors are included in such calculations, efforts to protect the natural environment and promote natural resource conservation are more than worth the effort and expense (Hawken, Lovins, and Lovins 1999; Lovins, Lovins, and Hawken 1999). Moreover, at the global level, the United States is not playing a major role in forging an effective international agreement to control climate change because of the political power of certain domestic industries, primarily the energy companies. Environmentalists accuse business of derailing efforts to pass legislation to protect the environment in Congress by the kinds of lobbying tactics they use and by the vast sums of money they contribute to certain House and Senate campaigns. Following the passage of environmental-protection laws, business frequently seeks to influence rulemaking in government agencies, principally in the EPA, and, if unsuccessful, challenges the laws in court.

In addition, environmentalists charge that business spends large sums of money to frame issues purposely in biased ways in order to affect public opinion. Firms do this, according to environmentalists, by manipulating media coverage and writing editorials that slant the truth (Devra Davis 2002). A number of large companies, including Koch Industries, ExxonMobil, Philip Morris, General Motors, General Electric, Archer Daniels Midland, and DaimlerChrysler, have developed and heavily funded several conservative think tanks such as the Cato Institute, Citizens for a Sound Economy, and the Federalist Society (C. Moore 2002). The Koch family, for example, contributed more than $21 million to the Cato Institute alone between 1977 and 1994 (C. Moore 2002). The money is primarily used to fund policy and scientific research, produce publications and mailings, and hire "neutral" experts to write articles and editorials that support business interests. Several think tanks have sponsored scientific studies that diminish the severity of environmental threats posed by air and water pollution, acid rain, and climate change. Findings from these studies are being used to undermine the precautionary principle, undercut adaptive management, and insist on "complete" scientific knowledge as a basis for environmental regulation. Policy and economic analyses conducted by industry-funded think tanks almost always contend that current and proposed environmental and natural resource rules and regulations are extremely costly and provide little or no benefit. In 1999 the Citizens for a Sound Economy Foundation, the funding arm of the Citizens for a Sound Economy, paid top attorneys to write "friend of the court" briefs arguing that the Clean Air Act was unconstitutional. The Claude Lambe Foundation, DaimlerChrysler, and General Electric helped fund this effort. The Lambe Foundation has also funded the Foundation for Research on Economics and the Environment (FREE) based in Bozeman, Montana (C. Moore 2002). FREE, a libertarian organization, conducts seminars for federal judges, including those that serve on the Circuit Court of Appeals in Washington DC, which reviews numerous environmental cases.

Business leaders reject these accusations and point to the progress the country has made since the early 1970s in improving air and water quality, conserving energy, keeping the price of energy relatively low, and encouraging the safe transportation and disposal of chemical waste. Companies have spent hundreds of millions of dollars to retool their plants and manufacturing processes in order to control emissions, save energy, and safely dispose of toxic waste. The reduction of sulfur dioxide ($SO_2$) emissions by power plants in the mid-Atlantic states has significantly reduced acid rain, thereby protecting forests, lakes, and streams in the United States and Canada. The timber industry has hired numerous ecologists and conservation biologists and is now managing forests wisely by protecting critical habitats (Winter 2002). Large agricultural firms are effectively managing soil erosion and are containing feedlot waste and chemical runoff from cropland. Unlike in the past, firms are cooperating more closely with government regulators and maintain that a "greening of industry" is currently taking place (United Nations Conference on Trade and Development Programme on Transnational Corporations 1993; Hoffman 2000; Prakash 2000; Robbins 2001; Marcus, Geffen, and Sexton 2002; Press and Mazmanian 2003). National business associations cite programs such as Energy Star, Responsible Care, Project XL, and 33/50 as evidence that corporations have adopted a new attitude toward protecting the environment and conserving the nation's natural resources (Marcus, Geffen, and Sexton 2002; Press and Mazmanian 2003). Clearly, both environmentalists and business leaders present a number of compelling arguments to support their positions.

No matter which side one takes, it is surprising that little empirical research has been done on the influence of business over U.S. environmental policy given the frequency with which large companies are the primary targets of federal environmental laws, the large amounts of money companies spend to comply with government regulations, and the millions of dollars business spends on election campaigns and lobbyists each year. Moreover, since 1970 the media have covered issues related to business and the environment on a regular basis. Hardly a week goes by that a conflict over environmental protection or natural resource conservation involving business is not part of the news. The few studies that have been conducted tend to be narrow, descriptive, impressionistic, and anecdotal. Previous research focuses on only a few unique businesses as case studies, treats business as a single entity, and ignores that companies belong to distinct industrial sectors. These studies also overlook the extent to which companies disagree with one another and take opposing positions on environmental policies.

Although most researchers believe corporations wield considerable power in American politics today, there is disagreement over just how dominant they really are and to what extent they can mold the government agenda. Some researchers contend that the recent rise in citizen groups, including environmental organizations, has successfully miti-gated the influence of the once powerful firms in politics and government (for example, Baumgartner and Leech 1998; Berry 1999). Other scholars, however, believe that business groups are still dominant players in Amer-ican politics in general, and in environmental politics in particular (for ex-ample, Korten 1995; Clawson, Neustadt, and Waller 1998; Libby 1998; Glazer and Rothenberg 2001). A main goal of this inquiry is to shed light on this debate and to draw conclusions about whether business exerts too much influence in the environmental policy arena and, by so doing, un-dermines democracy and the well-being of the public.

De-Shalit (2000) argues that government *must* play a pivotal role in environmental protection in democratic, pluralist societies. Although classical liberals embrace pluralism and tolerate actions reflecting self-interest in democratic nations, he believes the environment is a unique case. According to him, "Environmental issues call for a politics of the common and the good, and consequently for interventionism" by govern-ment (2000, 92). Therefore, "A sense of community is needed since social and environmental responsibilities in the environmental era ought to take precedence over self-interested profit-making motivation" (2000, 92). In De-Shalit's view, the unique nature of environmentalism, with its focus on protecting and furthering the common good, calls for a limited policy-making role for industry and significant intervention by national govern-ment. A strong case can also be made, however, for limiting the govern-ment's role to rulemaking so as to internalize the costs and decisions of individual actors as opposed to government regulating aggressively (direct command-and-control regulation) (Freeman 2006).

### Summary and the Study Plan

This book contains seven additional chapters. Chapter 2 analyzes business, interest groups, and environmental policymaking. Chapter 3 de-velops a general theoretical framework to explain the role of corporations in American environmental policymaking. The framework outlined in this chapter forms the basis for the analyses reported in the chapters that fol-low. The framework identifies possible political and economic variables that might account for the ability of business to affect decisions concern-ing environmental issues in Congress and elsewhere. It also includes important theories of issue definition, framing processes, and agenda setting. Theories concerning the internal operation and characteristics of firms are briefly introduced as well. An overview of the study's research design is presented at the end of that chapter. Chapter 4 contains a quantitative analysis of agenda setting in Congress, and Chapter 5 investigates the influence of business in the EPA, certain natural resource agencies, and the federal courts. The findings reported in Chapters 4 and 5 justify the need to explore the influence of business over environmental and natural resource policy in specific situations. Therefore, Chapter 6 examines the role of industry in three cases concerning environmental regulation (General Electric's pollution discharge of polychlorinated biphenyls [PCBs] into New York State's Hudson River and the efforts to control acid rain and climate change in the United States). Chapter 7 discusses the role of industry in three natural resource policy issues (attempts to amend the General Mining Law of 1872, the restoration of the Florida Everglades, and the protection of the northern spotted owl and old-growth forests in the Pacific Northwest). The justification for selecting these cases is provided in the research design section of Chapter 3. The final chapter offers a summary of the study's major findings, discusses the implications of those findings with respect to the theoretical framework, and attempts to determine whether business has an unfair advantage in environmental policymaking and, as a consequence, undermines democracy and the public welfare. The last chapter concludes with suggestions for future research.

Early forms of corporations were found in Europe by the seven-
teenth century. These corporations were government-chartered businesses
created to attract private investors to further a specific public mission.
The United States, in fact, was settled by one such corporation, the Massachusetts Bay Company, which was chartered by King Charles I in 1628
for the purpose of settling the New World. Use of the corporation model
to facilitate private investment in public services prevailed more than 150
years later in the United States. Early corporations were typically state-
chartered entities established to perform specific public services, such as
digging canals, constructing bridges, and providing financial services. In
return for these services, the state granted the corporations permanence,
limited liability, and the right to own property.

Of course, the nature and characteristics of American corporations have changed considerably over time. As a result of experience and
good research, corporations are generally run more efficiently and effectively today. Compared to their earlier predecessors, firms are much
larger, wealthier, and play an important role as a pressure group in the
political system. Exactly how influential they are in politics is a matter of
perspective and debate.

This chapter reviews the evolution of corporate interests in America
as well as the literature on interest groups and business in politics.

The main purpose of this chapter is to examine the role of business in public policymaking in general, and in environmental policymaking in particular. Specifically, what do previous studies tell us about how much influence business interests have over the contents of environmental and natural resource policy? There is an ongoing debate between those who believe business has a major advantage and those who feel that citizen groups have successfully mitigated the increasing power of corporate America.

## The Evolution of Business Interests in America

From the start, U.S. corporations were established under state law, thus the individual state where an entity was incorporated had the power to require adherence to state laws on the creation, organization, and dissolution of corporations. Incorporation grants an entity a separate legal identity from its shareholders for the purpose of assuming liability for its debts and obligations, as well as a life independent of the natural life of its officers, directors, or shareholders. The corporation is not specifically recognized by the U.S. Constitution and derives many of its rights and protections through a series of U.S. Supreme Court decisions.

America transformed itself from a largely rural and agricultural society into a major industrial and manufacturing power between the Civil War and the stock market crash of 1929 (Korten 1995; Lehne 2001). Ensuing pervasive economic changes disrupted traditional cultural and political relationships, reshaped citizens' daily lives, and challenged the nation's institutions to manage drastically altered social conditions (Lehne 2001). Following the introduction of power-driven machinery, the development of new technologies, and the emergence of the factory system, 60 percent of the nation's workers were employed in industry by 1900 (Lehne 2001). The size of individual businesses also grew substantially during this period, with the railroads becoming the first big businesses, followed soon after by the oil companies (Engler 1977). The United States became the first nation in the world to have its economy dominated by large corporations.

Government attempted to rein in the excesses of "big business" but with mixed success. Legislatures passed laws regulating railroads, food-processing companies, and other industries, while both federal and state governments enacted legal standards for corporate conduct in such areas as working conditions, transportation services, and banking. According to

Lehne, however, "landmark pieces of legislation from this period such as the Interstate Commerce Act of 1887 and the Sherman Antitrust Act of 1890 resembled declarations of traditional values rather than clear elaborations of legislative programs" (2001, 11). As Korten observes:

> These were the days of men such as John D. Rockefeller, J. Pierpont Morgan, Andrew Carnegie, James Mellon, Cornelius Vanderbilt, Philip Armour, and Jay Gould. Wealth begat wealth as corporations took advantage of the disarray to buy tariff, banking, railroad, labor, and public lands legislation that would further enrich them. (1995, 58)

The stock market crash of 1929 and the Great Depression of the 1930s signaled an end to passive government intervention in the economy and in people's daily lives. The economy—and the people who depended on it—desperately needed help, and the federal government quickly moved in to offer assistance. Changes in legal doctrine through the passage of new laws and decisions by the U.S. Supreme Court also facilitated increased government intervention, particularly in regulating business practices and the economy. The result was a sharp increase in the size of the federal government; both federal government expenditures and federal civilian employment rose dramatically during this time (Lehne 2001). Government also expanded because of its willingness to provide Americans with a wide variety of social services, including education, health care, social security, and housing.

Today, multinational operations, product diversification, and professional management are major parts of large American corporations. The service industry has replaced manufacturing as the driving force behind economic growth. Mergers of large companies are fairly common, often inviting scrutiny and legal action by antitrust officials. Although major corporations play a significant role in the American economy, small firms are the ones that create a large percentage of the new jobs and about half of all industrial innovations (Lehne 2001). Small business employment is concentrated in the retail sector, whereas major corporations employ the largest percentage of people in manufacturing. Both big business and small business leaders frequently complain about what they feel are burdensome government regulations, including environmental laws.

The role of business in the American economy has changed dramatically since the colonial days. The country moved from an agrarian economy characterized by trading and small firms to an economy dominated financially by huge, diversified firms that possess significant wealth and political influence. The role of American government changed from passively promoting economic growth to promoting selected industries (for example, the railroads, oil companies, defense, and nuclear power) and attempting to sustain the economy.

According to Vogel (1978), only in the United States did the emergence of the large corporation predate the growth of substantial government oversight. Whereas European and Japanese leaders helped finance and establish large business enterprises, American corporations developed with less government assistance. Compared to other industrialized countries, business and American government have had an adversarial rather than a cooperative relationship, particularly since World War Two. This has particularly been the case with regard to environmental issues.

Business has long enjoyed a privileged position in our economy and in our society. Recognizing the importance of big business, government has protected and promoted its interests more often than not since the formation of the United States. Whether and, if so, to what extent environmental quality and the nation's natural resources have been unduly sacrificed in order to support corporate America and generate economic growth is a question this study seeks to answer.

### Interest Groups and the Policy Process

During the 1950s and 1960s political scientists engaged in a vigorous debate over pluralism and the role of interest groups in democratic society. Among the questions they were most concerned about were: Do we have a system where competing groups contest one another in a fair and equitable manner, or do we have a system where a few powerful interest groups—led by a small number of elites—shape policy to further their interests at the expense of the public good? Also, to what extent, if at all, do citizens have a meaningful say in government decision making? Studies by Bauer, Pool, and Dexter (1963), Milbrath (1963), and Scott and Hunt (1965) suggested that interest groups, including those associated with business, wielded far less influence than was generally attributed to them. Yet, studies by Cater (1964), McConnell (1966), and Lowi (1969) indicated that interest groups, led by "big business," were indeed undermining democracy and the public welfare.

Mancur Olson (1965) suggested that the explanation for these different appraisals could be found in the nature of collective-action problems and the advantages wealthy, private interest groups had in organizing and lobbying government compared to noneconomic, public interests (for example, the young and homeless). His seminal work revealed the dilemmas of organizing for collective action, and it challenged the pluralist perspective (as represented by the early writings of Bentley [1949], Commons [1950, 1959], Latham [1952], and Truman [1958]) that all potential interests were equal and would have a fair chance of participating in the American political system. Olson contended that while business-oriented groups possessed significant advantages in resources and organization and were likely to mobilize, those groups with many potential members seeking only collective benefits had a substantial disadvantage and were unlikely to unite. Hence, the battle between interest groups would never be equal and fair. Certain interests would be privileged at the expense of other interests, and this power differential would be reflected in government policy.

Olson accepted the idea that increased societal complexity led to the emergence of new interests as earlier researchers argued, but he questioned the contention that the emergence of new interests necessarily causes the creation of new organized interests. Shared interests, he maintained, are necessary but not sufficient for the establishment of organized interests. Thus, simply because a group of citizens shares an interest does not mean they will automatically organize to protect or promote that interest. According to him, significant obstacles to organized interest formation and survival exist, including the costs involved in time, effort, and money to form and maintain a group, the free-rider problem, and the reluctance of citizens to join organized interests because of their tendency to think that one person cannot make a difference.

Although subsequent research findings challenged elements of Mancur Olson's theory of interest group formation and survival, his recognition that there exist obstacles to organizing interests has important political implications (Nounes 2002). First, his theory suggests that large portions of the broad public will remain unorganized and, therefore, unrepresented by interest groups. Second, the organized interests that do exist do not necessarily represent the various interests that comprise society. Affluent groups in America, for example, tend to have unique concerns.

As recent research demonstrates, on the one hand, many more segments of society with shared interests have been able to overcome the barriers to interest group formation and continued existence than Olson's theory would have predicted (see, for example, Baumgartner and Leech 1998; Berry 1999). On the other hand, business has had no difficulty overcoming the obstacles to interest group formation and survival. On the contrary, Olson believes the largest and wealthiest corporations have enjoyed unprecedented access to the halls of power and have wielded significant influence over public policy in the United States. Unless a radical change in the American political system takes place, business will continue to exert considerable influence well into the future.[1]

### The Emergence of Neopluralists

Recent research on citizen groups and the influence of business over public policy, including environmental policy, challenges Olson's theory of collective action. Berry (1999), for example, analyzes three different sessions of Congress—1963, 1979, and 1991—in an effort to identify which groups were active on which issues and to determine how interest group politics and legislative policymaking has changed over time. In essence, his research attempts to document "the efforts of interest groups to influence the legislative process" (1999). According to Berry, it has been difficult to determine how citizen groups have fared compared with corporations and trade groups with which they contend, in part because the subject has rarely been studied. He examines 205 separate domestic social and economic policy issues that were addressed in a congressional hearing and received at least minimal attention in the press. He prepared a legislative case history for each of the 205 policy issues taken up by Congress during the combined three sessions. His findings are instructive for research reported in this book. Berry reports that since the early 1960s the agenda of American politics has shifted from issues that are exclusively material to a focus on issues that involve quality-of-life concerns, such as the environment. In other words, using Inglehart's (1977) terminology, he believes postmaterial concerns have replaced material concerns within society. He also finds that citizen groups, especially those on the left, have been the primary political force behind this trend. Citizen groups, he argues, are popular and have been remarkably successful in influencing public policy. Clearly, Mancur Olson's (1965) theory would not have predicted this trend.

According to Berry, "Most of those who have studied interest groups have concluded that there is a persistent dominance by business" (1999, 6). Yet, he finds that this was not the case during the three sessions of Congress he studied. He correctly observes that business is not unified on every policy issue and that since the 1960s the general interest group population has become larger, broader, more diverse, and increasingly influential. Indeed, Mark Smith (2000) reports that business has been unified only on a relatively small number of bills since the 1950s. Berry believes that his findings "are important not because they improve our understanding of contemporary interest group politics but because they bear upon the level of representation that various constituencies receive in Washington" (1999, 15).

Many critics maintain that interest groups subvert democracy, in part by pressing Congress to pass too much "special-interest" legislation that benefits the few at the expense of the majority and in part by blocking legislative initiatives they oppose even when those measures are favored by, or would benefit, the broad public. In addition, critics contend that campaign contributions by interest groups undermine democratic government and degrade the American electoral system. In contrast, Berry (1999) rejects these arguments, saying that interest groups help to link citizens to government: "They empower people by organizing those citizens with similar interests and expressing those interests to policymakers. In this regard, the growth of citizen groups reflects an expansion of organizing around interests that have too often received too little attention in Washington" (1999, 15). Berry carefully avoids saying that business interests are no longer a force in American politics, but he does argue that their influence has significantly declined.

One can question Berry's findings and conclusions on several grounds. First, he only focuses on three unique points in time over a period of three decades. There is no way to determine whether any significant changes in conditions took place between each time period and what effect these changes might have had on interest group dynamics and politics and the legislative process. Second, as Baumgartner and Leech (1998) point out, it is extremely difficult to measure and demonstrate with certainty whether interest groups, rather than other factors, are responsible for government policy. In many cases, for example, intense media coverage and broad public concern more than citizen group lobbying may have prompted Congress to pass the legislation he analyzes in his research. (M. Smith [2000] concludes exactly this in his research.) Third, Berry does not investigate how successful business organizations have been in influencing rulemaking by government agencies and litigation in the courts, areas of research this study addresses. Finally, as Berry admits, he does not examine the ability of business groups to block potential legislation. These concerns aside, his study's findings represent an important challenge to previous research and common assumptions about the role of interest groups in American politics, and they have significant implications for research on the influence of business interests over environmental policy.

Interestingly, Berry's (1999) findings and conclusions are a throwback to some of the positions of the early pluralists, namely that interest group politics is equitable and fair. For this reason, Berry and his contemporaries, such as Baumgartner and Leech (1998) who also share this view, are referred to as *neopluralists* in this volume. Specifically, neopluralists argue that the increasing number and size of citizen groups has furthered democracy and the public good by involving a broad range of interests in policymaking and by substantially countering the influence of business in the political system. The neopluralists, like the early pluralists, point to the positive aspects of group pressures on politics and government. Scholars who believe that public opinion also provides a check on the power of business are considered neopluralists as well (for example, M. Smith 2000). The degree to which environmental groups and public opinion mitigate business influence in environmental policymaking is examined in the present study.[2]

### Determining Influence

Baumgartner and Leech (1998) review the voluminous literature on contributions and lobbying activities by PACs. Both topics have received close attention by scholars and the media over the last three decades and are salient subjects in the interest group literature. The authors critique the literature on the influence of PAC money and conclude, "It is a mess" (1998, 14–15). Specifically, the studies conducted in this area tend to cover too many disparate issues and are fragmented and inconclusive.

In Baumgartner and Leech's (1998) view, the research on lobbying is equally confusing. Studies in this field contain too many contradictions and too many diverse theoretical frameworks and methodological approaches. As a result, the research community is "left with a bewildering array of findings rather than a coherent set of results" (1998, 16).

As Salisbury (1994) notes, the attempt to identify and measure influence is the common thread that ties together much of the research on interest groups in recent decades. A major reason why researchers focusing on PACs, lobbying, and other interest group activities have not been more successful, however, is because of the difficulty of defining, operationalizing, and documenting power and influence (Ainsworth 2002). From Mark Smith's perspective, "Scholars widely concur that power is a slippery concept, a conclusion reflected most notably in the massive literature attempting to define, describe, and understand it. Given an element of ambiguity in what power really means, it is extremely difficult to prove whether any particular actor has exerted power; the best one can do is to marshal evidence" (2000, 87).

In discussing the difficulty in identifying and measuring influence, Baumgartner and Leech (1998) point out the problem of including all relevant factors in a model. "This is particularly difficult," they argue, "when dealing with such concepts of what a vote of a member of Congress might have been in the absence of any lobbying or when attempting to insure that all relevant facts that might have influenced the member's decision have been identified and measured" (1998, 37). They question whether the concept of influence can be measured. They summarize their highly critical review of the literature by observing:

> To the extent that we attempt to define influence narrowly and in the context of a single decision, we inevitably fail in two ways. First, the models are rarely specified fully and are therefore doomed to fail. (This is especially true of the empirical models as opposed to the formal specifications, which are sometimes more complete.) Second, we are led to the adoption of overly narrow definitions of what lobbying is and how influence is wielded in politics. Most importantly, it leads us to study lobbying only at the very last stage of the decision-making process. Ironically, many scholars agree that this is where the possible exertion of influence is at its lowest point. (1998, 38)

Their concerns will be kept in mind as the study progresses.

### The Business Advantage?

Mark Smith's (2000) provocative investigation explores the widely held assumption that business dominates the policymaking process when it is unified on specific policy issues, thereby undermining democracy. Using the policy positions of the U.S. Chamber of Commerce as a guide, he identifies 2,364 unifying issues that were considered by Congress between 1953 and 1996. His list of unifying issues encompasses a wide range of policy areas including employment policy, labor-management relations, and clean air regulation. Agenda building in Congress over time is his dependent variable. Among the independent variables he analyzes are "public mood" (Stimson 1999), public attitudes toward corporations, partisan composition of Congress, "presidential leadership opening" (that is, when partisan turnover in Congress runs in the president's favor), corporate PAC funding, and the state of the economy. Mark Smith finds that

> unity does not increase the direct influence of business and reduce democratic control by the citizenry. Instead, unity coincides with the opposite results. Issues marked by a common business position are precisely those for which government decisions are affected most strongly by election outcomes and the responsiveness of officeholders to their constituents. Policies match the collective desires of business only when citizens, through their policy preferences and voting choices, embrace ideas and candidates supportive of what business wants. To bolster its odds of winning in politics, business needs to seek backing from the broad public. (2000, 8)

According to Mark Smith (2000), therefore, only when the public supports the unified positions of business on policy issues does business achieve its legislative goals. When the public opposes the positions of business, however, Congress tends to follow the public will even though business is unified. Since all unifying policy issues are highly ideological, partisan, and salient, Congress nearly always follows the public on these issues. He concludes by stating, "The long-standing debates over unity among pluralists, elite theorists, and ruling class theorists have focused our attention in the wrong place. Widespread scholarly concerns about business unity are misplaced, for unifying issues are marked by the highest, rather than the lowest, degree of democratic control by the citizenry" (2000, 200). Smith's interpretation of his findings places him in the neopluralist camp along with Baumgartner and Leech (1998) and Berry (1999).

Smith (2000) also argues that researchers should focus their attention on cases where single firms or small groups of companies or industries pursue their own specific interests without involving the rest of American business or when firms are significantly divided over an issue due to tension within the business community. These alignments, in addition to when companies are unified, should account for nearly all the scenarios when business tries to promote or hinder government actions. In investigating the influence of business over environmental policymaking, the present study examines these alignments as well as when business is unified.

One can question Mark Smith's (2000) conclusions about the effect of public opinion on congressional agenda building when business is unified on several grounds. First, as even Smith (2000) admits, it is rare that business is unified on policy issues. Studies by Vogel (1978) and Wilson (1990) show that the American business community is fragmented compared to business communities in other developed nations. Smith himself calculates that during the period of his analysis American business was unified on only 7 *percent* of all issues (2000, 70). Therefore, the number of times democracy is served during the five decades he examines is indeed small. Second, business unity is not static and can rapidly break down for any number of reasons (McFarland 1998). Similarly, as Stimson (1999) shows, public opinion and the public mood are subject to critical shifts over time. Third, it is difficult to demonstrate with certainty that public opinion is directly influencing how Congress votes on unifying issues. It is also possible that, in cases where Smith finds congruence between public opinion and business interests on unifying issues, every sector of the country—not only the public and business but all opposing interest groups as well—strongly supports a particular action by Congress. If Congress is not willing to abide by a consensus of all citizens, leaders, and interests throughout the nation on a proposed policy, then when can it ever be expected to follow the will of the people? On those occasions where public opinion runs counter to a unified business lobby, it could be that opposing interest groups are equally dug in and unified against business, thereby leading to the defeat of business in Congress. Unfortunately, Smith does not measure the intensity of support or opposition from other interest groups in his research. He does, however, note the importance of counter mobilization in his book. His failure to consider the varying contexts surrounding the passage of specific bills where business is unified significantly limits his ability to explain his findings. Finally, no attempt is made to learn about the internal culture and organizational dynamics of companies and to solicit the views of corporate managers (that is, top- and middle-level managers) on the lobbying tactics and strategies they pursued to influence agenda building in Congress. Such an investigation might shed light on whether business lobbyists adopted different approaches depending on the politics surrounding an issue. Conceivably, these choices—in addition to other factors—may explain their success or failure in the legislative process. Nevertheless, Smith's findings are significant and deserve further scrutiny, particularly in distinct policy areas like the environment and in cases where business is thought to be divided on the issues. This study includes many of the independent variables and the dependent variable Smith analyzes in his research to assess the influence of business over environmental policymaking in the Congress and elsewhere in government.

Baumgartner and Leech (1998) also ask whether business possesses a major advantage in the policymaking process in their research. They observe that nearly all analyses of the interest group community over time find that different types of organizations grow at different rates. Previous studies have disagreed, however, on the significance of these varying growth patterns. In an extensive study, Schlozman and Tierney (1986), for instance, find that although many new types of organizations have formed since 1960, these new groups do not comprise a more significant component in the interest group community. In contrast, they report that the business bias in the pressure community is increasing dramatically, providing business with a bigger advantage in agenda building. According to the two researchers, companies make up nearly 50 percent of the organizations represented in Washington DC. In addition, more than 75 percent of the groups represent business or professional interests of some kind. In their view, "If anything, the distribution of organizations within the Washington pressure community is even more heavily weighted in favor of business organizations than it used to be" (Schlozman and Tierney 1986, 388).

Baumgartner and Leech (1998) argue that while many researchers agree with Schlozman and Tierney (1986) that business is a key player in the interest group community, fewer agree with them that the business advantage is increasing over time (see, for example, Boyte 1980; Hadwiger

1982; Walker 1983; W. Browne 1988). There are two reasons for this. First, Schlozman and Tierney's own data show a more recent growth of nonbusiness interests in Washington. (These data agree with Berry's [1999] findings.) Second, the two researchers do not use a complete set of comparable data on which to base their results. Therefore, "the evidence that business dominance has increased since the 1960s is limited at best" (Baumgartner and Leech 1998, 107).

Nevertheless, a number of recent studies underscore the continued unique importance of business in American politics. As Libby (1998) explains, in a market economy government does everything it can to maintain good economic performance, including providing extensive "inducements" such as favorable tax, monetary, rail, highway, air, and tariff policies (see also Lindblom 1977). Libby asserts, "Thus business elites are more than simple representatives of special interests: they perform a quasi-public function that political leaders regard as indispensable. In other words, business elites are first among equals in the world of interest-group politics" (1998, 4). Korten (1995), Clawson, Neustadtl, and Weller (1998), Lehne (2001), Nounes (2002), and others offer many examples of how business dominates numerous aspects of American politics, including legislative, bureaucratic, and judicial agenda building. In the environmental policy arena specifically, Glazer and Rothenberg (2001) reveal how the American automobile companies have consistently opposed government regulation to reduce emissions and increase the fuel efficiency of their vehicles. As deadlines approach, the typical response by these companies has been that meeting regulatory goals is neither technologically nor financially feasible and that, without a postponement, they will need to reduce production and lay off thousands of workers. Lindblom (1977) and others believe that despite the decline of corporate influence during the 1960s and 1970s, other interest groups still cannot compete with the wealth and resources of business. Indeed, Rozell and Wilcox (1999) report a sharp rise in campaign contributions by corporate PACs during the last three decades, far outpacing the amount contributed by other interest groups. Therefore, Vogel (1996) contends that business, compared to other groups, exerts a significant influence in American politics.

Fellowes and Wolf's (2004) research reexamines the influence of business campaign contributions on congressional voting behavior. They argue that previous analyses have not fully considered the different funding mechanisms campaign contributors use to channel funds to legislators or the diversity of legislative policy instruments (for example, favorable tax bills and regulatory relief) used to reward contributors. Their study examines both individual and PAC campaign contributions from business groups and creates several indexes of macrobusiness policy votes in the 105th House of Representatives. Their findings reveal that "aggregate business campaign contributions do influence macro-level pro-business tax and regulatory policy votes—much more than mere access into the policy process or an occasional low-profile vote" (2004, 321). These results support a theory of "tactical rationality" that predicts representatives employ varied policy instruments to balance the benefits and costs associated with rewarding business campaign contributors. By carefully calculating the benefits and costs associated with the employment of diverse policy instruments and acting accordingly, they minimize the electoral risk of appearing in a quid pro quo relationship with corporations. Following this strategy allows them to attract large contributions to remain in office and cultivate favor among party leaders. This explains why business groups regularly contribute considerable sums of money to candidates each election cycle, but, on the surface, appear to gain no policy advantage from their sizeable investment (2004, 321).

In support of Baumgartner and Leech's (1998) position, Baumgartner and Jones (1993) report significant changes in the environmental interest group sphere and show dramatic growth in the numbers of environmental groups and the resources available to them. Based on their analysis, the number of environmental organizations nearly tripled from 1960 to 1990, and the combined staff reported by those groups increased nearly ten times. This surge in environmental group membership is one of the most important reasons for the enactment of so many major environmental laws during the 1970s and 1980s, often over the protests of powerful business lobbyists.

Since 1990, however, the size and resources of environmental groups have fluctuated, the competition over membership, donations, and credit for successful initiatives has intensified, and disagreements among groups have emerged (Bosso 2005). During the 1990s citizen groups became extremely sophisticated and effective at contacting Americans and persuading them to become members of their groups. Use of the Internet and advanced computer technologies aided them in this effort (Kraft and Wuertz 1996; Bosso and Collins 2002; Duffy 2003). Barring a major environmental crisis, one wonders whether the membership pool for environmental groups has bottomed out and whether there is any more room for existing groups to expand dramatically or for the addition of large environmental groups in the interest group system. In fact, several groups have been criticized for accepting substantial funding from corporate donors, a move that may be attributed to a falling off of contributions by individuals (Dowie 1995). The Nature Conservancy, for example, accepted $140 million in corporate funding (from Cadillac, Georgia-Pacific, Merrill Lynch, and others) in 2003 alone (Nature Conservancy 2003, 74). Further, environmental groups have not always been united on major policy issues, and continued disagreements about trade, immigration, population growth, environmental justice, and other issues might undermine their ability to collaborate and influence citizens and policymakers in the future (Dowie 1995). Thus, the worst may be over for business lobbyists. Vogel (1989), McFarland (1991, 1998), and others correctly observe that the influence of business, like other interest groups, surges and declines with changes in the nature of the times. It seems, however, that business organizations have more staying power and are more resilient over time than other interest groups in American politics.

Prior to the enactment of major campaign finance reform in 2002, Clawson, Neustadtl, and Weller (1998) analyzed the extent to which campaign contributions by business are a way of gaining access to elected leaders. Although this access is invaluable, "it does not—and is not expected to—*guarantee* [their emphasis] a quid pro quo" (1998, 6). Instead, from their standpoint,

> business uses campaign contributions in a way few other groups do, as part of an "access" process that provides corporations a chance to shape the details of legislation, crafting loopholes that undercut the stated purpose of the law. Other groups do this on rare occasions; business does so routinely. Businesses are far more likely than other donors to give to *both* [their emphasis] sides in a race. (Clawson, Neustadtl, and Weller 1998, 13; see also Nounes 2002)

In terms of environmental legislation, Clawson and his colleagues (1998) argue that corporations have done very well politically; environmental laws have cost them a fraction of the money needed to improve air and water quality, manage the disposal of hazardous and toxic wastes, and meet federal regulatory standards. Specifically concerning the Clean Air Act of 1990, they contend that business lobbied for and got a weak, ineffective, and unenforceable law (see also Cahn 1995; Gonzalez 2001).[3] Once the Clean Air Act was enacted, the fight continued at the EPA over specific standards, particularly those concerning acid rain regulations. According to Clawson, Neustadtl, and Weller (1998), business did lose on the proposed tough new rules for soot and smog adopted during the Clinton administration, but only after an intense lobbying campaign by polluters. The three investigators conclude, "The disparity in power between business and environmentalists looms large during the legislative process, but it is enormous afterward" (1998, 10). As they show, business often redirects its lobbying efforts toward the EPA (or a natural resource agency) after Congress has passed and the president has signed an environmental bill. It is therefore necessary to assess the role of business once the rulemaking process begins (Kerwin 2003). As Baumgartner and Leech (1998) point out, only a very few studies have pursued this line of inquiry. This study investigates the influence of business over rulemaking involving environmental and natural resource issues.

### Lobbying Administrative Agencies and the Courts

Lehne (2001) has closely examined the nature and extent of business lobbying in administrative agencies. His observations have important implications for business lobbying at the EPA and agencies that manage natural resources, such as the Forest Service, Bureau of Land Management, and Fish and Wildlife Service. Government agencies perform three functions in the policy process that affect companies. First, as experts, agencies frequently contribute their views and analyses when legislative programs are being formulated. Second, agencies translate statutory generalities into detailed administrative rules (that is, rulemaking). Third, agencies decide how administrative rules are applied to individual cases (Lehne 2001, 155). The often technical nature of legislation and a lack of public opinion and media attention provide business with an excellent opportunity to influence policy and rules. Further, many bureaucratic decisions affect individual companies rather than classes of firms, giving each company a better chance to triumph in front of an agency than before Congress. Given the circumstances and conditions surrounding administrative decision making, it is not surprising for Uslaner to remark, "Cabinet departments and all manner of independent agencies . . . are gold mines for lobbyists" (1998, 206).[4] Clearly, environmental groups rarely have the resources to mount an effective opposition to such business efforts in the agencies (Furlong 1997).

When important decisions by government agencies do not favor the interests of corporations, businesses will often seek litigation. The courts, therefore, are another institutional venue in which business lobbying takes place (Lehne 2001). Many large corporations boast impressive in-house legal staffs to study laws and proposed regulations and, when advantageous, pursue litigation to protect their interests. Although litigation concerning environmental rules and regulations is fairly common, little systematic research has been done on how successful business has been in court. Scholars have found, however, that business is frequently a major player in environmental litigation and often gets its way (McSpadden 2000; O'Leary 2006). Any accurate assessment of the influence of business in the environmental policy arena should, in addition to other things, consider the success of corporations in the judicial system. Accordingly, this study conducts such an analysis.

### The New Role of Business in Environmental Policymaking

Cooperation and collaboration between business groups and government increased during the 1990s, with certain companies publicly announcing that they now wish to go "beyond compliance" and join the "greening of industry" movement (N. Miller 2002). Taking advantage of this change in perspective on the part of corporate America, the EPA launched a number of voluntary government programs to encourage even more companies to follow this path. The 33/50 program was begun in 1991, just prior to President Clinton taking office, with the goal of reducing releases of seventeen high-priority chemicals by 33 percent by 1992 and 50 percent by 1995. According to the U.S. General Accounting Office, the program has achieved a moderate level of success (Press and Mazmanian 2003). The Energy Star program, which began in June 1992, certifies energy-efficient appliances, electronic equipment, personal computers and computer equipment, and many other products. By 2001 there were more than eleven thousand Energy Star–compliant products widely used in the United States and in other nations, resulting in considerable energy and cost savings (Press and Mazmanian 2003). Project XL (eXcellence and Leadership) was launched in November 1995 as an attempt to reward superior corporate environmental performers with greater statutory and regulatory flexibility. The program permits industry a certain degree of latitude in seeking cleaner, cost-effective environmental management strategies. According to Beardsley, Davies, and Hersh (1997), the program has had few environmental benefits and requires new authorizing legislation to enhance its limited incentives for participation. The Common Sense Initiative (CSI) was designed to move environmental protection beyond the traditional command-and-control, pollutant-by-pollutant approach to a novel industrial sector-by-sector approach aimed at developing integrated, comprehensive strategies for protecting air and water quality and land (U.S. EPA 1998). An analysis by Coglianese and Allen (2004) reveals that, despite claims by federal government officials, only a handful of the projects developed under CSI have produced technological innovations, prevented pollution, or resulted in any other significant policy change. Instead, most of the projects resulted only in the development of educational material or the collection of information. In 2002 and 2003 the EPA established the Design for the Environment (DfE) program and the Sector Strategies program, respectively.[5]

Industry, too, has taken the initiative and has developed voluntary programs that attempt to improve its environmental management practices. The Responsible Care program, for example, was instituted by the Chemical Manufacturers Association (CMA) in the wake of the explosion at a chemical plant in Bhopal, India, in 1984 (Garcia-Johnson 2000). Responsible Care is a comprehensive program containing a variety of elements from community education and emergency response to pollution prevention, process safety, and employee health. The CMA openly admits that the purpose of this program is to quiet criticism of their industry by improving the environmental, health, and safety performance record of their members (N. Miller 2002). Garcia-Johnson (2000) argues that multinational companies in the United States–based chemical industry are successfully exporting corporate voluntarism in the form of environmentalism through Responsible Care. This program, however, has had mixed success in the United States to date. Regardless of their motives, in recent years industry has indeed shown some willingness to address difficult pollution and natural resource problems on its own (see, for example, United Nations Conference on Trade and Development Programme on Transnational Corporations 1993; Hoffman 2000; Prakash 2000; Robbins 2001; Winter 2002).

Although business and government have welcomed this new era of cooperation, collaboration, and initiative, environmental groups have been quite skeptical about the new relationship between business and government as well as the so-called greening of industry. This skepticism was fueled by certain events that took place during the George W. Bush administration. Following on the heals of the Enron Corporation debacle, for example, the Bush administration was forced to release thousands of documents in spring 2002 detailing the work of the Energy Task Force, headed by Vice President Richard Cheney, whose main job was to develop a national energy plan (Simon, Sanders, and Shogren 2002; Van Natta and Banerjee 2002). Among other things, the documents starkly revealed frequent meetings and close collaboration between the U.S. Department of Energy and the nation's largest oil, coal, natural gas, and nuclear power companies and associations (Simon, Sanders, and Shogren 2002; Van Natta and Banerjee 2002). A large majority of the firms consulted were major donors to President Bush's 2000 presidential campaign (Simon and Shogren 2002). Environmental groups were excluded from these consultations despite the fact that future energy policy decisions would directly impact the environment. Not surprisingly, this incident added to the doubts already shared by many environmentalists about the close relationship between business and government in general, and the Bush administration in particular.

Such occurrences and the limited success of the new "beyond compliance" voluntary efforts have led to charges by environmentalists of "greenwashing."[6] Some environmentalists, for example, have accused Ford's launching of the 2005 Ford Escape electric and gasoline powered hybrid sports utility vehicle (SUV), which averages 31 miles per gallon, as an attempt by the automaker to appear "in harmony with nature," while a vast majority of its fleet is comprised of fuel-inefficient automobiles and "gas-guzzling" SUVs (Johnson 2004). In addition, the Shell Oil Company has spent a great deal of money on advertisements about its association with the Flower Garden Banks National Marine Sanctuary. Nevertheless, the oil company still drills for oil and natural gas in the Gulf of Mexico where the sanctuary is located. Pacific Lumber, a large logging company, is trying to redefine itself by changing its name to the more agreeable Palco and is simultaneously widely advertising its new "environmental commitment." However, the firm continues to clear-cut forests (Johnson 2004). Likewise, British Petroleum spent more than $180 million in 2000 to introduce its new name, BP, to the public and adopted the environmentally friendly slogan, "beyond petroleum," in an effort to promote itself as an alternative energy company. Yet, its Web site clearly states that the company's main activities are the exploration and production of crude oil and natural gas, refining, and the manufacturing and marketing of petrochemicals.

Most environmentalists believe the new voluntary programs and initiatives are largely symbolic. As Press and Mazmanian (2003) astutely observe, while many business managers are willing to alter and improve their operations in the short run, few are willing to make the necessary changes to promote the establishment of sustainable societies in the long run. The two researchers identify four major reasons why industry is reluctant to embrace even the most rudimentary level of greening:

1. Despite financial benefits, many managers view P2—pollution prevention—as an extension of existing costly and burdensome regulatory programs.
2. Accounting systems are still inadequate to measure the costs and savings of pollution prevention.
3. P2 involves changing production processes, which introduces risks that some plant managers are reluctant to take.
4. Investments in waste reduction programs compete with other demands on capital that are thought by managers to be of more strategic importance. Top management of many companies, while supporting the concept of pollution prevention, is not involved closely enough in promoting its implementation. (Press and Mazmanian 2003, 278)

It is unlikely that these obstacles will be overcome in the near future. Company managers will first have to undergo a significant value transformation before they will be willing to change their practices and participate actively in the development of sustainable communities. Among other things, there will need to be a substantial change in the culture and internal characteristics of most of today's largest corporations before a paradigm shift can take place. Rather than asking how much new approaches will cost or how much can be saved, business managers must begin to ask themselves what will happen if they take no action to improve environmental quality and conserve natural resources.

### Ecological Modernization

The term "ecological modernizaton" was first introduced in the early 1980s by Huber (1982) and by Janicke (1985). The idea received international attention in 1984 at the Organization for Economic Cooperation and Development's Conference on Environment and Economics. Hajer (1995) considers the Brundtland Report (World Commission on Environment and Development 1987) an important document on ecological modernization. Environmental degradation, Hajer (1995) says, is viewed as a structural problem that can only be effectively addressed through the economic system, but not in a way that necessitates a radical alteration of the political-economic scheme. Rather, pollution control strategies and other environmental protection approaches must be built into the redesign of the scheme. Ecological modernization is based on the premise that "the capitalist political economy needs conscious reconfiguring and far-sighted action so that economic development and environmental protection can proceed hand-in-hand and reinforce one another" (Dryzek 1997, 143). In comparing ecological modernization with sustainable development, Dryzek argues that "ecological modernization has a much sharper focus than does sustainable development on exactly what needs to be done with the capitalist political economy, especially within the confines of the developed nation state" (1997, 143).

Ecological modernization is achieved not through an adversarial process, but by bringing government and business together within a cooperative framework. Government intervenes by imposing design criteria and other policy measures on industry. Industry itself cooperates enthusiastically in the formulation and implementation of environmental policy (Dryzek 1997). Industry benefits because less pollution means more efficient production; problems are addressed in the present and not in the future when they will be more costly to solve; workers are pleased that they are employed by a "green" company; and profits are made by producing and selling green goods and services as well as pollution-prevention and -abatement products (Dryzek 1997).

In Robbins's (2001) view, ecological modernization is a historical phase of modern industrial society. It draws on the risk-society model that suggests contemporary "postscarcity" society is increasingly defined by distributions of environmental risk instead of distributions of wealth. Underpinning this model of society is the uncertainty of risks and the potentially devastating consequences from living with the effects of unforeseen environmental problems (Robbins 2001). Although proponents of ecological modernization agree that scientific uncertainty and contemporary global risks exist, they are optimistic about the ability of government, science, technology, and industry to resolve serious environmental problems.

Further, ecological modernization suggests that industry has become increasingly aware of the negative effects of pollution and that the best way out of the global environmental crisis is for society to become even more modernized. Ecological crises can be addressed in a rational manner by soliciting the help of a wide array of knowledgeable people, including corporate managers, natural scientists, economists, politicians, legal experts, and others (Robbins 2001). By working together, these individuals can accurately measure the extent of a community's pollution problem, develop the appropriate response, and formulate and implement the required technological solution in a cost-effective manner (Alperovitz 2005). This, in turn, will allow environmental protection and economic growth to continue. As Robbins explains, "Ecological modernization theorizes the ways in which environmental and economic contradictions (characteristic of many debates in the 1960s and 1970s) have been decoupled, integrated and converged to create a plan for the continued development of modern industrialized societies that includes both growth and environmental responsibility (characteristic of the 1980s, 1990s and beyond)" (2001, 25).

The proponents of ecological modernization maintain that technology, not nature, is out of control. If properly directed, technology can provide the answers to many of the world's environmental difficulties. Ecological modernization provides society with choices concerning how to use technology to protect the natural environment and further economic growth simultaneously (Robbins 2001). By working closely together, business and government can solve almost any environmental or natural resource problem. To the extent that ecological modernization is actually practiced, it has the potential to correct capitalism's uncontrolled and unlimited consumption of natural resources.

Deep ecologists, however, are uneasy with the notion of ecological modernization because it threatens to divert criticisms away from industrial society (Christoff 1996; Mol 2001; Dryzek et al. 2003; York and Rosa 2003). It has the potential to co-opt the moral and ethical imperatives that originally inspired and continue to drive the environmental movement, which is perhaps why it appeals to both industry and government. As a privileged discourse among many competing discourses, environmentalists worry that it can postpone critical discussions (and actions) concerning the root causes of present-day environmental degradation.

Whether ecological modernization, which places considerable emphasis on institutional learning, collaboration, and compromise, can evolve quickly enough (or at all) to avert serious environmental and natural resource problems in the future is uncertain. Political obstacles, such as the incentive for elected officials to satisfy short-term needs at the expense of long-term considerations so they can be reelected, stand in the way of meeting the goals of ecological modernization. In addition, the continued globalization of capitalism is likely to place greater demands for increased economic growth and higher standards of living that, in turn, will make it even more difficult for society to balance environmental quality, natural resource conservation, and economic development. In certain situations bargaining and compromise will not produce the kinds of decisions necessary to solve critical environmental issues, such as the protection of endangered species or the rapid depletion of particular nonrenewable resources. Such actions will require society to adopt comprehensive, long-term plans that address population growth and distribution, land-use patterns and habitat protection, energy consumption, economic expansion, water resource access and use, food-production needs, and various other environmental challenges (Alperovitz 2005). Whether effective and affordable "green" technologies can be developed and implemented quickly enough to allow all nations to attain higher standards of living, superior environmental quality, and, ultimately, sustainable societies is doubtful. In the end, consumers may be the ones who have to shoulder the financial burden of environmental protection and natural resource management.

Ultimately, a significant value transformation must first occur before we can achieve intergenerational equity and sustainable societies. Values reflecting the dominant social paradigm (for example, materialism, high rates of consumption, and uncontrolled growth) must be replaced by values reflecting the new environmental paradigm (for example, harmony between economic growth and environmental protection, greater reliance on renewable resources, and the need for high levels of environmental quality and quality of life) (Milbrath 1989). Such a value transformation must take place not just in industry and government but in all segments of society, including the general public.

### Summary

Previous studies of the role of business in public policymaking and in environmental policymaking report conflicting findings over how much influence business interests have over the contents of environmental and natural resource policy. Many researchers believe that business interests do have a major advantage in policymaking, while others feel that citizen groups have successfully halted the increasing power of corporate America. The research reported in this book offers critical insights into this debate.

Chapter 3 provides an understanding of the ways in which business shapes the government agenda and environmental policy by developing a general theoretical framework that explains how business influences policy at the individual company level, the industrial sector level, and the aggregate level. The theoretical framework reflects the critical role government institutions play in agenda building and environmental policymaking. The discussion now turns to possible theoretical explanations concerning how business affects policy.

# 3 Theories of Issue Definition, Framing, and Agenda Building

Researchers tend to emphasize different theoretical factors in their explanations and analyses of corporate behavior. Internal company characteristics, for example, are considered by those who analyze organization and management theory, sociological institutional theory, and stakeholder theory (for example, Prakash 2000; Robbins 2001). By contrast, those who examine theories of issue definition, framing, and agenda building focus on variables that normally lie outside the corporation and interest group (for example, Snow et al. 1986; Kingdon 1995; Druckman 2004). Although this study reviews theoretical principles concerning internal management dynamics, the question of how much business interests influence environmental policymaking at the national level is best answered by theories that highlight the importance of outside social, political, and economic forces.

A broad empirical approach is pursued in this investigation. This research analyzes the influence of business interests over agenda building in the environmental policy domain by conducting a quantitative analysis of corporate influence in Congress, the bureaucracy, and the judiciary. Case studies in which business plays a significant role in salient environmental controversies are examined as well. Although quantitative investigations yield generalizable findings, they tend to ignore context. Case studies permit good in-depth analysis; however, they produce findings that are often limited in the extent to which they can be generalized. By pursuing both these avenues of inquiry, this study takes advantage of the separate and counterbalancing strengths of the two different methodological approaches and, as a result, paints an extensive portrait of business influence in the environmental policy sphere.

In order to provide contextual background for the theoretical discussion, the discussion below first examines general issues regarding politics, economics, and environmental policy types and scenarios. Various theories concerning internal company management dynamics are briefly addressed. Then a number of political and economic variables that might account for the success of business in Congress and in other policymaking venues, such as government agencies and the courts, are reviewed. This is followed by a review of theories involving issue definition and framing processes and agenda building. The study's research design is presented at the end of the chapter. The analysis begins with a discussion of the key aspects of politics and economics that are relevant to business and environmental policymaking.

## Economics and Political Reality

As the previous chapter indicated, capitalism has been the dominant economic system throughout America's history. With its emphasis on the importance of private property and profit making, capitalism has provided the United States with unprecedented economic growth and a consistently high standard of living. By rewarding those who develop new manufacturing approaches and technologies, a strong economic incentive structure has arisen, leading to the development of many new inventions, products, advances in health care, and other highly valued benefits to society. The affluence of the United States is primarily due to an abundance of natural resources and close adherence to capitalist principles.

The American government and economic system was initially established to allow citizens and companies to develop freely as entrepreneurs and achieve the greatest economic wealth possible. By facilitating business success through a variety of tax policies, subsidies, and other financial incentives, corporations have been encouraged to grow in size and power over time with minimum interference from government. The result has been the development of generally cost-effective, efficient, and highly profitable corporations that employ millions of workers on a consistent basis (Lehne 2001).

The overall success of American business has led to the conventional wisdom that the private sector can do everything better than government. Most people believe that companies are run more effectively and efficiently and at lower cost compared to government. Those who perpetuate this view tend to overlook the large number of businesses that have filed for bankruptcy or that have been bought out by other companies because they were performing poorly and losing money. Apparently, the huge savings and loan collapse in the 1980s and the failure of a number of large corporations at the turn of the twentieth century have done little to alter these prevailing assumptions. While business is more apt than government to operate efficiently and effectively, it does not have a monopoly on achievement, especially in the area of providing social welfare. To be sure, the corporate world has had a mixed record in protecting and promoting the health, safety, and general well-being of society.

As neoclassical economic theory suggests, companies are unitary actors that seek to maximize profits (Hirshleifer 1988; Prakash 2000). Accordingly, businesses pursue only those strategies and projects that can be shown, ex ante, to be potentially profitable. Corporate managers estimate future benefits and costs and adopt projects that meet or exceed a given rate of return. Such projects are considered potentially profitable. Investment decisions are strategically made based on whether they will maximize the wealth of shareholders. This objective is widely shared among company leaders and normally leads to consensus among managers as to which direction the company should take (Prakash 2000).

Gonzalez (2001) argues that economic elites, more than anyone else, shape the content and implementation of American environmental policy to their economic and political advantage. Using Barrow's (1993) research as a guide, he defines economic elites as those persons who own or manage corporations. He notes that they represent between 0.5 and 1.0 percent of the population and are "the upper class and the upper echelon" of the business community (Gonzalez 2001, 14). Their vast wealth and income permits them to exercise substantial influence over government decision making, particularly within the environmental sphere. Although disagreements exist among economic elites, they are able to resolve their differences through various social institutions, "policy-planning networks," and other mechanisms quietly behind the scenes. In direct opposition to the traditional pluralist perspective, Gonzalez contends that economic elites have dictated the way government has managed the national forests and national parks, often with the intent to serve their narrow self-interests. They also are responsible for the enactment of basically ineffective wilderness preservation policy and national clean air policy.

Despite Gonzalez's (2001) efforts to provide evidence to support his arguments, his position is generally one sided. Although his study contains a number of perceptive insights, analysts (including pluralists and neopluralists) might contend that he exaggerates the power economic elites wield in American society by downplaying the oftentimes countervailing impact of the media, citizen groups, competing elites (public and private), federalism, and the government's system of checks and balances. If anything, environmental policymaking is a highly dynamic, complex process involving a wide array of independent and often competing actors and groups at different levels of government. Today, most environmentalists tend not to believe that policy is being formulated and implemented by a small, clandestine group of wealthy individuals. Most also do not call for a complete overhaul or the elimination of the capitalist system. Reflecting the central thrust of ecological modernization, they instead argue that the country can have both environmental protection and economic growth with the aid of science and technology.[1] Ehrlich and Ehrlich (1996), for instance, maintain that the United States can have stronger environmental protection and continued growth of the GNP, that environmental regulations do not reduce the competitiveness of American industry, and that stricter environmental regulations do not cost American jobs by forcing industries to relocate in nations with weaker regulations.

Business leaders, too, seem to have backed away from their earlier extreme claims and dire predictions concerning the U.S. adoption of environmental protection programs. Based on previous research, Press and Mazmanian note how certain companies have "evolved from being heavy polluters to conscientious pollution abaters by significantly reducing emissions, better managing wastes, reformulating products and production processes in order to use fewer natural resources and energy, and making goods recyclable, more durable, and less toxic" (2003, 287). This has occurred in leading-edge companies because of "visible involvement of corporate leadership in developing and promoting new management philosophies and infiltration of upper management by younger executives and women" (Press and Mazmanian 2003, 287).[2]

Despite these observations, a majority of companies have ignored government appeals and inducements and have not voluntarily improved their environmental record to any significant extent. One possible explanation for this might lie in the way universities train future business executives. The author of this study analyzed the graduate curriculum of the thirty top-ranked business schools in the country in 2002 (usnews.com 2003) to determine whether and, if so, to what extent students receive training in environmental studies. Among the thirty top business schools, only two have joint programs with an environmental law (Dartmouth) or environmental studies program (Duke) and only seven offer an environmental policy course. The remaining twenty-one schools do not offer any courses or training in the environmental field. The data suggest that a high percentage of individuals who receive a Master of Business Administration (MBA) or an equivalent graduate degree from the nation's elite business schools are never exposed to the kinds of environmental issues and problems they will face in the corporate world. The narrow training in business administration they receive most likely reinforces a strong desire for profit and leads to greater intransigence on environmental issues. These findings cast a dark cloud over future hopes for widespread support for environmental policy and regulation within the business community.

Economists explain why more firms have not gone beyond environmental compliance voluntarily by invoking the classic externalities problem (see, for example, Freeman 2006). Corporations have almost no incentive to pay for pollution abatement costs and lessen their impact on the environment so long as society does not hold them accountable. Press and Mazmanian observe:

> From a competitive standpoint, it makes little sense for them to voluntarily take on the added expenses of pollution abatement or production line modification. The central message of the economic analysis is that greening will not come voluntarily. It will take hold if the problem of acting progressively when others do not—the classic problem of collective action—is solved for the firm. (2003, 287–88)

Economists offer a variety of policy recommendations intended to internalize unwanted environmental externalities, including emissions taxes or fees and instituting emissions-trading programs (Freeman 2006).

For these policy proposals to work, however, their cost to companies involved will need to be considerable. Yet, in Press and Mazmanian's view,

> imposing such costs requires strong and effective environmental regulations, monitoring, and enforcement—that is, a dedicated, powerful government. This is the dilemma of the economists' prescriptions. Though their research may be analytically persuasive and their remedies internally consistent, they offer few avenues for overcoming the political hurdles and business costs of implementing their recommendations, making their adoption highly improbable and minimizing their effectiveness, especially on the global scale required. (2003, 288)

Whether this conundrum can be resolved in time to prevent serious harm to the environment and protect the country's natural resources is uncertain.

### Institutional Venues for Lobbying Activities

Within the environmental policy arena business groups often seek to protect their interests either by actively opposing proposals for new rules and legislation or by attempting to weaken existing regulations and standards. The mining industry, for example, has been successful at defeating efforts to revise the General Mining Law of 1872. Under this old legislation mining companies pay extremely low or nonexistent mining fees and royalties on use of public lands (Lowry 2000; Klyza 2001). In 1998 mining lobbyists and their congressional supporters in western states were able to beat back Clinton administration attempts to reform the law (C. Davis 1998). There are numerous other examples, including congressional rejection of stricter fuel-efficiency standards for automobiles, SUVs, and light trucks in 2002. Environmental groups pushed hard for the adoption of tougher fuel-efficiency requirements, while the automobile industry and automobile unions opposed the effort.

Although many battles over environmental regulations are fought in Congress, many others take place within the bureaucracy or the federal courts. During the Reagan administration, for example, various industrial sectors led an attack on the Clean Air and Clean Water Acts and the 1980 Comprehensive Environmental Response, Compensation, and Liability Act (CERCLA or Superfund). While much less successful in Congress, business was able to help persuade the incoming administrator of the

EPA, Anne M. Gorsuch (later Burford), and the new secretary of interior, James G. Watt, to review and in many cases rewrite the rules and procedures of their agencies to accommodate industries such as mining, logging, chemical, manufacturing, oil, coal, and natural gas (Vig 2003). Strict guidelines concerning deregulation and cost-benefit analysis were instituted, and the budgets and staff of the EPA and the Council on Environmental Quality were significantly cut (Vig 2006). Reagan viewed environmental protection as being fundamentally at odds with economic growth and prosperity, thereby permitting business to exert considerable influence over bureaucratic decision making. Obviously, who controls the White House plays a large role in determining the influence of business inside government agencies.

The federal courts have also been an institutional venue where business lobbyists challenge environmental standards and guidelines (O'Leary 1989, 2006; Fiorino 1995; McSpadden 2000). Business frequently shifts the conflict to the courts when they fail to defeat environmental measures in Congress and later in government agencies (Fiorino 1995). Of course, undertaking legal action is expensive, and business and environmental groups normally pursue this avenue selectively and when a great deal is at stake. To the contrary, McSpadden observes, "With their superior legal and economic resources, major corporations and trade associations have asked the courts to reinterpret environmental laws in a more probusiness light" (2000, 148). Business and industry have taken the EPA to court over environmental laws such as the Clean Air Act, Clean Water Act, and Superfund (McSpadden 1995). Likewise, the U.S. Fish and Wildlife Service has been brought into court over the implementation of the Endangered Species Act. In addition to the Federal District Trial Courts, the Circuit Court of Appeals for the District of Columbia has been frequently involved in environmental litigation because it is the seat of the federal government (Fiorino 1995). Exactly how well business interests have fared in federal court is addressed in this research.

### Types of Environmental Strategies Firms Pursue

Prakash (2000) maintains that firms today are less reluctant to implement environmental laws and are increasingly likely to adopt "beyond-compliance" environmental approaches that are tougher than the requirements of extant policies. He does not provide any empirical data, however, to support this observation. His study addresses why and how external factors (for example, governmental agencies, nongovernmental international organizations, industry-level associations, and customers) assist or prevent supporters (among managers) of beyond-compliance approaches to persuade their firms to adopt these approaches. Prakash (2000) considers ten cases where the two companies in his investigation, Baxter International Incorporated and Eli Lilly and Company, adopted beyond-compliance environmental programs. The managers within these firms, and not the firms themselves, are his units of analysis.

Assuming firms are profit maximizers, they can be expected to pursue environmental strategies that will, ex ante, equal or exceed their estimated profit following evaluation. From a managerial perspective, Prakash (2000) believes environmental strategies can be classified based on two conditions: whether they meet or exceed the ex ante profit criteria following evaluation, or whether they are legally required or are beyond-compliance.[3] Four types of strategies can be identified using these conditions:

Type 1: beyond compliance and meet or exceed the profit criteria;

Type 2: beyond compliance but cannot or do not meet the profit criteria;

Type 3: required by law and meet or exceed the profit criteria; and

Type 4: required by law but cannot or do not meet the profit criteria. (Prakash 2000, 3)

Firms are expected to adopt Type 3 and Type 4 environmental strategies because they are required by law to do so. In addition, companies have a strong incentive (that is, making money) to adopt Type 1 environmental approaches; therefore, they are expected to pursue such avenues. Prakash (2000) argues that managers are most likely to disagree on the economic advantages of Type 2 decisions. As a consequence, companies will only follow these strategies for reasons other than profit (for example, they could influence environmental rules and guidelines if they themselves adopt such measures and gain "first-mover" advantages). Given the importance placed on profit generation in the economic system in the United States, however, one would hypothesize that the more costly a voluntary environmental strategy is to a firm, the less likely it will implement it.

Prakash (2000) is most interested in the question, why do companies selectively adopt beyond-compliance environmental strategies and programs? He addresses this question by examining how managers perceive and interpret external pressures and act on them. He deals exclusively with Type 2 environmental strategies in his analysis of Baxter International Incorporated and Eli Lilly and Company. Both are multinational firms and are in the health care industry. Prakash's goal is to discover why some managers are able to persuade their companies to pursue beyond-compliance strategies, while other managers are unsuccessful at doing so. His findings are reported and discussed later in the chapter.

At the international level, the United Nations Conference on Trade and Development Programme on Transnational Corporations (1993) has collected survey data on the general management orientations of companies with operations in more than one country and with annual sales in excess of one billion dollars. The main purpose of the study is to measure the current state of international corporate environmental management. Many companies based in the United States participated in the survey. According to the study, a number of multinational corporations now address environmental management issues, and top management tends to be the prime initiator of environmental initiatives in corporations.

The data from this research show that corporations have chosen markedly different ways of tackling the environmental challenge. Based on the answers provided by the respondents, there are four different management approaches being utilized: compliance-oriented management; preventive management; strategic environmental management; and sustainable development management. Briefly, compliance-oriented management is the lowest level in the evolution of corporate management practices and is oriented toward compliance with existing laws and standards. (Profit aside, this approach mirrors Prakash's [2002] Type 3 and Type 4 strategies.) Preventive management goes beyond mere compliance and seeks pollution prevention and the reduction of resource use. Strategic environmental management integrates environmental protection in the overall business strategy of a corporation and attempts to seize the business opportunities of expanding green markets. Finally, a small number of multinational companies have begun to consider their role in sustainable development in a fundamental way and have adopted business practices to protect the global commons. No doubt, the last management type is the preferred model among those who are concerned the most about the future of the world's ecosystem. Unfortunately, only very few American firms pursue this management approach.

### Types of Business Alignments

As discussed in the previous chapter, Mark Smith (2000) classifies policy issues based on the alignments among firms. As he explains, when business organizes around major policy issues, these issues are considered unifying issues. Legislators seek public input because these issues tend to be highly politicized (that is, these issues tend to be ideological, partisan, and salient among the public). This increases public influence and decreases the influence of business in the legislative process. Business interests triumph when they are on the same side as public opinion or when they are successful in shaping public opinion. Companies experience defeat when public opinion runs counter to their positions.

Smith (2000) classifies other policy issues as either particularistic or conflictual. Particularistic issues are where individual firms or small subgroups of companies pursue their own specific interests without involving the rest of business. A single company or a narrow sector of industry enters a policy debate and lobbies government. As Smith (2000) observes, this perspective can be traced back to Cater (1964), McConnell (1966), and Lowi (1979), who maintain that policymaking takes place within insulated spheres. These institutional settings, referred to as "subsystems," "subgovernments," or "iron triangles," allow for a small number of private- and public-sector players to reach mutually beneficial decisions by cooperating with one another (M. Smith 2000). Since most of these types of interactions take place in the political background, companies are able to exert considerable influence on matters most important to them and often succeed in accomplishing their objectives. The lumber industry or mining companies, for example, often approach the U.S. Forest Service or the Bureau of Land Management, respectively, to obtain favorable rules or exemptions. Since particularistic issues vary widely and, by definition, are highly specific in nature, companies normally do not oppose each other.

The overall cumulative impact, however, substantially privileges American business. In fact, Godwin and Seldon (2002) argue that researchers have underestimated this type of lobbying by corporations and have overestimated coalition behavior of corporate lobbyists.

Conflictual issues are characterized by tensions within the business arena (M. Smith 2000). Anywhere from two individual companies to different groups of firms might disagree on policy goals and will battle one another. Whereas fossil fuel companies oppose regulations on greenhouse gas emissions, for example, the nuclear power industry generally favors them (Nuclear Energy Institute 2004). The ability of opposing interests to expand the scope of conflict can help determine their success or failure in the policymaking process (Schattschneider 1960).

Although Mark Smith (2000) focuses on the business community in his analysis, his typology is also applicable to the environmental movement and other interests in American politics. Environmental groups, perhaps even more than business, have joined forces and presented a united front on such issues as clean air and water policy. Nevertheless, there have been times when they have taken different positions on salient issues (for example, the North American Free Trade Agreement and the Restoration Plan for the Florida Everglades, both conflictual issues) (Vos 1997). In some instances a single environmental organization or a small group of similar organizations has pursued a specific issue (for example, ocean dumping and nuclear waste disposal, both particularistic issues). In addition to other factors, whether environmental groups are united or not (as well as whether business is united or divided) is likely to determine the success or failure of their proactive and countermobilization efforts. Whether environmental groups are united, conflicted, or operating in isolation will be noted at appropriate points in the study.

### The Theoretical Framework

Figure 3.1 presents a general outline of the theoretical framework that is used to analyze the influence of business over environmental policymaking in this study. A set of theories and explanations are provided under the broad topics of internal company management dynamics, political and economic variables, and issue definition and framing processes. In most cases these theories and explanations have important implications

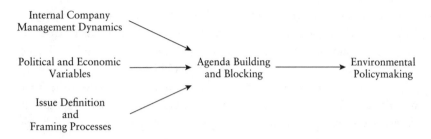

FIGURE 3.1.  Theoretical Framework for Analyzing the Influence of Business over Environmental Policymaking

(as suggested by the arrows) for the development of the public (or issue) agenda and the government (or formal) agenda. Likewise, several theories of agenda building and agenda blocking should help explain how firms mold environmental policy. The theories listed under the four categories identified in Figure 3.1 should provide critical insights into corporate influence over environmental policy.

The theoretical framework shown in Figure 3.1 is not directly tested in this research. Rather, the purpose of the figure is to provide readers with a summary of the overarching theoretical perspective employed in this investigation. The individual theories that fall under the general headings in the figure are applied at appropriate points in the study. Readers are encouraged to refer back to Figure 3.1, as well as the tables containing the different theories under each category included in this chapter, as they move through the analysis.

### Internal Company Management Dynamics

Most interest group studies analyze companies as a population and pay almost no attention to the critical internal management dynamics of individual firms. As the September 11, 2001, attack on the World Trade Center in New York City vividly showed, companies are not faceless, impersonal entities; they are comprised of hard-working people who have families, friends, and a life outside the workplace. Managers who help run companies generally are well-educated and well-trained individuals who hold particular attitudes, values, and philosophical viewpoints like everyone else. These are the people who make the important and difficult decisions and help steer their firms toward profitability without harming their public image. Managers basically determine the extent to which their companies improve environmental quality and conserve natural resources.

Often, corporate officers must take sides in policy debates and decide on the tactics and strategies to use to influence Congress, federal agencies, and other parts of the government in order to protect and promote their interests. The path corporate managers choose to follow is not based on an exact science of politics but rather on educated estimates of how to influence government officials and institutions most effectively at the lowest cost. Although much can be gained by studying the general business population or business sectors, researchers must also analyze the internal dynamics and decision-making process of individual companies if they hope to paint a full picture of why and how business affects public policymaking, including environmental policymaking.

Prakash (2000) investigates how sociological institutional theory, stakeholder theory, and the new institutional framework might explain whether managers support the adoption of beyond-compliance initiatives in cases where profit is not a significant criterion (his Type 2 strategy). Institutional theory emphasizes the impact of external institutions on the decisions made by managers (see, for example, Scott 1987; Oliver 1991; Hoffman 1997).[4] As opposed to neoclassical economics that emphasizes the institutions of markets and governments, institutional theory considers other social institutions as well. Companies are not profit maximizers, and their decisions reflect external pressures for legitimacy (Prakash 2000). Whereas neoclassical economics emphasizes the importance of maximizing the wealth of shareholders, stakeholder theory suggests that companies adopt strategies taking into account the preferences of multiple stakeholders (for example, Clarkson 1995; Donaldson and Preston 1995). In this vein, companies have societal responsibilities other than increasing the wealth of shareholders and decide to pursue certain approaches because they are simply "the right things to do" (Prakash 2000). Lastly, new institutionalists treat decisions by managers as institutions and companies themselves as organizations. Thus, Prakash (2000) considers the Type 2 strategies he examines in his study as a specific category of institutions. New institutionalists do not treat businesses as unitary actors and make a distinction between companies and individual actors in explaining decision making. Based on his analysis, Prakash finds mixed support for social institutional theory and stakeholder theory and more compelling evidence for the new institutional framework in explaining why the two companies he studies adopt beyond-compliance strategies.

Robbins (2001) investigates whether the theoretical orientation of the sociology of management can account for the "corporate greening" of four firms, Atlantic Richfield Corporation Chemical Company-Europe, Ben and Jerry's Homemade, Incorporated, The Body Shop International, and the Royal Dutch/Shell Group of Companies.[5] Under the general rubric of the sociology of management he includes rational choice theory, organizational theory, and corporate culture. In rational choice theory, managers seek to maximize their personal preference satisfaction by maximizing benefits to themselves and minimizing costs. Applying rational choice theory to environmental issues and policy, managers are likely to believe that environmental regulations are obstacles to profit maximization, especially in the short run. As a result, they will attempt to block regulations or, failing that, ensure that the regulations are minimal in order to promote wealth creation (Robbins 2001). The component concept of bounded rationality suggests that, though intending to act rationally, managers are prevented from doing so because they frequently do not possess all of the required information to make truly informed, therefore rational, decisions (March and Simon 1958). Collecting accurate data in a timely fashion is necessary to overcome bounded rationality. In deciding which environmental strategies to implement, managers will try to achieve goals that they consider attainable rather than an overall "maximizing goal." Rational choice theory is derived from classical economics theory and closely mirrors central elements of neoclassical economics theory.

Corporate responses to environmental problems occur within corporate structures that need to be understood as well (Robbins 2001). Using Weber's (1947) work as a starting point, organizational sociologists analyze a variety of managerial styles and institutional forms. Whether a company is more hierarchical and centralized or whether it is more vertical and decentralized may have a bearing on its ability to change current practices and develop and implement new, beyond-compliance environmental programs. Much depends on whether sympathy for instituting environmental initiatives is emanating from the bottom up or from the top down.

TABLE 3.1
*Theories of Internal Management Dynamics
and Corporate Strategies*

| Theories | Main Elements |
|---|---|
| Sociological Institutional Theory | Emphasizes impact of external institutions, including social institutions, on decisions by managers. |
| Stakeholder Theory | Decisions by companies reflect the preferences of multiple stakeholders. |
| New Institutional Theory | Treat decisions by managers as institutions and companies as organizations. Businesses are not viewed as unitary actors, and a distinction is made between companies and individual actors in explaining decision making. |
| Rational Choice Theory | Regulations are obstacles to profit maximization. Bounded rationality suggests that managers will not act rationally because they do not possess all the required information to make truly informed, rational decisions. |
| Organizational Theory | The analysis of a variety of managerial styles and institutional forms, for example, hierarchical and centralized or decentralized. Is sympathy for instituting environmental initiatives emanating from bottom up or top down? What impact does this have on corporate decision making? |
| Corporate Culture Theory | What are the norms or way of life in a company? Is there one dominant culture or several subcultures present in a company? |

SOURCES: Prakash (2000) and Robbins (2001).

Corporate culture, according to Robbins (2001), refers to a set of norms or a way of life in a company. As he explains, "These norms might revolve around the exercise of authority and power, expectations about formality in the workplace, working hours and even appropriate dress for the job" (2001, 32). While there may be one dominant culture in a company, other subcultures may exist within different sections. Prakash (2000) does not directly consider organizational structure or corporate culture in his analysis.

Table 3.1 summarizes the major elements of the theories discussed in Prakash (2000) and Robbins (2001). As the table shows, each researcher provides a somewhat different explanation for how the internal dynamics of companies and the orientation of company managers can account for corporate environmental strategies. This study incorporates their theories in its theoretical framework and applies them in the analysis of one of the six case studies, the contamination of the Hudson River by the General Electric Company. To varying degrees, the theories offered by Prakash (2000) and Robbins (2001) help explain agenda building and corporate behavior and influence in this dispute.

### Possible Explanatory Variables of Business Influence in Congress

In addition to determining how much corporations influence agenda building on environmental issues in Congress, this study examines under what conditions they are likely to be more or less effective in their appeals. Based on previous research, several possible political and economic factors may explain why business tends to be more influential on some environmental legislative issues and less influential on others. This section discusses potential political and economic variables that may account for the ability of business groups to affect agenda building and, consequently, policy outcomes between 1970 and 2000. Although the main focus of the discussion is on Congress, some of the variables examined below may also explain agenda setting and business influence in the EPA, natural resource agencies, judiciary, and case studies.

#### Public Opinion

Mark Smith's (2000) research suggests that public opinion accounts for the level of success of business in the legislative process. In attempting to explain the finding that business victories across various policy domains tend to bunch together in one year and their defeats tend to occur in another year, his work indicates that the liberal-conservative dimension of public opinion helps explain the success or failure of business on unifying issues. Business generally endorses conservative policies that limit or do not require government intrusion. The public, by contrast, has been known to fluctuate between liberal and conservative perspectives on the appropriate size and scope of government. In other words, the public has been known to be more liberal and support more government action during some eras and to be more conservative and oppose government intrusion in other eras. Stimson (1999) refers to this as the "public mood."

As much as any issue arena, efforts to protect the environment and natural resources nearly always require government intervention. Thus, a given public mood might help or hinder the cause of business on environmental issues. More specifically, based on Smith's (2000) analysis, one might hypothesize that business will be more successful in thwarting attempts to adopt environmental regulations during a conservative period and less successful during a liberal era.

Public attitudes toward corporations within a particular period might also impact the ability of business to affect environmental policy. As Smith (2000) points out, citizens can possess either positive or negative opinions about specific corporations and business in general. People are likely to hold positive views when they believe that firms employ competent managers, further the well-being of society, and behave in an ethical manner. People are likely to hold negative views when they think firms have too much power, exploit consumers and workers to boost profits, and behave in an unprincipled way. The business scandals at the end of the twentieth century, for example, may have significantly enhanced negative public attitudes toward corporations. Since most environmental policy proposals will infringe on corporations in some way, one can hypothesize that legislators and policymakers will be more likely to support environmental initiatives in periods when the public holds unfavorable attitudes toward industry.

### Congressional and Presidential Elections

Which party controls Congress is likely to determine how successful business is in opposing environmental legislation. In the past, with some notable exceptions, Democrats have tended to be more supportive of environmental legislation than Republicans. This observation is also true for party identifiers within the electorate. However, party cleavages in Congress (and state legislatures) over environmental policy initiatives are deeper and wider than in the broad public (Kamieniecki 1995). Thus, one can hypothesize that business will be triumphant in opposing environmental legislation during times when Republican strength in Congress is at a maximum.

Given the powers of the presidency (for example, veto power, agency appointments, and determining policy priorities and direction), which party controls the White House is important as well (M. Smith 2000). This is especially true when partisan turnover in Congress favors the president. In such instances the president obtains added leverage due to the expanded congressional ranks of his party. Cooperation between the executive and legislative branch is easier to achieve, and this can influence agenda building on environmental issues in Congress. Mark Smith (2000) refers to this favorable setting as a "presidential leadership opening."

### Campaign Spending

Since the passage of the 1974 amendments to the Federal Election Campaign Act, companies and business organizations have helped finance federal elections by establishing PACs. Numerous companies and trade associations formed their own PACs in the 1980s, and the amount of money contributed to election campaigns has grown substantially. Most researchers believe contributions to political campaigns do not determine how legislators will vote. Instead, large donations to election efforts provide groups and wealthy individuals access (Baumgartner and Leech 1998; Lehne 2001). Although access is different from a quid pro quo, it does increase the chance that corporate PACs will have some say over the contents of legislation (or whether certain laws are adopted). According to Mark Smith:

> If corporate PACs do directly affect legislative decisions, the impacts could be felt on particularistic or conflictual issues rather than unifying ones. A winning candidate who received contributions from a certain company's PAC, for example, could reward the company through a narrow policy benefit irrelevant to the rest of the business community. (2000, 120)

This research analyzes the possible impact corporate contributions have on the ability of business to shape agenda building on environmental issues in Congress, with special attention paid to particularistic and conflictual issues. The amount of money contributed to political campaigns by environmental groups is likewise considered (as a measure of countermobilization). Whether and, if so, to what extent campaign contributions by business interests and environmental organizations affect agenda building in the six case studies of environmental and natural resource disputes is also explored in this study.

### Countermobilization

The literature on the role of business in American politics addresses the important impact of countermobilization on policymaking. Mark Smith (2000), for example, observes that countermobilization leads to increased media coverage and greater dissemination of information about the issues. This, in turn, raises public awareness and involvement, which can help derail certain initiatives and promote competing legislative measures. In such cases issues cannot be decided within policy subsystems, and multiple institutions must become involved. In addition, Hansen and Mitchell's (2000) analysis of the political activity of domestic and foreign corporations in national politics shows that countermobilization is a significant indicator of increased, reactive lobbying activities by large business groups.

Neopluralists such as Baumgartner and Leech (1998), Berry (1999), and Mark Smith (2000) argue that public opinion and citizen groups, as a countervailing force, have contained and often thwarted efforts by business and industry to oppose or weaken legislation. Countermobilization on the part of environmental groups, for example, is credited with the passage and continued enforcement of clean air and clean water legislation as well as other major environmental laws (Baumgartner and Jones 1993). Berry's case studies indicate that citizen groups, including environmental organizations, "succeeded through rather undramatic, traditional lobbying and not because of outside events that created opportunities for them to get their issues considered. Mother was right: hard work pays off" (1999, 69). The conclusions of neopluralist scholars are based on studies of Congress; they do not analyze the bureaucracy (or the courts). In assessing the ability of business to influence environmental policy since 1970, it is hypothesized that countermobilization will be important in determining both legislative and bureaucratic outcomes.

### Economic Conditions

Vogel's (1989) research points to the significance of economic conditions in determining the relative influence of business over national legislative policy. The present and near future state of the economy can especially have a bearing on the willingness of congressional legislators to support environmental policies. Congress is likely to take into account the state of the economy if the private sector must spend substantial sums of money in order to comply with new environmental regulations. Such large expenditures might financially weaken companies and, in turn, hurt the nation's economy. (At least business interests are likely to make this claim.) Since the economic welfare of the nation can have an important impact on the reelection success of legislators (and other elected officials), they will generally avoid taking actions that will undermine the economy. One can therefore anticipate that members of Congress will be more willing to support business and oppose environmental legislation when the economy is doing poorly than when the economy is doing well.

In addition to the status of the national economy, one must also consider the impact of regional, state, and local economic conditions on environmental policymaking. Businesses that employ many people and dominate the economy of a particular area of the country can influence state and local politics and gain support of members of Congress from that region. This can lead to serious tension between narrow regional interests and what best serves the nation. This is especially likely to be true in disputes involving natural resource issues. Therefore, this study analyzes the effect of both national and regional economic and political conditions on agenda building.

Table 3.2 lists the political and economic factors that might affect agenda building and corporate influence over environmental policy. The research issue each variable represents is noted in the table as well. The variables in the table should assist in explaining the circumstances in which business interests are likely to prevail on environmental and natural resource policy issues.

### Issue Definition and Framing Theory

Entman (1993, 1996) believes that researchers typically do not define framing clearly and that much is left up to the reader to understand. In an effort to correct this situation, he offers a number of insights into framing. According to Entman, "A *frame* operates to select and highlight some features of reality and obscure others in a way that tells a consistent story about problems, their causes, moral implications, and remedies" (1996, 77–78).[6] He explains that frames have four locations in the communication process: the communicator, the text, the receiver, and the culture (1993). Communicators make judgments in deciding what to say,

TABLE 3.2

*Political and Economic Variables that Can Affect*
*Agenda Building and Corporate Influence over*
*Environmental Policymaking*

| Variables | Research Issues |
| --- | --- |
| Public opinion | Does public support for or opposition to business goals matter? |
| Party control | Does the partisanship of Congress, the president, and other government officials affect their level of support for business? |
| Campaign spending | Is the amount of money corporate interests contribute to election campaigns related to their ability to shape environmental policy? |
| Countermobilization | Can environmental groups mitigate the influence of business in environmental policymaking by funding campaigns and lobbying in general? |
| National versus regional politics | Is there significant conflict between national and regional interests? If yes, to what degree? What is the impact? |
| Economic conditions | Do national and/or regional economic conditions promote or hinder the ability of business to get its way on environmental policy issues? |

guided by schemata that organize their belief systems. Texts contain frames that are defined "by the presence or absence of certain keywords, stock phrases, stereotyped images, sources of information, and sentences that provide thematically reinforcing clusters of facts or judgments" (1993, 52). The frames that influence the thinking and conclusions of receivers may or may not reflect what is in the text and the framing intentions of communicators. Culture usually comprises a set of common frames exhibited in the discourse and thinking of most citizens in a social grouping. He concludes by observing, "Framing in all four locations includes similar functions: selection and highlighting, and use of the highlighted elements to construct an argument about problems and their causation, evaluation, and/or solution" (1993, 53). In the end, frames call attention to some elements of reality while obscuring other aspects, which might lead certain segments of society to have different reactions (Kahneman and Tversky 1984; Entman 1993).

### The Impact of Framing on Policymaking

Entman (1996) conducts a frame analysis of the press coverage of certain provisions of The Job Creation and Wage Enhancement Act and some related bills that emerged from the Contract with America, a set of positions and proposals put forward by Republicans in 1995 after they assumed control of Congress. These bills contained changes that would increase the role of scientific risk assessment, cost-benefit analysis, and economic efficiency in developing and enforcing environmental and public health or safety regulations. He shows how the media (television, newspapers, and magazines) launched an all-out attack against these bills and produced many more negative news stories and especially editorials than positive ones. The negative media coverage influenced the congressional legislative agenda, and many of the Contract with America initiatives were not enacted into law.

Libby (1998) discusses the importance of framing for understanding interest group politics and policymaking. He shows how the framing of the issues and problems by the chemical industry led to the defeat of the 1990 California "Big Green" proposition, the boldest, most ambitious, and wide-ranging environmental policy ever considered in the United States. The chemical industry was able to defeat the proposition by claiming that the measure was not based on "hard" science and was too costly and complex to implement.

Schneider and Ingram (1993) offer a theory of how the social construction of target populations influences the policy agenda, the choice of policy tools, and the rationales that legitimate policy decisions. Their framework makes an important contribution to the debate over which groups benefit from policy, which groups are burdened, and why powerful groups do not always win. Their research indicates that much policy debate really is about language, symbols, and image. This point is also made in writings by Luke (1989) and Dryzek (1990, 1997).

### Framing Strategies

Research by Zaller (1992) suggests that political elites control the framing of issues. The frames conveyed by such elites can influence public opinion and how the public views political controversies. This occurs because, among other things, citizens are not generally well informed and cognitively active. Framing, as a consequence, strongly affects their responses to communications (Iyengar 1991; Druckman 2004). Business leaders, as well as leaders of other interest groups, attempt to take advantage of a generally uninformed and often unaware public by strategically framing environmental issues in a way favorable to their interests. This study analyzes the extent to which this takes place in the environmental policy arena.

Sociologists have paid a great deal of attention to theories concerning framing processes, primarily within the context of the mobilization and maintenance of social movements (see, for example, McAdam, Tarrow, and Tilly 1997). They have thus presented valuable insights into how issues are strategically defined and framed (for example, Goffman 1974; Snow et al. 1986; Snow and Benford 1988). In contrast to previous studies in political science and public policy, this research employs the relevant theoretical principles from the sociology literature to explain the ability of business to affect agenda building and national environmental policy.

Goffman (1974) was one of the first scholars to highlight the critical nature of issue definition and frame analysis. He defines "frame" and "frame analysis" in the following manner:

> I assume that definitions of a situation are built up in accordance with principles of organization which govern events—at least social ones— and our subjective involvement in them; frame is the word I use to refer to such of these basic elements as I am able to identify. That is my definition of frame. My phrase 'frame analysis' is a slogan to refer to the examination in these terms of the organization of experience. (1974, 10–11)

He expands this definition by stating that a primary framework is developed by "rendering what would otherwise be a meaningless aspect of the scene into something that is meaningful" (1974, 21). His work is primarily about the organization of experience. His objective is to isolate several of the basic frameworks of understanding extant in American society for comprehending events and to investigate the particular vulnerabilities to which these frames are subject. Among the topics he explores are fabrication, illusion and deception, and misframing. He also examines "keying," which is the act of transcribing something meaningful from a primary framework to something else, and the layering of a frame, which is when something to be modeled is placed on top of an existing model.

Snow and colleagues (1986) extend and refine Goffman's (1974) frame analytic perspective by proposing and elaborating on four types of frame alignment processes: frame bridging, frame amplification, frame extension, and frame transformation. Frame bridging, the most common form of alignment, is "the linkage of two or more ideologically congruent but structurally unconnected frames regarding a particular issue or problem" (1986, 467). Such bridging can occur at either the organizational level or at the individual level and is effected mainly by group outreach and information diffusion through interpersonal or intergroup networks, the mass media, the telephone, direct mail, and the Internet. Common Cause and the National Rifle Association, for example, have taken advantage of ideologically congruent but untapped and unorganized sentiment pools (Snow et al. 1986). Frame amplification concerns "the clarification and invigoration of an interpretive frame that bears on a particular issue, problem or set of events" (Snow et al. 1986, 469). Value amplification and belief amplification are two kinds of frame amplification. Value amplification involves the identification, idealization, and elevation of one or more values presumed basic to certain people but which have not inspired collective action for a variety of reasons (Snow et al. 1986). Beliefs are presumed relationships between two things or between some thing and a trait of it, and they are ideational elements that cognitively foster or impede action in pursuit of desired goals (Snow et al. 1986). Beliefs concerning the seriousness of a problem, issue, or grievance in question; beliefs regarding the locus of causality or blame; stereotypic beliefs involving antagonists or target of influence; beliefs concerning the probability of change or the efficacy of collective action; and beliefs addressing the necessity and propriety of taking a stand are among the kinds of beliefs found in the social-movement literature. Political activity is often contingent on the amplification or transformation of one or more of these sets of beliefs.

Frame extension is when an interest group must extend the boundaries of its central framework so as to include interests or viewpoints that are incidental to its main objectives but of substantial salience to potential supporters (Snow et al. 1986). In other words, the interest group tries to widen its base of support by portraying its goals or activities as addressing or being in line with the values or interests of potential supporters. Thus, a coal company battling new restrictions on carbon dioxide emissions might expand its base of support through the use of frame extension by appealing to other fossil fuel companies and firms that use fossil fuels for their backing.

In the context of frame transformation, the programs, causes, and values that some groups promote may not resonate with, and sometimes

may even appear antithetical to, conventional lifestyles or rituals and extant interpretive frames (Snow et al. 1986). When this happens, new values may have to be planted and nurtured, old meanings or understandings
eliminated, and erroneous beliefs or "misframings" reframed in order to
increase support. In such cases a transformation of frame is required, initially referred to as "keying" by Goffman (1974).

### Argument, Persuasion, and Rhetoric

The separate but complementary literature addressing argument,
persuasion, rhetoric, and policy may also provide possible explanations
as to how business interests are able to frame issues and influence environmental policy. Majone (1989), for example, attempts to reconstruct
policy analysis on the basis of rhetorical categories by viewing the policy
actor as a generator of arguments, capable of distinguishing between
good and bad rhetoric. The central issue he addresses is how policy actors pursue their goals within existing constraints, and how they try to
change these constraints in their favor. He points out that "political parties, the electorate, the legislature, the executive, the courts, the media, interests groups, and independent experts all engage in a continuous process of debate and reciprocal persuasion" (1989, 1). Policymakers arrive
at moral judgments and policy choices through the process of argumentation. Majone observes that "policy actors not only pursue their goals
within existing institutional, political, and cultural constraints, but
also strive to change these constraints in their favor" (1989, 113–14).
Those interests that are able to bring forth compelling and persuasive
evidence, whether in the form of facts, data, information, science, or
something else, will normally tend to control policy debates and the political agenda.

Riker (1996) conducts a fascinating analysis of the rhetoric and
heresthetic of the campaign of 1787 and 1788 to ratify the U.S. Constitution. "Heresthetic" is a word Riker (1996) derived from a Greek root
for choosing and deciding; it refers to the way in which the choice process is structured. He first conducts a comprehensive qualitative and
quantitative examination of the content of the campaign's rhetoric. His
investigation finds distinct rhetorical patterns in the campaign, including
an emphasis on negative themes. He reports a notable failure by both the

Federalists and the Antifederalists to address all the issues of the campaign, or even to address the same issues.

In an effort to explain this failure, Riker (1996) presents a theoretical analysis of the strategy of rhetorical interaction. His observations lead to the derivation of the Dominance Principle and the Dispersion Principle. The Dominance Principle applies in cases where an interest successfully dominates in the volume of rhetorical appeals on a particular theme, and as a result, the other side abandons appeals on that theme. The Dispersion Principle suggests that when neither side dominates in volume, both sides abandon the appeal. Stated another way, the Dominance Principle is applicable when one side is more persuasive and wins the argument on an issue, the other side stops to discuss it, and the victorious side continues to exploit it. Under the Dispersion Principle, both interests fail to persuade and win the debate on an issue. Instead, the two sides cease to discuss the issue and search for some other, potentially more effective issue. This investigation seeks to determine whether and, if so, to what extent Riker's (1996) two principles explain how business affects agenda building and environmental policy.

Riker (1996) employs both historical analysis and rational actor theories of political choice in his exploration of the heresthetic of the campaign. Although the rhetorical context was crucial in formulating the issues of the campaign, the Federalists' heresthetical maneuvers were critical to their narrow victory. The most important maneuver was the holding of a Constitutional Convention and beginning anew, as opposed to merely revising the Articles of Confederation. As a consequence, the Federalists controlled the choices that could be made. Following an examination of the relation between rhetoric and heresthetic, Riker concludes, "Both were necessary for the Federalist victory; rhetoric, to build support for Federalist positions; and heresthetic, to structure the choice process in such a way that that level of support would be sufficient" (1996, 11). Table 3.3 summarizes the theories concerning issue definition and framing presented in Snow et al. (1986) and Riker (1996).

### Theories of Agenda Building

Scholars tend to emphasize different theoretical concepts in their explanations of agenda building.[7] Researchers, for example, focus on the

TABLE 3.3
*Theories of Issue Definition and Framing Processes*

| Researchers | Main Elements of Theory |
| --- | --- |
| Snow et al. (1986) | Extend and refine Goffman's (1974) frame-analytic perspective by offering four types of frame-alignment processes. *Frame bridging*: most common form, the linking of two or more ideologically congruent but structurally unconnected frames regarding a particular issue or problem. *Frame amplification*: the clarification and invigoration of an interpretive frame that bears on a particular issue, problem, or set of events. Value and belief amplification are two kinds. *Frame extension*: an interest group extends the boundaries of its central framework to include interests or viewpoints that are incidental to its main objectives but of substantial salience to potential supporters. *Frame transformation*: new values are planted and nurtured, old meanings or understandings are eliminated, and erroneous beliefs or "misframings" are reframed in order to increase support. |
| Riker (1996) | Heresthetic is the way in which the choice process is structured; rhetoric is what is said. *Dominance Principle*: where an interest successfully dominates in the volume of rhetorical appeals on a particular theme and the other side abandons appeals on that theme. *Dispersion Principle*: when neither side dominates in volume, both sides abandon the appeal. |

importance of issue definition (for example, Cobb and Elder 1983; Baumgartner and Jones 1993; Rochefort and Cobb 1994; Leech et al. 2002; Jones and Baumgartner 2004), the identity and characteristics of political actors (for example, Kingdon 1995), belief systems and policy learning (for example, Haas 1992; Sabatier 1993), and symbols and language (for example, Petracca 1992; Schneider and Ingram 1993; Litfin 1994; Kamieniecki 2000). Bachrach and Baratz (1962, 1963) were the first to argue that "nondecision making" on the part of government officials is also part of the agenda-setting process. Further, Bachrach and Baratz (1962) and later Cobb and Ross (1997a) highlighted the significance of denial of agenda access or "blocking" in their analyses.

Most researchers only address a narrow set of theoretical principles in their studies of agenda setting and, by doing so, offer incomplete and often contradictory explanations for policy change. The agenda-building process is a dynamic and complicated phenomenon, and one must consider a variety of factors simultaneously to explain policy change fully. Accordingly, this section reviews the theoretical literature on agenda building and discusses those theoretical concepts that might explain how business influences the government's environmental policy agenda.

### Importance of Issue Definition

Previous research contains different theoretical approaches to agenda setting. One theoretical approach centers on the nature of the problems or harms themselves, such as whether they are serious or mild, new or recurring, short-term or long-term, and health effects or economic effects. Cobb and Elder (1983), for example, believe the key to understanding agenda building does not lie in the content of issues but rather in the nature of conflict itself. According to Cobb and Elder, "The issues in a conflict will vary along several dimensions," and "how an issue is defined . . . will have important bearing on the nature and eventual outcome of a conflict" (1983, 96). Their five dimensions of issues include the degree of specificity, the scope of social significance, the extent of temporal relevance, the degree of complexity, and the degree of categorical precedence. In addition to these issue characteristics, they also note the importance of the length of time that is required before an issue fully captures the public's attention. They hypothesize that conflicts that rapidly develop and are abstract, socially significant, long-term in scope, nontechnical, and unprecedented are most likely to gain agenda status.

Baumgartner and Jones (1993, 2002) expand on Cobb and Elder's (1983) earlier work through their study of the process of issue definition and issue development over long periods of time. The two analysts argue that issues attract attention through a process of "punctuated equilibria." New programs initially develop as "policy monopolies," protected by positive "policy images" and "institutional venues" controlled by supporters. Like their predecessors, these systems may be rejected when criticism of policies develops and a "countermobilization" takes place. As Baumgartner and Jones explain, "Much of the political world is never at equilibrium, but that points of stability are created and destroyed at critical junctures throughout the process of issue development" (1993, 22). Political leaders are always seeking to either construct a "policy monopoly" or destroy one in order to achieve their ends. Their approach to the study of policy agendas is linked to the definition of policy images (the issue-definition process) and the structure of political institutions.[8]

### Identity and Characteristics of Political Actors

Some analyses focus on the identity and characteristics of political actors, including leaders, interest groups, professionals, and bureaucrats. Studies in this area rely on attitudes, resources, and opportunities of actors to explain the emergence of policy problems and their particular formulations at any point in time. Kingdon (1995), for example, posits that there are three process streams flowing through the policymaking system—streams of problems, policies, and politics. The three process streams are largely independent of one another, and each evolves according to its own dynamics and rules (Kingdon 1995). At certain critical junctures, however, the three streams are joined, and "the greatest policy changes grow out of that coupling of problems, policy proposals, and politics" (1995, 19). Kingdon explains, "Solutions become joined to problems, and both of them are joined to favorable political forces" (1995, 20).

This coupling is most likely to occur when policy windows of opportunity are open either by the emergence of compelling problems or by events in the political stream. As a result, agendas are established by problems or politics, and program alternatives are developed in the policy stream. "Policy entrepreneurs," according to Kingdon (1995), are responsible for gaining the attention of important people, for coupling solutions to problems, and for coupling both problems and solutions to politics. The likelihood of items rising on a "decision" agenda is increased if all three streams are coupled together. Elected officials and their appointees (rather than career bureaucrats or nongovernmental actors) play a crucial role throughout this process.

### Belief Systems and Policy Learning

The advocacy coalition framework developed by Sabatier (1993) also contributes to our knowledge of agenda setting and policy change. It emphasizes the importance of shared belief systems among a diverse set of policy actors to form advocacy coalitions, promote specific interests, and influence public policy. Through serious policy debates with competing coalitions over time, advocacy coalitions acquire knowledge and learn about the dynamics of specific policies. This policy-oriented learning leads to changes in thought and behavior, resulting in improved public policy.

Haas (1992), too, discusses how policy actors can learn new patterns of reasoning and pursue new policy interests at either the domestic or international level. In his view, networks of knowledge-based experts, which he refers to as "epistemic communities," play a crucial role in "articulating the cause-and-effect relationships of complex problems, helping states identify their interests, framing the issues for collective debate, proposing specific policies, and identifying salient points for negotiation" (1992, 2). An epistemic community, according to him, is a network of professionals with recognized expertise and competence in a given field and an authoritative claim to policy-relevant knowledge and information with that field or issue area. These experts share a set of normative and principled beliefs, causal beliefs, notions of validity, and a common policy enterprise. Haas argues that "control over knowledge and information is an important dimension of power and that the diffusion of new ideas and information can lead to new patterns of behavior and prove to be an important determinant of international policy coordination" (1992, 2–3).

### Symbols and Language

Another school of thought emphasizes the use of symbols and language to promote or block an issue from reaching the public agenda.[9] Litfin (1994), who like Haas (1992), explores agenda building at the international level, pursues this type of inquiry in her study of the role of scientific knowledge in the development of the Montreal Protocol on Substances that Deplete the Ozone Layer and its subsequent revisions. Relying on in-depth interviews with participants and primary-source documents from the negotiating process, she conducts a contextual analysis of the pivotal role science played in the framing of the treaty. As Litfin explains:

> The cultural role of science as a key source of legitimation means that political debates are framed in scientific terms; questions of value become reframed as questions of fact, with each confrontation leading to the search for further scientific justification. Paradoxically, the demand for legitimation results in a process of delegitimation. Moreover, facts

must be expressed in language, and they require interpretation. Facts deemed relevant are always chosen selectively, depending on the interests of the communicator and the audience. This is where knowledge brokers come in—as intermediaries between the original researchers, or the producers of knowledge, and the policymakers who consume that knowledge but lack the time and training necessary to absorb the original research. (1994, 4)

She argues that the ability of knowledge brokers, who generally operate at low or middle levels of governments, to frame and interpret scientific information is a major source of political power. In Litfin's view, "Knowledge brokers are especially influential under the conditions of scientific uncertainty that characterize most environmental problems" (1994, 4).[10]

Table 3.4 lists the different theories of agenda setting and the main elements of each theory. The theories tend to differ in terms of emphasis and scope. Clearly, researchers vary markedly in their explanations of which factors shape the agenda-building process.

The theoretical literature on agenda building intersects and diverges at various points. Litfin (1994) generally agrees that facts and ideas are often reinterpreted and manipulated in the agenda-setting process. She is highly skeptical of the motives of politicians and scientists, never suggesting that many might be altruistic in the way they approach their work and the challenges they face. To a certain degree, Sabatier's (1993) notion of advocacy coalitions resembles Haas's (1992) idea of epistemic communities. The emphasis on professional expertise and the importance of shared belief systems and values are apparent in their definitions and treatment of advocacy coalitions and epistemic communities. Sabatier's advocacy coalition, however, suggests the existence of a much broader group of actors than Haas's epistemic community. On the surface one might see a similarity between epistemic communities, Kingdon's (1995) "policy entrepreneurs," and Litfin's (1994) "knowledge brokers." If one looks more closely, however, Haas and Litfin believe that scientists play a critical role in agenda setting; in contrast, Kingdon sees them as simply providing answers for important political leaders in the policy stream. Whereas Baumgartner and Jones (1993) and Sabatier view policy change taking place over many years, often decades, Cobb and Elder (1983) seem to view agenda setting taking place within a fairly narrow time frame. In addition, Haas and Sabatier integrate the notion of causation in their theories. In

TABLE 3.4
*Theories of Agenda Building*

| Researchers | Main Elements of Theory |
|---|---|
| Cobb and Elder (1983) | Key to understanding agenda building does not lie in the content of issues but in the nature of conflict itself. Their dimensions of issues include degree of specificity, the scope of social significance, the extent of temporal relevance, the degree of complexity, the degree of categorical precedence, and the length of time an issue fully captures the public's attention. |
| Baumgartner and Jones (1993) | Issues attract attention through a process of "punctuated equilibria." "Policy monopolies" are protected by "policy images" and "institutional venues" controlled by supporters. Political leaders seek to either construct or destroy a "policy monopoly" in order to achieve their ends. Their study of policy agendas is linked to the definition of policy images and the structure of political institutions. |
| Kingdon (1995) | Three process streams flow through the policymaking system: streams of problems, policies, and politics. Policy change occurs when the streams are joined, often when policy windows of opportunity are open. "Policy entrepreneurs" gain the attention of important people, couple solutions to problems, and couple both problems and solutions to politics. |
| Sabatier (1993) | The advocacy coalition framework emphasizes the importance of belief systems among a diverse set of policy actors to form advocacy coalitions, promote specific interests, and influence policy. Over time advocacy coalitions accumulate knowledge and learn, leading to changes in thought and behavior resulting in improved policy. |
| Haas (1992) | "Epistemic communities" are networks of knowledge-based professionals with recognized expertise and competence in a given field and an authoritative claim to policy-relevant information with that field. Experts share a set of normative and principled beliefs, causal beliefs, notions of validity, and a common policy enterprise. Their words and actions lead to policy change. |
| Litfin (1994) | Emphasizes the use of language and symbols to promote or block an issue from reaching the public agenda. In order to achieve legitimation, political debates are framed in scientific terms. "Knowledge brokers" operate at low or middle levels of government and wield considerable power. |
| Hirschman (1991) | Business groups make three kinds of arguments in their attempt to derail laws: (1) *the perversity thesis*, any effort to introduce change will only make conditions worse; (2) *the futility thesis*, any attempt to improve conditions will cost too much and will do |

TABLE 3.4
*(continued)*

| Researchers | Main Elements of Theory |
|---|---|
|  | little to correct the problem; and (3) *the jeopardy thesis*, any attempt to improve conditions will only produce new problems worse than the current ones. |
| Cobb and Ross (1997b) | Divide strategies that interest groups use to keep new issues off the formal agenda into four categories based on the resources they must expend: *low-cost strategies*; *two medium-cost strategies* (discredit the issue position of the group or the group itself or show symbolic concern in addressing the problem); and *high-cost strategies*. |

contrast, Kingdon's work seems to suggest a far more dynamic, complicated process taking place in multidimensional space, thereby making it difficult to isolate cause-and-effect relationships.

Further, Haas (1992) and Litfin (1994) differ on the interpretation and role of scientific knowledge in agenda building and politics. Haas suggests that epistemic communities forge a political consensus on the basis of "objective, value-free science." Litfin, in contrast, maintains that knowledge is not simply a body of concrete and objective facts; accepted knowledge is deeply implicated in questions of framing and interpretation, which generally reflect perceived interests. How knowledge is framed, she argues, can have a substantial impact not only on the listing of alternative policies but also on which course of action is eventually chosen. Most studies ignore the crucial roles of language, rhetoric, discourse, and argumentation in policymaking in general, and in agenda setting in particular.

Research by Cobb and Elder (1983), Baumgartner and Jones (1993), Sabatier (1993), and Kingdon (1995) has significantly added to our understanding of agenda building in the context of American politics. At the international level, research by Haas (1992) and Litfin (1994) provides additional critical dimensions of agenda setting. The logic and theoretical principles on which these studies are based should be applicable to agenda building within different branches of American government and, used in combination, should offer a full picture of policy change. Knowledge of how issue and formal agendas are set can render important insights into policy formulation, implementation, and legitimation processes regardless of whether policy change is continuously incremental, such as in public transportation, or fairly radical, such as sometimes in national defense policy. This analysis, therefore, employs the central theoretical concepts presented in the agenda-building literature (for example, policy monopolies, epistemic communities, policy entrepreneurs, and knowledge brokers) to explain the ability of business groups to influence the government's environmental policy agenda. Given the complexity of the agenda-setting process in environmental policy, it is necessary to apply various theories in combination to account for the ability of business to shape the government's environmental agenda.[11]

### Agenda Denial

Indeed, the burden of agenda setting often falls on the shoulders of proactive environmental groups to define the issue, garner public support, and persuade Congress to enact important environmental legislation. Although environmental organizations are often the initiators of new proposals for policy change, business groups also lobby for new legislation and revisions in existing or proposed laws and rules. In addition to lobbying frequently for agenda status of their issues, however, there are times when business and environmental groups also try to prevent the favored issues and proposals of each other from attaining agenda status in the public sphere and the government sphere. Schattschneider (1960) was one of the first scholars to argue that the ability to deny an issue from reaching the government agenda is an indication of power. As he observes, "A conclusive way of checking the rise of conflict is simply to provide no arena for it or to create no public agency with power to do anything about it" (1960, 71). In his view, "All forms of political organization have a bias in favor of the exploitation of some kinds of conflict and the suppression of others because *organization is the mobilization of bias* [his emphasis]. Some issues are organized into politics while others are organized out" (1960, 71).

In another early work, Bachrach and Baratz (1962) argue that there are two faces of power: one where individuals or groups effectively initiate a policy proposal, and one where individuals or groups effectively limit decision making by preventing policy issues from being considered for adoption. According to them, "To the extent that a person or group—consciously or unconsciously—creates or reinforces barriers to the public airing of policy conflicts, that person or group has power" (1962, 949). They add, "To measure relative influence solely in terms of the ability to initiate and veto proposals is to ignore the possible exercise of influence or power in limiting the scope of initiation" (1962, 952). Few studies on interest groups, however, pay serious attention to this facet of political influence and politics.[12]

Cobb and Ross's (1997a) research is an exception to this glaring oversight in the literature. They use Edelman's (1964) early work as a foundation on which to explore the process of agenda blocking. Edelman presents ways in which conflict expansion is sometimes achieved and other times thwarted. He discusses how political leaders and interest groups provide symbolic benefits to unorganized interests while securing tangible paybacks for themselves. In Edelman's (1964) view, this is accomplished through symbolic manipulation, which is used to define priorities as well as direct attention toward or away from specific problems and issues. In pursuing this approach, he focuses on the role of language and the ability to connect policy concerns with deeply held cultural symbols.

Based on this logic, Cobb and Ross (1997b) present a theoretical framework for the study of agenda setting and agenda denial that focuses on symbolic processes—and not just the role of material resources—in explaining why issues are denied agenda access. The main reason that issues are excluded from the political agenda, in their view, is the active effort of those whose interests would be harmed by the initiator's success. Cobb and Ross (1997b) believe that in order to understand agenda block- ing, attention must be paid to the political uses of what they call "cultur- ally rooted resources." Cultural processes, particularly those that explain the dynamics of issue identification and symbolization, account for why individuals or groups succeed or fail at agenda blocking. Interest groups can keep certain issues off the public or governmental agenda by strategi- cally defining or redefining issues and by deftly employing political sym- bols. Agenda denial takes place by connecting political claims to deeply rooted cultural concerns. In this way, political and cultural definitions of problems limit the consideration of new policy issues.

This study examines the degree to which corporations and busi- ness groups have been able to keep certain environmental problems off the government's agenda by controlling how they are defined. At the very least, and despite the best efforts by environmental organizations, this strategy may have prevented the formulation and implementation of strict environmental programs and regulations (that is, issue containment) in the past. Applying Hirschman's (1991) terminology, business groups have often made three kinds of arguments in their attempt to derail tough, new environmental laws: (1) the perversity thesis—any effort to introduce change will only make conditions worse; (2) the futility thesis—any attempt to improve environmental conditions will cost too much money and will do little to correct the problem; and (3) the jeopardy thesis—any attempt to improve environmental conditions will only produce new problems worse than the current ones. How successful business interests are in using these and other similar kinds of arguments to deny or limit agenda access is explored in this book.

Cobb and Ross's (1997a) study highlights the significance of cultural and symbolic strategies intended to define a problem in such a manner that a group can block an issue from attaining agenda status and achieve success in the long run. They divide strategies that interest groups can use to keep new issues off the formal agenda into four categories based on the resources (that is, time, effort, and money) they must expend. Low-cost strategies include nonrecognition of the problem, denial that a problem exists, and refusal to recognize the groups that are promoting an issue. Medium-cost strategies involve two different types of issue avoidance. An attempt is first made to discredit the issue position of the group or the group itself. Such an effort might include, for example, the reversal of roles by claiming victim status, use of deception by releasing false data and information, disputing the facts of the case, stating the issue is not a legitimate public concern, and claiming that concerns are isolated incidents and the problem is not that serious. If this fails to derail the initiators, an effort is then made to show symbolic concern in addressing the problem. This approach can include invoking community norms, such as loyalty, engaging in showcasing or tokenism by narrowly defining the problem and indicating something is being done to address it, co-opting leaders or the group's symbols (for example, the Wise Use Movement), creating a commission to study the problem, or postponing a decision. High-cost strategies normally involve economic threats, threats to withhold electoral support, legal threats or actions (for example, lawsuits and injunctions), and even physical threats or actions (for example, physical beating and murder). Cobb and Ross (1997b) argue that if initial low-cost approaches fail, opposing groups will pursue increasingly costlier and aggressive strategies.

After analyzing agenda denial in seven case studies, they find that medium-cost strategies are especially common among opponents and that the adoption of high-cost strategies is rare. They conclude, "The politics of contemporary agenda denial is primarily about the nuts and bolts of alternative issue definition—government agencies and interest groups in a battle over political and cultural definitions of what is at stake" (1997c, 218). The degree to which individual companies and business groups have employed the strategies outlined by Hirschman (1991) and Cobb and Ross (1997b) in the environmental policy domain, and how successful they have been in doing so, is reported in this study. Table 3.4 contains the main elements of the explanations of agenda blocking presented in Hirschman and Cobb and Ross.

### The Study's Research Design

As King, Keohane, and Verba (1994), Mahoney (2000), Sekhon (2004), Tarrow (2004), and George and Bennett (2005) recommend, this study utilizes a combination of quantitative and qualitative methodologies to address the central questions raised in Chapter 1 concerning the influence of business over environmental and natural resource policymaking in the United States. First, the study pursues a quantitative analysis of legislative outcomes on environmental policy issues in Congress between 1970 and 2000. The research uses the political and economic explanatory variables and the same measure of the dependent variable—legislative outcomes as an indicator of agenda setting—found in Mark Smith (2000). The final disposition of legislative issues is determined using a variety of sources, identified in Chapter 4. Unifying, particularistic, and conflictual policy issues are considered separately in the analysis.

Various data sources are relied on in the quantitative segment of the study. Internet sites provide up-to-date information on topics such as corporate policies and activities, results of public opinion polls over time, and contributions to election campaigns. Among the published directories of organized interests consulted in this study are the *Encyclopedia of Associations*, the *National Directory of Corporate Public Affairs*, *National Trade and Professional Associations of the United States*, and the *Washington Representative Index*. Other sources of information are noted in relevant sections of the study. Multiple regression analysis is used to identify the significant explanatory variables of agenda building on environmental issues in Congress.

The research also explores the influence of business in the bureaucracy, specifically in the EPA, the Fish and Wildlife Service, and the Forest Service, and the federal courts. Written comments submitted to the EPA, FWS, and Forest Service following a notice of proposed regulations in the *Federal Register* are analyzed in the study. The number and type of groups and the content of their arguments are investigated. Finally, the frequency with which companies litigate and succeed in the U.S. Circuit Court of Appeals for the District of Columbia is examined.

Mancur Olson (1965) provides a theoretical rationale for investigating companies within individual industrial sectors. In explaining how business groups can be influential in a democracy that operates according to majority rule he states, "The high degree of organization of business interests, and the power of these business interests, must be due in large part to the fact that the business community is divided into a series of (generally oligopolistic) 'industries,' each of which contains only a fairly small number of firms" (1965, 143). He further explains how small groups share strong, common interests, have certain political advantages, and are more likely than large groups, such as business as a whole, to influence government decisions.[13] More recent studies by Prakash (2000), Press and Mazmanian (2003), and others argue for the need to analyze companies within specific business sectors.

Accordingly, the cases examined in this study involve companies that represent varied and distinct industrial sectors, including science and technology, energy production and consumption, agriculture, mining, and logging. The following six case studies are examined in this inquiry:

- General Electric's pollution discharge of PCBs into the Hudson River in New York State and EPA's decision that the company must remove the pollution from the river.
- The effort to control acid rain in midwestern and northeastern states by significantly reducing sulfur dioxide ($SO_2$) emissions in those states.
- The debate over climate change in the United States.
- The failed attempts to amend the General Mining Law of 1872.

- Agriculture, the sugar industry, developers, and the battle to restore the Florida Everglades.
- Forest management, logging, and the northern spotted owl.

As Mahoney (2000), Gerring (2004), Ragin (2004), and George and Bennett (2005) advise, the case studies were selected based on certain methodological objectives and previous research (on interest groups and environmental policy). Among the sampling criteria used were: pollution control versus natural resource management; geographic dispersion; the salience of the conflict; and the nature of the combatants. The environmental policy literature distinguishes between regulatory policy and the management of natural resources because they are subject to different political, administrative, and institutional processes. The nature of the politics, actors, and objectives within the two policy areas differs as well. The cases themselves are geographically dispersed, primarily to control for variation in local and regional political culture. Disputed issues tend to differ in local, regional, and national scope. In addition, an effort was made to select at least one controversy that reflects each of Mark Smith's (2000) categories of unifying, particularistic, and conflictual policy issues. There has been widespread agreement within American industry, for example, that the United States should oppose international efforts to control greenhouse gas emissions. Thus, climate change represents a unifying issue. The case involving the timber industry and the northern spotted owl represents a particularistic issue, while the case concerning efforts to reduce $SO_2$ emissions and control acid rain represents a conflictual issue (that is, the battle between companies that mine high-sulfur coal in the East versus companies that mine low-sulfur coal in the West). Furthermore, following the advice of King, Keohane, and Verba (1994), Mahoney (2000), Gerring (2004), Ragin (2004), George and Bennett (2005), the companies and policy issues vary across the case studies. As Prakash (2000) recommends, the companies are all large American businesses with considerable revenues and sales. All the cases encompass salient controversies (that is, they affected many people and received media attention), and they represent interesting illustrations of several analytic issues raised to this point in the discussion (for example, bottom-up democratic mobilization, situations of inequality of the forces involved, evidence for or against beyond compliance, and neopluralist findings concerning the importance of citizen groups and public opinion). Conflicts were not selected, a priori, based on whether business won or lost. The particular environmental and natural resource controversies analyzed in this research should provide a good balance between comparability and variability across the case studies (King, Keohane, and Verba 1994; Mahoney 2000; McKeown 2004).

Finally, and most importantly, the analysis of the case studies will permit a thorough examination of the different theoretical concepts and perspectives introduced in this chapter. The analysis should provide valuable knowledge about, for example, the effect of certain political and economic variables on agenda building (for example, public opinion and national versus regional economic conditions). In addition, the case studies will shed light on critical aspects of theories pertaining to issue definition and framing processes and agenda building (proactive and denial).

A number of sources are relied on to provide data and information concerning the various case studies. These include personal and telephone interviews with company managers, key environmentalists, journalists, and government officials. Government documents and company documents (to the extent they are made available) provide additional sources of information for this research. Data and information from other sources, including scholarly publications, newspaper and magazine articles, Internet sites, and polling data (where available), are also used in this investigation.

This study focuses almost exclusively on the influence of business over environmental policy at the federal level. Of course, interest groups, especially business, also lobby state and local governments for favorable treatment. Instances where such activity impacts national policy are noted in this research. Although an analysis of interest group activity solely within state and local jurisdictions would probably prove interesting and fruitful, such an inquiry is beyond the scope of this inquiry. Nonetheless, the findings of this investigation should provide an important theoretical and empirical basis for conducting an analysis of interest group lobbying in state and municipal governments in the future.

One of the most difficult challenges of the present research is how to define and measure the influence of interest groups (and other policy actors). It is extremely difficult to determine the level of influence with precision, and most researchers examine interest group access instead. This study adopts this strategy as well. In an effort to explore the concept of influence in greater depth, however, the author takes a risk and also identifies low, medium, and high levels of influence in instances where the data are sufficient and such conclusions are warranted. Specifically, the level of influence of business interests, as well as environmental groups and other public and private actors, is roughly measured by the effort exerted by such interests and the extent to which business got what it wanted. In other words, how much time and money do companies devote to an issue, and to what extent do they achieve none, some, or all of their stated goals? Since many environmental and natural resource controversies can last a long time, it is possible for business groups to get their way at some points and lose at other points. This must be considered prior to formulating a general conclusion as to how influential such groups have been in a given conflict. As is always the case, it will be left up to the reader to decide whether the evidence presented in the analysis supports the interpretations provided by the author.

By the end of the study readers will have an accurate picture of how much business molds federal environmental policy. The data analysis should provide critical findings as to whether environmental groups have mitigated the dominance of business in policymaking in all branches of government, as the neopluralists contend, or whether business is still influential. Given the unique combination of theoretical perspectives introduced in this chapter and the blending of different methodological approaches recommended by Susskind, Jain, and Martyniuk (2001) and others, the study's findings should provide researchers with important insights into theories concerning issue definition, framing processes, and agenda building, particularly as they relate to the way firms shape national environmental policy. The results should also indicate whether certain political and economic variables (for example, public opinion, the state of the economy, campaign spending, and so on) account for the success of business in Congress and elsewhere in government.

The focal point for agenda building in environmental policy has been the Congress. Since the beginning of the environmental movement, Congress has developed, enacted, and amended numerous laws to control pollution (for example, the Clean Air and Water Acts), manage toxic materials and hazardous waste (for example, Resource Conservation and Recovery Act and Superfund), and conserve natural resources (for example, Endangered Species Act and National Forest Management Act). Democrats outside the South along with a handful of northeastern Republicans have made environmental protection a priority, and they have generally taken strong stands on critical issues in this important policy arena.

In the 1970s, as a result of protests led by environmental groups and extensive media coverage of the nation's serious pollution problems, the public quickly became aware and concerned about a variety of environmental threats. The Democratic controlled Congress enacted a number of tough, new environmental laws during that decade (Kraft and Vig 2006). Rising criticism of federal environmental programs by industry and the two-term presidency of Ronald Reagan substantially slowed the progress of environmental policymaking in Congress in the 1980s. The dominance of the Republicans in the U.S. House of Representatives and the U.S. Senate since the mid-1990s has also stalled further progress and has forced proponents to devote much of their time to defending existing environmental regulations (Eilperin 2004a; Kraft 2004). Republican control of Congress coupled with the two-term presidency of George W. Bush at the turn of the twentieth century has nearly brought a halt to the adoption of effective environmental and natural resource programs. For the most part, only proposed legislation designed to repeal or significantly weaken major environmental programs (for example, the Endangered Species Act, the Clean Air Act, and various forest conservation laws) tend to be placed on the congressional agenda. Thus far, continued strong public support for pollution control and natural resource conservation has made it difficult for congressional opponents to overturn landmark environmental legislation.

Since the early 1970s business interests have spent hundreds of millions of dollars to lobby Congress and prevent stricter environmental regulations from becoming law. Environmentalists, commentators, and scholars (see, for example, Milbrath 1989; Cahn 1995; Korten 1995; Ehrlich and Ehrlich 1996; Dryzek 1997; Brown 2001; Gonzalez 2001; Devra Davis 2002; Press and Mazmanian 2003) argue that corporations wield too much influence in Congress and often try to block environmental initiatives, even in cases where scientific studies show that there is a demonstrated need to protect public health and the national interest. In their view, business frequently gets its way.

This chapter analyzes the influence of business interests over the congressional agenda on environmental and natural resource issues. Specifically, the chapter addresses the following research questions:

1. How often and in what manner does business take positions on environmental legislation?
2. How consistent are business positions on environmental legislation?
3. Is business success constant, or does it vary systematically across different stages of legislative agenda setting and across different patterns of business alignments?
4. To what extent can various political and economic variables explain the success of business influence?

Data on the different positions business has taken on environmental and natural resource legislation in Congress between 1970 and 2000 are presented in order to answer the first two questions. The study seeks to answer the third question by examining the empirical components of the environmental legislative agenda and the positions of business within this sphere. This is accomplished by conducting a factor analysis of various indicators of agenda building in Congress. Multiple regression analysis is then employed to investigate how political and economic variables affect the advancement of environmental legislation when business aligns in certain ways. The results of this inquiry are used to address the fourth question. The implications of the overall findings are discussed near the end of the chapter. Before presenting the data analysis, the study briefly comments on the general complexity of agenda building in Congress.

### The Complexity of Legislative Agenda Building

Legislative agenda setting is a highly complex process and difficult to analyze. Legislative proposals vary markedly in terms of how far they make it through Congress, and only a small percentage of bills actually become law. Researchers disagree as to why this is the case, and their studies suggest that a variety of factors explain why certain legislative measures are enacted while others are not. In order for bills to pass through both houses of Congress and become law, they must successfully make it through a mine field of political obstacles and veto points. Clearly, bills differ in their level of salience and, hence, the attention they receive from potential opponents (and supporters). The level and nature of media coverage and public scrutiny can accelerate or derail the progress of legislative proposals. Given the long and often contentious battle over environmental and natural resource issues, it is safe to assume that legislative agenda building involving these issues is at least as complex as legislative agenda building in other policy spheres.

An example of the multifaceted nature of agenda building concerning environmental legislation in Congress is the extraordinary effort by Republican Senator Christopher Bond from Missouri to protect employment in his state by restricting California's ability to improve air quality. Under the Clean Air Act of 1990, California must meet federal air quality standards for a number of major pollutants by 2010. In order to achieve this goal, the state has adopted numerous rules and regulations addressing a wide variety of sources of pollution. At the end of 2003 Senator Bond introduced a measure that would block efforts by California to reduce the pollution emitted by small gasoline engines in machines such as lawn mowers, tractors, forklifts, and chain saws (Shogren and Polakovic 2003). The amendment was attached to an omnibus bill to fund a number of different government agencies. The amendment would give the EPA the sole authority to regulate gasoline engines that are fifty horsepower or less, and it directed the agency to propose new regulations for the engines by the end of 2004. Senator Bond argued that California's regulation would drive twenty-two thousand manufacturing jobs in the United States abroad. Briggs & Stratton Corporation, the world's largest manufacturer of these engines, contended that revamping its production facilities to satisfy California clean air rules would be so expensive that it would have to close its facilities, two of which are in Missouri, and move production overseas. The company spent $520,000 during an eighteen-month period lobbying Congress to act on this issue (Shogren and Polakovic 2003). Democratic Senator Dianne Feinstein of California argued that the amendment would deprive California and other states of an essential tool to meet clean air standards and strongly opposed the measure. Although the amendment was adopted by the Senate, Senator Bond was later forced to revise the amendment for the final version of the omnibus bill so that California could regulate the use of small engines. At Bond's urging, the EPA is studying whether catalytic converters, which reduce harmful emissions by as much as 75 percent, do not pose a potential fire threat in lawn mowers.

### The Data

A major effort was undertaken to identify environmental legislation, including natural resource bills, considered by Congress between 1970 and 2000. The *Congressional Quarterly Weekly Report* (*CQ Weekly* since 1998), *Congressional Quarterly Almanac*, and the Congressional Information Service's online index of congressional hearings and documents were used to find legislation in this policy area. Environmental legislation identified in Appendix 1, Major Federal Laws on the Environment, 1969–2002 in Vig and Kraft (2003) was included in the data set.[1] Included in the research were bills that reached the agenda but went no farther, passed one house of Congress but not the other, or were enacted into law. In the end, 1,124 pieces of legislation were identified and included in

TABLE 4.1

*Number of Environmental and Natural Resource*
*Bills Considered by Congress Each Year,*
*1970–2000*

| Year | Number of Bills | Year | Number of Bills |
|------|------|------|------|
| 1970 | 51 | 1986 | 24 |
| 1971 | 45 | 1987 | 33 |
| 1972 | 91 | 1988 | 41 |
| 1973 | 49 | 1989 | 22 |
| 1974 | 47 | 1990 | 34 |
| 1975 | 25 | 1991 | 38 |
| 1976 | 40 | 1992 | 49 |
| 1977 | 30 | 1993 | 36 |
| 1978 | 46 | 1994 | 45 |
| 1979 | 27 | 1995 | 26 |
| 1980 | 32 | 1996 | 22 |
| 1981 | 23 | 1997 | 18 |
| 1982 | 44 | 1998 | 37 |
| 1983 | 40 | 1999 | 19 |
| 1984 | 63 | 2000 | 6 |
| 1985 | 21 | | |
| N = 1124 | | | |

the data set. A complete list of the bills analyzed in this chapter is available from the author.

Table 4.1 reports the number of environmental and natural resource bills considered by Congress each year between 1970 and 2000. Congress considered the largest numbers of bills during the 1970s. Of the 1,124 legislative proposals selected for analysis in this study, about 40 percent were placed on the congressional agenda during this time. Approximately 31 percent of the 1,124 legislative proposals were reviewed by Congress in the 1980s, and a slightly smaller percentage (about 29 percent) was reviewed by Congress in the 1990s. Level of agenda-building activity in Congress coincides, therefore, with the periods in which higher and lower numbers of major environmental and natural resource bills were signed into law.

The 1,124 legislative proposals considered by Congress between 1970 and 2000 vary widely in nature, scope, type, and salience. As Table 4.2 demonstrates, the bills cover very different areas of pollution control and natural resource management. Many pieces of legislation seek to limit

TABLE 4.2

*Categories of Environmental and Natural Resource*
*Bills Considered by Congress, 1970–2000*

| Categories | Percent |
|---|---|
| Clean air policy | 3.2 |
| Clean water/water resources/flood control | 12.4 |
| Climate change/ozone layer/global issues | 2.5 |
| Coastal protection | 2.6 |
| Education/research | 5.2 |
| Endangered species | 1.4 |
| Energy production/conservation | 8.4 |
| Environmental policy/regulation assorted | 5.3 |
| Forest management | 3.5 |
| Habitat management/conservation/wetlands | 4.1 |
| Hazardous and solid waste | 6.7 |
| Information collection/dissemination | 1.1 |
| Land use management/preservation/reclamation | 9.8 |
| National parks/monuments | 5.9 |
| Natural resources management, assorted | 9.6 |
| Noise pollution regulation | 1.0 |
| Ocean protection/resources | 3.0 |
| Pesticides regulation | 1.0 |
| Public works | 1.2 |
| Toxic substances control | 1.9 |
| Wilderness protection | 4.4 |
| Wildlife/marine life protection | 6.4 |
| Totals | 100.6 |
| | (1,124) |

different types of emissions, control hazardous and solid waste and toxic substances, and protect a variety of public lands, wilderness areas, and natural resources, including forests, wildlife, minerals, and sources of energy. Legislative proposals to control water pollution and manage water resources are the most frequent. A closer look at the data shows that attempts to manage hazardous and solid waste were more numerous in the 1980s and 1990s than in the 1970s. Otherwise, legislative activity within the categories listed in Table 4.2 does not vary significantly across time. Although a certain number of legislative proposals are clearly national (and some international) in scope, many more tend to focus on a particular region, state, or locality. A majority of the 1,124 legislative measures tend to address natural resource issues rather than pollution control. Lastly, the proposed bills differ markedly by salience, with only a relatively small number (fewer than forty) being salient or highly salient (that is, are listed in Appendix 1 of Vig and Kraft 2003).

### Typology of Business Alignments

Next, the study seeks to determine the positions business groups take on separate legislative issues over time. Mark Smith (2000) classifies legislative policy issues into three general types based on how business interests align. According to him, unifying issues, the main focus of his empirical analysis, denotes when business interests form a consensus on policy issues. This happens only in a small percentage of the cases. Particularistic issues are where individual companies or small subgroups of companies pursue their own distinct goals without involving the rest of the business community. This type of legislative issues reflects the idea that policymaking takes place within insulated spheres. Godwin and Seldon (2002) contend that analysts underestimate this sort of lobbying by firms and overestimate coalition behavior of corporate lobbyists. Finally, conflictual issues are characterized by tensions between companies. In such cases, firms possess competing self-interests, disagree on policy objectives, and battle one another in the political arena. Prakash (2000), Robbins (2001), Press and Mazmanian (2003), and others suggest that conflict between corporations over environmental policy has been on the rise in recent years. This has occurred because more companies are involved in "green" industries and therefore seek tougher environmental regulations to promote their business. Also, according to these analysts, major companies have become increasingly concerned about the environment and have tempered their progrowth positions on certain policy issues (for example, renewable energy and climate change).

Using Mark Smith's (2000) typology of business alignments as a guide, data were collected on the different positions companies, trade associations, and business groups took on environmental and natural resource legislation considered by Congress between 1970 and 2000. Several sources were used to collect these data. In addition to the *Congressional Quarterly Weekly Report*, major newspapers such as the *Los Angeles Times*, *New York Times*, and *Washington Post* were consulted to determine the positions of individual companies, trade associations, and business groups on each of the 1,124 proposed bills. Local and regional newspapers (for example, the *Oregonian*) also were reviewed at appropriate points. A search was made to find information and press stories that mentioned specific legislative proposals and the position of business interests on those proposals. The positions of business interests were coded based on a content analysis of all available sources of information. Because of a lack of accurate information, no attempt was made to measure systematically the level of involvement and level of support or opposition to proposed legislation. Determining the positions of business interests on legislation, particularly legislation of low salience, is no easy task, and some error is likely to occur. Nonetheless, a concerted effort was made to find all information on alignments. The resulting data should provide a fairly good estimate of where firms stand on environmental and natural resource bills during the period examined in this study.[2]

Care was taken to make sure that the general intent of the proposed bills was to improve environmental quality or protect natural resources. The names of a number of bills suggest that they attempt to protect the environment; however, a closer examination of their contents reveals that they fail to do this. Such legislative proposals were excluded from the analysis. A more vexing problem is whether to consider business in support (or in opposition) of environmental policy when legislation seeks to roll back standards or change the conditions of implementation. In these cases a bill may still help improve environmental quality but not to the extent that environmentalists demand or stipulated in prior legislation. For example, a number of environmentalists strongly favor a complete halt to the use of pesticides and believe that anything less is unacceptable. Also, early clean air and water legislation contained unattainable standards and goals and had to be revised accordingly in subsequent amendments by Congress. Determining business support or opposition in these and other similar and often ambiguous circumstances is likely to depend on the specific context of the proposed legislation and, as such, is open to interpretation. It would be almost impossible to derive an accurate and reliable measure of business position for these legislative proposals, and no attempt was made to develop a separate indicator for these select bills. Instead, the position of business was determined on proposals that sought to improve environmental quality and natural resource management more generally without examining the specific context of each bill and dissecting the unique circumstances surrounding its contents and intentions.

Table 4.3 shows the position of companies, trade associations, and other business groups on proposed environmental and natural resource legislation between 1970 and 2000. Business interests do not take a

TABLE 4.3
*Position of Business on Environmental Legislation,*
*1970–2000*

| Position | Percent |
|----------|---------|
| Unified against | 3.6 |
| Unified support | 8.3 |
| Particularized against | 3.6 |
| Particularized support | 4.8 |
| Conflictual | 0.5 |
| Took no position | 79.3 |
| Totals | 100.1 |
|  | (1,124) |

position on almost 80 percent of the bills considered by Congress within this policy domain. Perhaps equally remarkable is that the business community, either as a whole or in part, opposes legislation in relatively few instances. Instead, industry is somewhat more likely to support rather than oppose environmental bills. In fact, when business interests are unified, they are twice as likely to support rather than oppose environmental legislation. Furthermore, companies are rarely divided over this policy issue. These findings hold even when environmental and natural resource bills are analyzed separately.

The data presented in Table 4.3 challenge certain conventional wisdom held by environmentalists, news commentators, political pundits, and researchers. The commonly held belief that business interests nearly always take a position on environmental legislation and nearly always oppose such legislation is clearly not true. In a large majority of the cases, business interests are not significantly impacted by environmental legislative measures, and they do not take a stand on these measures. When they do, they tend to support—not oppose—such legislation. Perhaps anticipating objections from congressional supporters of business, sponsors of environmental bills probably draft legislation with the interests of business in mind in order to avoid conflict and increase the chances their bills will advance. It is also possible that business interests had rejected earlier proposals in private communications but were willing to embrace the revised legislation because objectionable provisions were eliminated and recommended changes were made. No doubt, such bargaining and compromise takes place prior to submitting legislation formally as well as after legislation is submitted for congressional approval. In some cases, corporations may even feel that new laws to protect the environment are needed. In addition, the data dispute Godwin and Seldon's (2002) assertion, at least in the environmental area, that particularistic actions by business are common. Such occurrences take place only a small fraction of the time. Overall, the results of the aggregate data analysis provide justification for closely examining agenda building within specific legislative contexts.

Berry (1999) investigates the extent to which legislation causes conflict within one industry and among two or more industries. After examining highly salient policy issues considered by Congress in 1963, 1979, and 1991, he finds that, averaged across the three years, about 28 percent of the legislation produced conflict within one industry and almost 30 percent produced conflict between two or more industries. The discrepancy between his findings and those reported here probably can be explained by the differences between the two data sets. Berry analyzes a broad range of social and economic policy issues that are highly salient at three distinct points in time. The data used in this research address proposed environmental and natural resource bills between 1970 and 2000 regardless of level of saliency. Since this study covers a different time period, analyzes a single policy domain, and contains only a small percentage of highly salient legislative proposals, the results of the two studies are probably not comparable. A review of the data employed in this study shows that conflict between companies occurred on both high- and low-salient bills.

The myths about corporate behavior in the environmental policy sphere are probably perpetuated by the close attention the media pay to disputes over important legislative issues and the role of business in these disputes. By focusing on the involvement of business interests in especially salient, bitter controversies, those viewing news stories come away with the belief that such involvement is common and ongoing. Instead, the findings suggest that corporations carefully pick and choose their battles over environmental issues, and they are most likely to enter a legislative fight when there is a great deal at stake for them. In such cases business groups are most likely to flex their muscles and lobby Congress hard to protect their interests. This often results in a public display of power and influence, thereby giving the lasting impression that business is ubiquitous within the policymaking process. Environmental groups usually attempt to counter the lobbying activities of business, further increasing media coverage and analysis. They often use the media to argue that business leaders have too much power and are trying to defeat critical policy proposals. Business groups probably win important environmental and natural resource debates often enough to fuel the idea that they continuously participate in the legislative process and, perhaps, generally get their way in this policy area. The data, of course, show that this is a gross exaggeration of what really happens in Congress. The in-depth case studies of salient environmental and natural resource controversies analyzed here provide important insights into the dynamics underlying the role of business interests in agenda setting in Congress.

An analysis was done to see whether there were any discernible patterns in the different positions business took on environmental and natural resource legislation over time. For the most part, business positions on legislation (including taking no position) tended to be randomly distributed and were not more prevalent at one point in time versus another. The argument that business has become more conflicted over environmental policy issues in recent years is not supported by the data. Indeed, such occurrences are random and rare. Furthermore, the different alignments of companies, trade associations, and business groups vary independently of one another over time. In other words, the positions that companies took on bills addressed by Congress since 1970 do not covary in any apparent fashion. The data suggest that, among other things, narrow self-interest and ever-changing political conditions influence how business interests view and react to environmental legislation at any particular time.

### Agenda Building in Congress

Richard Smith (1995) reviews the small amount of research that has been conducted on agenda building in Congress. Drawing on interviews with numerous federal officials and almost two dozen case studies of policy initiation and noninitiation, Kingdon (1984, 1995) finds that interest groups play a key role in agenda building across different policy areas. In particular, more than 90 percent of congressional representatives say that interest groups play a vital role in the legislative process. He argues that promotion of agenda items is not the only way that groups influence the agenda; they also devote time to negative blocking activities.

Baumgartner and Jones (1993) make similar observations in their analysis of agenda setting in Congress and other branches of government. Neustadtl (1990) reports that campaign contributions by business interests do not have a major impact on legislation concerning corporate America.[3] Haider-Markel's (1999) research on congressional voting, however, indicates that the process and factors behind agenda building differ from the influences over actual voting on the floor.

Mark Smith utilizes multiple indicators to measure agenda building in Congress, primarily "because no single measure could adequately cover the entire scope of legislative actions" (2000, 81). His indicators address critical facets of lawmaking, including what is placed on the agenda, who wins floor votes, and who succeeds in terms of enacted bills. His analysis includes all stages of the legislative process, from the earlier ones where most legislation dies to the later ones where some bills eventually become law. To capture the full range of agenda-building activity, he creates six annual measures:

1. *Agenda composition*: Of the total number of agenda items (that is, all bills or provisions marked by either business support or opposition that receive formal consideration in Congress), the proportion supported by business.

2. *Out of committee*: Of the total number of business-related items reaching some stage beyond the committee level (that is, bills that were reported and/or received a floor vote), the proportion supported by business.

3. *Passed one chamber*: Of the total number of business-related items passing either the House or the Senate or both, the proportion supported by business.

4. *House margins*: Of all relevant votes on the floor of the House, the average proportion of voting members taking the pro-business side.[4]

5. *Senate margins*: Of all relevant votes on the floor of the Senate, the average proportion of voting members taking the pro-business side.

6. *Enactment scorecard*: Of the total number of business-related items signed into law, the proportion supported by business (2000, 81–82).[5]

Each measure is scored so that higher values represent policy decisions more favorable to business. Mark Smith (2000) multiplies all six measures by 100 to generate scores with theoretical ranges between 0 and 100. He uses these indicators to measure agenda building in Congress on those issues business is unified. This study adapts his indicators of agenda building for all the business alignments analyzed in this chapter.

Smith (2000) finds that the six indicators of legislative action closely track one another and vary similarly over time (that is, between 1953 and 1996). Although one might consider studying each facet of the legislative process independently for theoretical reasons, he correctly reasons that the high intercorrelation of the six measures will result in the same findings. As he says, "If business fares well at one stage, it fares well at all stages" (2000, 84). He conducts a principal components factor analysis to examine the dimensionality of the six measures, and he finds, not surprisingly, that a one-factor solution fits his data well. He extracts a latent dimension from his data by rescaling the first measure, agenda composition, in order to take it through a linear transformation. Since the measures share nearly the same mean, variance, and pattern over time, it does not matter which one is chosen to provide the reference metric. He chooses to use the first indicator for the sake of simplicity. To calculate the value for each year, he multiplies the original factor scores by the standard deviation of agenda composition and then adds its mean. The newly derived scale can theoretically vary from 0 to 100. The resulting scale is used as the dependent variable throughout most of his analysis.

In order to see whether business success is constant or whether it varies systematically across different stages of legislative agenda setting and across different patterns of business alignments (the third research question posed at the beginning of the chapter), a principal components factor analysis of Mark Smith's (2000) six indicators of agenda setting was conducted for each position business took on environmental and natural resource legislation between 1970 and 2000. Since business is seldom divided in their position on legislation, the analysis excludes the few cases where companies are conflicted over bills. Tables 4.4 and 4.5 present the results of the factor analyses. Similar to Smith's research, the data yield a single dimension when business is unified in support of environmental legislation.[6] At first glance, agenda setting appears to be bidimensional when business is unified against, particularized against, and particularized in support of initiatives in Congress.

TABLE 4.4

*Factor Analysis of Six Indicators of Agenda Setting
When Business Is Unified on Environmental
Legislation, 1970–2000\**

| Agenda Setting Indicators | UNIFIED AGAINST FACTORS | | Unified Support Factor |
|---|---|---|---|
| | 1 | 2 | |
| Agenda composition | .864 | .417 | .927 |
| Out of committee | .904 | .340 | .922 |
| Passed one chamber | .894 | .357 | .925 |
| House margins | .243 | .914 | .675 |
| Senate margins | .282 | .910 | .744 |
| Enactment scorecard | .897 | .092 | .772 |
| Variance explained | 72.66% | 17.22% | 69.48% |
| Eigenvalues | 4.36 | 1.03 | 4.17 |
| N = 31 | | | |

\* Figures in the table represent factor loadings for those factors with eigenvalues of 1.00 or above following varimax rotation with Kaiser normalization.

TABLE 4.5

*Factor Analysis of Six Indicators of Agenda Setting
When Particular Businesses Oppose or Support
Environmental Legislation, 1970–2000\**

| Agenda Setting Indicators | PARTICULARIZED AGAINST FACTORS | | PARTICULARIZED SUPPORT FACTORS | |
|---|---|---|---|---|
| | 1 | 2 | 1 | 2 |
| Agenda composition | .776 | .477 | .800 | .165 |
| Out of committee | .384 | .869 | .897 | .325 |
| Passed one chamber | .281 | .895 | .908 | .265 |
| House margins | .952 | .007 | .178 | .928 |
| Senate margins | .899 | .167 | .105 | .866 |
| Enactment scorecard | −.065 | .728 | .752 | −.080 |
| Variance explained | 58.57% | 22.91% | 55.95% | 22.34% |
| Eigenvalues | 3.51 | 1.38 | 3.36 | 1.34 |
| N = 31 | | | | |

\* Figures in the table represent factor loadings for those factors with eigenvalues of 1.00 or above following varimax rotation with Kaiser normalization.

In each of the three scenarios where agenda building is bidimensional, however, the second factor is much less pronounced as indicated by the relatively small eigenvalues (barely above the 1.00 level) and percentages of explained variance. New scales representing each of the three second factors listed in Tables 4.4 and 4.5 were created the same way

Mark Smith developed his single measure of agenda setting for unifying business support. Thus, House margins were used to create a measure representing the second dimension for unified against and particularized support. Out of committee was used to create an indicator of the second dimension for particularized against. A criterion variable analysis was then conducted to see whether the second factors for unified against, particularized against, and particularized support, respectively, were theoretically legitimate components of agenda building within the domain of environmental and natural resource legislative policy (Zeller and Carmines 1980). A bivariate correlation analysis between the three newly created scales and theoretically important political and economic variables (for example, public attitudes toward corporations, partisan composition of Congress, employment rate, and so on) yielded no significant relationships. As a consequence, the three second factors were eliminated from the research, thereby leaving a single factor to represent each of the three respective business positions.

The results of the factor analyses suggest different patterns in agenda building across the different business alignments. As the data in Tables 4.4 and 4.5 show, the same indicators of congressional agenda building do not load high on each factor for the four possible types of alignments. Although all indicators load high on the unified support factor, measures of House and Senate margins do not load high on the factors for unified against and particularlized support. Furthermore, measures of out of committee, passed one chamber, and enactment scorecard do not load high on the particularized against factor. These findings reveal that agenda-building activities differ over time depending on the nature of the business alignment with respect to environmental and natural resource legislation. The findings also indicate that the four alignments are different and should be analyzed separately. Overall, the results show that the agenda-setting process in Congress is extremely complex, and no one theory of agenda building can explain legislative policy outcomes.

### Independent Variables

A number of political and economic variables analyzed by Mark Smith (2000) are used in this research to explain why business interests influence agenda building on environmental legislative issues (the fourth research question noted at the beginning of the chapter). The theoretical rationale for including these variables in this research, along with the anticipated findings, was discussed in the previous chapter. The independent variables address important conditions that might account for the ability of business to affect legislative policy outcomes between 1970 and 2000.

### Political Variables

Mark Smith (2000) finds that public opinion is central to determining the level of success of business in the legislative process. In a nutshell, companies prevail when public opinion is generally conservative. One expects this to be the case in the environmental issue area since legislation in this arena often requires government to adopt new rules and regulation and change policy. Stimson's (1999) measure of "public mood," an indicator of the liberal-conservative dimension of public opinion, is used in Smith's research and in this study.[7] Higher values denote liberal public preferences and support for stronger government.[8] Stimson's (1999) indicator of public mood is complimented by a measure of public attitudes toward corporations.

Since 1977 the Harris Poll has asked a national sample of Americans how confident they are in selected institutions, including "major companies." The percent reporting "a great deal of confidence" each year between 1977 and 2000 is included in this analysis.[9] Mark Smith (2000) reports this item is strongly correlated with an extracted dimension based on responses to a large number of survey questions dealing with "big business" and corporations since 1953. This particular item is used because it covers more years since 1970 than any of the other items in Smith's study. Percentages fluctuate between a low of 11 percent in 1992 and a high of 28 percent in 2000.

Other political variables included in the analysis are party control of Congress and presidential leadership opening. The partisan composition of Congress resulting from elections is measured by the Republican proportion of the total Republican and Democratic seats.[10] Individual measures for the House and Senate are averaged to create the party control of Congress measure. In addition to this measure, Smith (2000) constructs an indicator of what he refers to as "presidential leadership opening." For Republican presidents with a leadership opening, the indicator is calculated as the Republican portion of congressional seats at time $t$ minus the Republican portion of congressional seats at time $t—2$. For Democratic presidents with a leadership opening, the indicator is measured as (the negative of) the Democratic portion of congressional seats at time $t$ minus the Democratic portion of congressional seats at time $t—2$. All presidents without an opening (that is, presidents whose party lost seats in the previous congressional election) are treated as equivalent and scored as zero.[11]

Data were also collected on campaign spending by PACs representing corporations and trade associations as well as on campaign contributions by environmental organizations. Data on campaign spending by business-related PACs are available since 1978. Information about campaign spending by environmental organizations is available since 1982. The Federal Election Commission provides data on campaign spending by business interests (www.fec.gov). Information on campaign spending by environmental groups comes from Orenstein, Mann, and Malbin (2002), www.opensecrets.org (the Center for Responsive Politics), and www. vote-smart.org. Additional data on campaign spending are derived from Gainor, Roybal, and Willis (1998) and Zuckerman (2002). Complete data on campaign contributions from environmentalists are difficult to obtain, and caution should be used when interpreting results from analyses involving this variable. Corporate PAC funding and campaign contributions by environmental groups are measured during the preceding election in order to reflect causality. Overall, these measures provide a general indication of the ability of business to mobilize its forces and of the ability of environmentalists to countermobilize if the need arises (and, of course, vice versa).

*Economic Variables*

Following Smith's lead, data on the following four measures of the economy are analyzed in this research:

1. *GDP*: The rate of growth in real Gross Domestic Product.
2. *Employment*: The percent of civilian job-seekers who are employed, calculated by subtracting the unemployment rate from 100.

3. *Growth in investment*: The rate of growth in real nonresidential fixed private investment.

4. *Index of leading economic indicators*: The annual change in the index of leading economic indicators. (2000, 155)[12]

Data for these economic measures are provided by Haver Analytics (2003). As Mark Smith observes, rate of growth in GDP and employment rate can be considered indicators of current prosperity. At the same time, growth in investment and the change in the index of leading indicators can be considered predictors of future prosperity.

### The Findings

A bivariate correlation analysis was conducted between the independent political variables and the outcomes of agenda building on environmental and natural resource bills for the four business alignments, unified against, unified support, particularized against, and particularized support. The analysis revealed no significant Pearson correlations between presidential leadership opening, campaign spending by business interests, campaign spending by environmental organizations, and each measure of agenda setting for each business alignment. These independent variables are therefore not considered further in this research. However, public mood, public attitudes toward corporations, and partisan composition of Congress are related in varying degrees to agenda building across the different business positions. Public mood and public attitudes toward corporations are not significantly intercorrelated, and partisan composition of Congress is only moderately correlated with public views about corporations ($r = .41$, significant at the .05 level).

An analysis was also conducted to determine whether the indicators of present and future economic conditions are intercorrelated and, if so, to what degree. Rate of growth in GDP, rate of growth in investment, and change in the index of leading economic indicators are highly intercorrelated with one another (that is, Pearson r is greater than .90 in each case). Rate of growth in GDP and employment rate, in contrast, are only moderately related ($r = .41$, significant at the .05 level). Both economic indicators are correlated with agenda building across the different business alignments and are included in the study. Rate of growth in investment and change in the index of leading economic indicators are excluded from the analysis due to their very strong correlations with rate of growth in GDP.

Indicators of agenda setting for business interests unified against environmental legislation, business interests unified in support of environmental legislation, particular business interests against environmental legislation, and particular business interests in support of environmental legislation are regressed on several political and economic variables. A goal of the analysis is to develop parsimonious regression models. Given Mark Smith's (2000) findings highlighting the importance of public opinion in the agenda-building process when business is unified on different policy issues, the impact of public attitudes toward corporations is singled out for special attention. In comparison to public mood, Smith's other measure of citizen opinion, this variable most directly taps people's views about business per se over time, and it is theoretically important in this study on environmental policy.[13] Thus, the following two regression equations are analyzed in this research for each of the four business alignments $Y_{t1-4}$:

$$Y_{t1-4} = c + \beta_1 \text{ Public mood}_t + \beta_2 \text{ Partisan composition of Congress}_t$$
$$+ \beta_3 \text{ GDP}_t + \beta_4 \text{ Percent employed}_t + \varepsilon_t \qquad \text{EQUATION 1}$$

$$Y_{t1-4} = c + \beta_1 \text{ Public mood}_t + \beta_2 \text{ Partisan composition of Congress}_t$$
$$+ \beta_3 \text{ GDP}_t + \beta_4 \text{ Percent employed}_t$$
$$+ \beta_5 \text{ Public attitudes toward corporations}_t + \varepsilon_t \qquad \text{EQUATION 2}$$

The results of the regression analysis of agenda building when business interests are unified against environmental legislation and when particular business interests are against environmental legislation appear in Tables 4.6 and 4.7. Employing ordinary least squares (OLS) estimates spanning the available years, none of the political and economic variables is related to agenda building in cases where business is unified in its opposition to environmental bills. In contrast, public attitudes toward corporations are a significant predictor of agenda setting when business interests are particularized and oppose environmental legislation. In other words, legislative proposals advance when citizens are confident about corporations in general in spite of opposition by individual firms or small clusters of companies. Partisan composition of Congress and GDP are

TABLE 4.6
*When Business Is Unified Against
Environmental Legislation*[a]

| Independent Variables | Unstandardized Coefficients | Standardized Coefficients | Unstandardized Coefficients | Standardized Coefficients |
|---|---|---|---|---|
| Public mood | −0.236 | −0.209 | −0.438 | −0.384 |
| | (0.237) | | (0.349) | |
| Partisan composition | 0.083 | 0.093 | 0.281 | 0.310 |
| of Congress | (0.205) | | (0.297) | |
| GDP | 0.000 | 0.276 | 0.001 | 0.255 |
| | (0.000) | | (0.001) | |
| Percent employed | 0.700 | 0.206 | 1.512 | 0.413 |
| | (0.673) | | (1.218) | |
| Public attitudes toward | | | −0.651 | −0.424 |
| corporations | | | (0.446) | |
| Constant | 14.75 | | 29.85 | |
| | (16.91) | | (28.81) | |
| Durbin-Watson statistic | 1.54 | | 1.43 | |
| N | 31 | | 24 | |
| $R^2$ | 0.16 | | 0.29 | |
| Adjusted $R^2$ | 0.03 | | 0.09 | |

*$p \leq .10$
**$p \leq .05$
[a] The figures in parentheses are standard errors. Significance tests are one-tailed.

TABLE 4.7
*When Particular Business Interests Are Against
Environmental Legislation*[a]

| Independent Variables | Unstandardized Coefficients | Standardized Coefficients | Unstandardized Coefficients | Standardized Coefficients |
|---|---|---|---|---|
| Public mood | −0.107 | −0.128 | 0.246 | 0.312 |
| | (0.167) | | (0.211) | |
| Partisan composition | 0.267* | 0.405* | 0.323* | 0.516* |
| of Congress | (0.144) | | (0.179) | |
| GDP | 0.000 | −0.242 | −0.001* | −0.742* |
| | (0.000) | | (0.001) | |
| Percent employed | −0.803 | −0.320 | −0.826 | −0.326 |
| | (0.475) | | (0.735) | |
| Public attitudes toward | | | 0.558** | 0.525** |
| corporations | | | (0.269) | |
| Constant | −1.991 | | −35.23* | |
| | (11.92) | | (17.39) | |
| Durbin-Watson statistic | 1.35 | | 1.57 | |
| N | 31 | | 24 | |
| $R^2$ | 0.24 | | 0.46 | |
| Adjusted $R^2$ | 0.12 | | 0.31 | |

*$p \leq .10$
**$p \leq .05$
[a] The figures in parentheses are standard errors. Significance tests are one-tailed.

TABLE 4.8
*When Business Is Unified in Support of
Environmental Legislation*[a]

| Independent Variables | Unstandardized Coefficients | Standardized Coefficients | Unstandardized Coefficients | Standardized Coefficients |
|---|---|---|---|---|
| Public mood | 0.600* | 0.355* | 0.994** | 0.618** |
| | (0.330) | | (0.482) | |
| Partisan composition of Congress | −0.034 | −0.026 | 0.226 | 0.177 |
| | (0.285) | | (0.410) | |
| GDP | −0.002** | −0.603** | −0.004** | −1.104** |
| | (0.001) | | (.002) | |
| Percent employed | 0.168 | 0.033 | 1.684 | 0.327 |
| | (0.937) | | (1.680) | |
| Public attitudes toward corporations | | | 0.330 | 0.153 |
| | | | (0.615) | |
| Constant | −25.56 | | −64.86 | |
| | (23.53) | | (39.74) | |
| Durbin-Watson statistic | 1.69 | | 1.72 | |
| N | 31 | | 24 | |
| $R^2$ | 0.28 | | 0.32 | |
| Adjusted $R^2$ | 0.17 | | 0.13 | |

*$p \leq .10$
**$p \leq .05$
[a]The figures in parentheses are standard errors. Significance tests are one-tailed.

also predictors of legislative outcomes. Thus, when Republicans hold a large share of seats in Congress compared to Democrats and when the GDP is declining, agenda building still takes place in situations where particularized business interests are against environmental legislation. According to the adjusted $R^2$, the variables in the equation explain 31 percent of the variance in the dependent variable when public attitudes toward corporations are included in the regression analysis.[14]

Tables 4.8 and 4.9 show the results of the OLS regression analyses of the same political and economic variables, when business is unified in support of environmental legislation, and when specific business interests support environmental bills. According to the data, public mood and GDP are significant predictors of agenda building when business is unified in support of environmental policy. Thus, increasing liberal tendencies among the public and declining GDP over time tend to result in agenda building when business demonstrates a consensus on legislative initiatives. The variables in the equation, however, only explain about 13 percent (adjusted $R^2$) of the variance in the dependent measure. As Table 4.9

TABLE 4.9
*When Particular Business Interests Support*
*Environmental Legislation*[a]

| Independent Variables | Unstandardized Coefficients | Standardized Coefficients | Unstandardized Coefficients | Standardized Coefficients |
|---|---|---|---|---|
| Public mood | −0.254 | −0.225 | −0.201 | −0.314 |
| | (0.235) | | (0.208) | |
| Partisan composition of Congress | −0.040 | −0.044 | −0.227 | −0.446 |
| | (0.203) | | (0.177) | |
| GDP | 0.000 | −0.043 | 0.001 | 0.727 |
| | (0.000) | | (0.001) | |
| Percent employed | −0.847 | −0.248 | −1.244* | −0.605* |
| | (0.667) | | (0.726) | |
| Public attitudes toward corporations | | | 0.193 | 0.223 |
| | | | (0.266) | |
| Constant | 22.09 | | 21.76 | |
| | (16.75) | | (17.19) | |
| Durbin-Watson statistic | 1.61 | | 2.76 | |
| N | 31 | | 24 | |
| $R^2$ | 0.18 | | 0.20 | |
| Adjusted $R^2$ | 0.06 | | 0.03 | |

*$p \leq .10$
**$p \leq .05$
[a]The figures in parentheses are standard errors. Significance tests are one-tailed.

shows, percent employed is negatively associated with agenda building when public attitudes toward corporations is included in the equation for particularized support among business interests. Percent employed is not a significant factor, however, when public opinion is omitted from the multivariate analysis. No other variables predict agenda setting when individual or small groups of companies support environmental legislation.[15]

### Discussion

The regression analysis yields important findings worthy of discussion. First, Mark Smith's (2000) major finding concerning public mood is not supported by the analysis of legislative outcomes involving environmental and natural resource issues. The public mood of the country does impact agenda building when business is unified in support of environmental legislation; however, the public tends to be more *liberal* rather than more *conservative* in such cases. Smith reports the opposite to be true: when the public is more conservative than liberal, unifying policy issues are more likely to advance in the agenda-building process. Smith, of course, examines a wide variety of legislative policy issues in his research. The progressive nature of environmental policy initiatives and the perceived need for government to implement them probably explains the reverse finding reported in this study. Otherwise, public mood is not related to agenda building in Congress when business interests are unified against environmental bills. The variable is also not a factor when particular firms are either for or against environmental policy.

Furthermore, public attitudes toward corporations, an important indicator of public opinion, affect legislative outcomes only when particular business interests oppose environmental policy proposals. Interestingly, environmental bills are likely to advance when public confidence in corporations is high even though a single company or a small group of companies opposes environmental legislation. This also tends to be the case when Republicans hold a greater share of the seats in Congress and when the GDP is declining. A closer look at these individual cases might reveal that individual companies or narrow industrial sectors are opposing legislation that is more generally believed to have no impact on or somehow may even be beneficial to the nation's business and economy overall. Or, perhaps pro-business Republicans are grateful that the legislation is not tougher and ignore the protests of a single company or a small minority of business interests. Otherwise, public views about corporations have no significant effect on congressional agenda building within the environmental policy sphere.

Finally, the findings have implications for the ongoing debate over environmental protection versus jobs. Except in one case, percent employed is not a significant predictor of agenda building on environmental policy in Congress. Thus, for the most part, business interests have been unable to influence the advancement of legislation during periods of relatively high unemployment when they oppose such legislation. This finding and the few significant predictors of agenda setting across the various business alignments (as particularly evident in Tables 4.6 and 4.9) suggest that the legislative policymaking process is highly complex and its outcomes are determined by factors that tend to differ from one context to another. No single model can adequately explain agenda building on legislative environmental issues even when the positions of business are examined separately. Thus, the unique political and economic circumstances surrounding each bill must be investigated. This is done as part of a comprehensive analysis of case studies of environmental and natural resource controversies in Chapters 6 and 7.

### Conclusion

This chapter analyzed how often and under what conditions business affects the congressional agenda on environmental and natural resource policy issues. The chapter began by presenting information about the different positions business took on environmental legislation introduced in Congress between 1970 and 2000. Next, the study examined the empirical components of environmental legislative agenda building based on positions of business within this policy sphere. The research then analyzed how certain political and economic variables affect agenda building in cases where business interests form different alignments. The implications of the findings were discussed at the conclusion of the chapter. Contrary to popular belief, the study showed that business interests do not frequently take a position on environmental legislation, and when they do they tend to support—not oppose—such legislation. As Kingdon (1995) correctly observes, legislative agenda setting is a dynamic, complex process, thereby making general patterns difficult to discern.

Once environmental legislation becomes law, business interests can turn their attention to the executive branch and attempt to influence the rulemaking process. Companies and trade associations, for example, can provide input on the development of environmental and natural resource policy during the public comment period following the proposal of new rules and regulations by the EPA and other agencies. If this fails, business groups can ask the federal courts to intervene and review the legality of certain rules and regulations. Very little research has been conducted on this aspect of agenda building within the environmental policy domain.

# 5 The Influence of Business in Federal Agencies and Courts

Actions taken in the bureaucracy and the courts often have a major impact on U.S. environmental policy. Within the executive branch, the EPA and natural resource agencies are frequently required by Congress to promulgate important rules and regulations concerning a particular section of legislation. Congress delegates this authority because it feels it does not have the time or the expertise to provide in-depth analysis of all the relevant implementation issues necessary to select regulatory strategies to achieve compliance and improve environmental quality (Cohen and Kamieniecki 1991; Cohen, Kamieniecki, and Cahn 2006). Occasionally, members of Congress cannot agree on specific rules and regulations and delegate that authority to pass along potential "hot potatoes." Stakeholders are invited to participate in the rulemaking process, and sometimes they strongly disagree with the final outcome. In such cases, the fight can shift from the agency to the courts. Opponents hope that they can change or nullify the rules and regulations handed down by the EPA or natural resource agencies by convincing a court that their grievances have legal merit.

Corporations actively participate in the rulemaking process involving environmental and natural resource issues. In cases where they have been unsuccessful in blocking or shaping congressional legislation, they often try to affect the formulation and implementation of specific provisions of the law. They attempt to influence rulemaking by offering information about the cost, underlying science and technology, and over-all effectiveness of different regulatory options. Companies and trade as-sociations, as well as environmental groups, have taken the EPA and nat-ural resource agencies to court when they have felt that final rules violate existing laws, regulations, or legal procedures.

This chapter explores the extent to which business influences the rulemaking process in the EPA and natural resource agencies. It also in-vestigates the level of success business has in the judicial system. The chap-ter begins with a discussion of rulemaking in the federal government by examining important, broad issues concerning the process. The purpose of this discussion is to provide a general background for the research that follows. The study then analyzes input by business and other groups dur-ing the public comment period following the formal proposal of environ-mental and natural resource rules. The intent is to see whether views con-cerning a proposed rule affect the contents of the final rule. Theories of issue definition and framing processes and agenda building are used to ex-plain the findings of this analysis. Next, the investigation examines the role courts play in environmental policymaking. The frequency with which business interests have prevailed in federal court is addressed at the end of the chapter.

### Congressional Delegation of Authority

Lowi (1979) offers an insightful and compelling indictment of con-temporary American government in general, and of congressional delega-tion of power to regulatory agencies in particular.[1] Although he does not object to delegation in principle, he does criticize delegation without guidelines and standards, a practice he attributes to widespread accept-ance of "interest-group liberalism." He later writes that the congressional delegation of authority "is an inevitable and necessary practice in any gov-ernment," and "no theory of representative government is complete with-out it" (Lowi 1987, 295). Nonetheless, "the delegation of broad and undefined discretionary power from the legislature to the executive branch deranges virtually all constitutional relationships and prevents attainment of constitutional goals of limitation on power, substantive calculability, and procedural calculability" (1987, 296). He reasons that every delegation of discretion away from electorally responsible levels of government to professional career administrative agencies is a calculated risk because politics will always flow to the point of discretion; the demand for representation would take place at the point of discretion; and the constitutional forms designed to balance one set of interests against another would not be present at the point of discretion for that purpose. (1987, 297–98)

As a consequence, liberalism is undoing itself because public policies are resulting in privilege and private goods going not to the deserving but to the best organized. As Mancur Olson (1965) points out, the best-organized interests are likely to be business groups. Those who are poorly organized (for example, people without health care) tend to receive comparatively little attention from government bureaucrats.

Fiorina (1982) questions the correctness of Lowi's explanation, pointing out that there are a number of good reasons for legislators to delegate regulatory authority (for example, lack of time or technical information). He demonstrates how these reasons are empirically supported by previous research. He then turns his attention to the role uncertainty plays in the literature on regulatory origin, and he offers various formal models of the role of uncertainty in the regulatory process.

### The Rulemaking Process

Despite Lowi's concerns, rulemaking has become an important component of public policymaking (West 1982, 1985; Cohen and Kamieniecki 1991; Cohen, Kamieniecki, and Cahn 2006). Numerous federal agencies, such as the EPA, the Forest Service, and the FWS are required by legislative mandates to draft and implement specific guidelines and regulations that are broadly referred to in enacted legislation. The Administrative Procedure Act (APA) of 1946, written by Congress to bring consistency and predictability to the decision-making processes of government agencies, states that a rule means the whole or part of an agency statement of general or particular applicability and future effect intended to implement, interpret, or prescribe law or policy. Rules provide the specific information often missing in laws, and rulemaking brings a capacity for adaptation to changing conditions that a statute alone would lack (Kerwin 2003). Rules originate in agencies, stipulate law and policy as directed by authorizing legislation, have either a broad or narrow focus, and attempt to influence future conditions. According to Kerwin:

> Increasingly, rulemaking defines the substance of public programs. It determines, to a very large extent, the specific legal obligations we bear as a society. Rulemaking gives precise form to the benefits we enjoy under a wide range of statutes. In the process, it fixes the actual costs we incur in meeting the ambitious objectives of our many public programs. (2003, 2)

The process of rulemaking, as Kerwin (2003) explains, is central to the formulation and implementation of public policy in the United States. It differs and is separate from the legislative and judicial process, but it is also a critical part of the overall policymaking effort.

The New Deal and the 1960s and 1970s were eras of sharp growth in governmental programs that required extensive rulemaking to meet ambitious goals (Kerwin 2003). In the 1980s the Reagan administration attempted to decrease substantially the number of rules and regulations that government was adopting and implementing. Despite the efforts of the Reagan administration, rulemaking actually expanded during the 1980s and 1990s. Today, despite criticisms and attempts at reform, rulemaking is an indispensable governmental process, and this is unlikely to change in the future. The manner in which rulemaking is carried out has significant implications for the functioning of democracy and the nation's well-being.

Although rulemaking was intended to be efficient, factually oriented, nonpolitical, and objective, it has become something quite different. Rulemaking appeared to grant bureaucrats an immense amount of freedom of action. Instead, they must adhere to a long list of procedural guidelines and are subjected to political pressure from different quarters including the White House, Congress, interest groups, and the public (West 1982; Magat, Krupnick, and Harrington 1986). The rulemaking process has become increasingly open and information driven, thereby providing stakeholders an opportunity to influence the final outcome of the process. Opportunities for participation have grown and diversified since the passage of the APA, and agencies are under pressure to take public comments seriously. The Office of Management and Budget (OMB) plays a crucial role in the rule-adoption process by reviewing new regulations and assessing their economic impact (Buff 1989; McGarity 1991a, 1991b, 1992).

Kerwin (2003) identifies and discusses eleven stages of rulemaking. They include origin of rulemaking activity, origin of individual rulemaking, authorization to proceed with rulemaking, planning the rulemaking, developing the draft rule, internal review of the draft rule, external review of the draft rule, revision and publication of a draft rule, public participation, action on the draft rule, and post-rulemaking activities. It is a mistake to assume that the rulemaking process has a clear start and finish; components of rules can be challenged and altered at any time.[2]

The APA suggests that there are three categories of rules: legislative or substantive, interpretive, and procedural (Kerwin 2003). Legislative or substantive rules are promulgated when, by legislative mandate or authorization, agencies draft what in essence is new law. Interpretive rules explain to the public how agencies interpret existing law and policy and do not create new legal requirements. Procedural rules outline the organization and processes of agencies and often concern matters of importance to the public. Rules can also be classified by the segment of society they influence and direct (that is, rules for private behavior).

### Negotiated Rulemaking

Regulatory negotiation, or "reg neg" as it is frequently referred to, offers competing interests a direct and meaningful role in rulemaking. A fairly recent concept, this idea began to take shape in the early 1980s with the changing political climate and as academics and practitioners began to write about the approach. Writings at the time discussed the rationale for regulatory negotiation, its likely benefits, the necessary conditions for success, and the obstacles to its execution (Kerwin 2003). Harter (1982), for example, severely criticized contemporary rulemaking for its adversarial process, distortion of information, foundation for litigation, and the lack of progress that had resulted. As a consequence, announcements of rules were often delayed and their quality was frequently poor. Affected parties were frustrated and disillusioned by the process, and compliance suffered as a consequence. Instead, Harter (1982) recommended the adoption of an alternative approach, one in which conflict was resolved through face-to-face negotiations, bargaining, and compromise. Agency officials would organize and participate in the negotiations rather than remain aloof from the process. In this way information would flow more freely, thereby producing higher-quality regulations in less time than in traditional rule-making. Stakeholders would also be much less likely to litigate after the rule was issued because they were part of the process and therefore would perceive the regulation to be legitimate (Wald 1997; Langbein and Free-man 2000). Compliance was predicted to increase, saving taxpayers money on enforcement costs (Harter 1982). In 1990 the federal government responded to these and other criticisms and calls for reform by passing the Administrative Dispute Resolution Act and the Negotiated Rule-making Act (Coglianese 1997; Harter 1997). In 1993 the National Performance Review, chaired by Vice President Al Gore, made a number of recommendations, including widening the use of "reg neg" to improve rulemaking (Gore 1993).

Since the adoption of regulatory negotiation by certain agencies, including the EPA, there has been considerable research of the process. Coglianese (1997), for example, analyzes the timeliness and litigation experience of rules developed using negotiation. He finds that negotiated rules are not produced more quickly than are rules developed using standard procedures. He also reports that rules developed using negotiation are, on average, challenged in court more frequently than those that result from traditional processes.[3] In another study, Langbein and Kerwin (2000) examine the quality of the experience of participants in both "reg neg" and conventional rulemaking. Based on their interviews with random sets of participants, they find that those involved in negotiated rulemaking give that process higher ratings on the quality of information it generated, the amount learned, economic efficiency, cost effectiveness, compliance, legality, overall quality, net benefits for the organization, and the personal experience of the respondents than participants in the conventional rulemaking process.[4] In contrast, Siegler (1997), who represents the American Petroleum Institute in regulatory negotiations, believes that "reg neg" is a cumbersome process "for everyone involved." Coglianese reports that "negotiated rulemaking has not lived up to its promising potential to save regulatory time or prevent litigation" (1997, 1335). He concludes that regulatory negotiation is not worth the additional time, money, and resources required for its operation. Overall, Coglianese (1999) and Coglianese and Allen (2004) argue that "reg neg" does not necessarily lead to improved policy design and more effective regulation.

*The Time It Takes to Make Rules*

As Coglianese (1997) and Kerwin (2003) point out, the time it takes to draft, adopt, and implement regulations can be significant. Often the regulatory process proceeds too slowly and compliance is postponed. Barke (1984) demonstrates how lengthy delays in the promulgation of rules have hurt the regulatory activities of the Interstate Commerce Commission and the Federal Communications Commission. West (1982) reports the same malady at the Federal Trade Commission. Durant (1984) arrives at a similar finding in his research on the EPA's efforts to bring the Tennessee Valley Authority into compliance with air and water quality standards. Sometimes agencies will act too quickly due to outside pressures. Thompson (1982) argues that Occupational Safety and Health Administration officials in the early 1970s were impatient in promulgating and enforcing new rules. However, firms can also forestall compliance through the use of delay tactics, unless such tactics are viewed as detrimental to the operation of the firms over the long haul (for example, by generating negative media attention or risking substantial long-term costs).[5]

The time it takes to make rules in government agencies, especially in the EPA, has been a topic of research. Kerwin and Furlong (1992), for instance, analyze the average time it takes to formulate rules in four major programs at the EPA: air, water, toxic substances, and waste. They report that rulemaking takes anywhere from slightly longer than two years to a little less than five years. Although it is difficult to say how much time the EPA should take in issuing rules since conditions vary from one policy context to another, Congress has grown frustrated by the pace of rulemaking in the agency and by 2003 had passed approximately one thousand statutory deadlines for the issuance of regulations under a variety of environmental laws.[6]

*The EPA and Rulemaking*

Despite earlier problems, the EPA has become quite efficient and effective at rulemaking.[7] McGarity, for instance, observes, "With the very notable exception of the turbulent early 1980s, the EPA has acquired a well-deserved reputation as one of the most intelligently run agencies in the federal government. While its output has never been high, it has . . . been of increasingly high quality" (1991b, 111). Over the years, the EPA has moved away from, for example, its practice of appointing a work group for all rules and has fashioned a new, more sophisticated tier system. Rules are now assigned one of three tiers depending on the rule's importance, its cross-environmental media implications, and the potential for controversy inside or outside of the agency. Kerwin (2003) believes other agencies in the federal government are likely to adopt this new EPA model.

In his examination of negotiated rulemaking in the EPA, however, Coglianese (1997) cites the failure of the Clean Fuel Negotiated Rule-making Committee to head off conflict concerning the requirements for re-formulated gasoline under the Clean Air Act of 1990. In its effort to secure consensus, the reformulated gasoline rule led to the adoption of MTBE. Immediately following its adoption, however, citizens complained about headaches and dizziness associated with the additive. Others complained about the increase in fuel prices. These complaints were widely covered in the media. Coglianese concludes, "To this day, press reports about the rule continue, though now they focus on cases of groundwater contamination with MTBE, a substance which is reported to be a possible carcinogen" (1997, 1293).

Harter (1997) argues that the EPA values negotiations and part-nering highly, and the agency strongly promotes negotiated rulemaking. The aim is to reach a consensus in rulemaking. Although there have been some complaints, most applaud the EPA's effort to pursue and improve negotiated rulemaking. More generally, and in opposition to Coglianese (1997), Harter (1997) believes that negotiated rulemaking has worked well throughout the bureaucracy.

### Soliciting Public Comments

The APA gives citizens a right to express their opinions before an agency adopts final rules. Participant requirements were enacted in the 1970s in order to correct imbalances in representation of participants (Schlozman and Tierney 1986; Gormley 1989; Kerwin 2003). The rule-making process generally follows a simple procedure called "notice and comment" in federal agencies. Agencies provide notice of a pending regulation (Notice of Proposed Rulemaking—NOPR) by publishing a proposed rule in the *Federal Register*. Any individual or organization may review this notice and submit written comments regarding it. In some cases public hearings are held where interested parties may speak and offer comments. The period during which comments are accepted by agencies will usually be either thirty, sixty, or ninety days. The time during the notice and comment period provides interest groups and citizens an opportunity to voice their views and possibly affect regulation.

Detailed instructions on how, when, and where an opinion may be expressed are noted for each proposed rule published in the *Federal Register*. Agencies also note the name and telephone number of a person to contact for further information. In addition, agencies frequently request comments from particular citizens, industry, academia, and other government agencies. When officials publish final rules in the *Federal Register*, they must respond to significant issues raised in comments and explain any changes made in response to them. Occasionally, agencies use the "notice and comment" process to keep constituents informed, solicit their opinions on specific policy or program issues, or obtain general guidance.[8]

In 2002 the EPA launched a new electronic system for record keeping and obtaining public comments on proposed rules. EPA Dockets (EDOCKET) is an online public docket and comment system created to expand access to documents in the agency's major dockets and increase public input. Dockets contain *Federal Register* notices, support documents, and public comments for rules the agency publishes and various nonregulatory activities. EDOCKET allows anyone to search, download, and print the documents in a docket, as well as submit comments about proposed rules online. This process has come to be known as "eRulemaking" (Shulman 2003). As one would imagine, this new way of soliciting comments, which has also been adopted by other government agencies, has made it much easier for interest groups and citizens to provide input on proposed regulatory actions.[9]

This aspect of "eRulemaking" raises a number of concerns and questions. While the process, at least in theory, makes it much easier for citizens to learn about and comment on regulatory proposals, it also allows well-funded and organized interests to deluge government agencies with comments expressing a single point of view, thereby inadvertently undermining the intent of public participation in the rulemaking process.

In particular, this process makes submission of form letters by members of interest groups extremely easy. Whether this new method of soliciting public comments reduces or actually increases conflict, however, is unknown. Moreover, to what extent, if any, do large numbers of comments from interest groups have an impact on the adoption of final rules? In other words, how much importance do agencies assign to the number of comments expressing the same opinion in exactly the same fashion? Are agencies able to pay for the extensive review of tens of thousands and sometimes hundreds of thousands of comments? What methodology do they use to sort and categorize responses? Does the additional information the agency receives justify the huge expense in maintaining and analyzing comments? In the end, do government agencies implement more acceptable and effective rules? These and other questions ought to be addressed in future research.

### Who Participates in the Rulemaking Process?

As Golden (1998) correctly observes, most research reveals little about who participates in the rulemaking process. Some studies analyze high-profile rules such as the Occupational Safety and Health Administration's cotton-dust guidelines (Bryner 1987) or the EPA's ozone regulations and standards under the Resource Conservation and Recovery Act (RCRA) (Landy, Roberts, and Thomas 1994). These studies, however, primarily focus on the role of OMB, Congress, and internal agency procedures. Other investigations center on a particular aspect of rulemaking. They examine, for instance, the use of cost-benefit analysis in agency rulemaking (for example, Bruff 1989; McGarity 1991) and regulatory review (for example, Bowers 1993; Furlong 1995; Portney and Berry 1995). Although these are important topics for research, such inquiries do not consider facets of rulemaking explicitly intended to foster direct accountability (Golden 1998).

A few researchers rely on survey research to examine who participates in agency rulemaking (for example, Kerwin 2003). They attempt to determine the degree to which interest groups participate in agency rulemaking and how much they feel they are influencing the process. As Golden (1998) points out, however, these studies are flawed because they focus on groups that are only located in Washington DC. It is possible that many groups that submit comments are situated beyond the beltway and represent types of organizations different from those in Washington DC. In addition, interest groups tend to overreport their influence and federal agencies tend to underreport pressure group influence (Golden 1998). Only an analysis of the changes sought by rulemaking participants and a measure of how much agencies alter their proposals in line with group positions can provide researchers with an accurate assessment of interest group influence in the rulemaking process.

In an attempt to learn more about interest group influence in rulemaking, Golden (1998) examines public comments on eleven regulations in three federal agencies, the EPA, the National Highway Traffic Safety Administration (NHTSA), and the Department of Housing and Urban Development (HUD).[10] Of the three, HUD is not a regulatory agency and is treated somewhat differently in the investigation. All the rules she analyzes were proposed and adopted during the first term of the Clinton administration. She tests traditional models of interest group relations with federal agencies, mainly those concerning iron triangles and agency capture, and the issue network model in her analysis. The three EPA rules she examines address national emission standards for hazardous air pollutants for industrial process cooling towers, testing and monitoring activities for hazardous waste management under RCRA, and voluntary participation in the acid rain program. The EPA received forty-three, sixty, and forty-eight comments, respectively, on these rules. After analyzing who participates in the rulemaking process in the EPA and the NHTSA, Golden reports:

> The strongest and most striking finding is the dominance of business commenters in the rulemaking process at the EPA and NHTSA. Between 66.7 percent and 100 percent of the comments received were submitted by corporations, public utilities, or trade associations. For five of the eight rules, citizen groups did not submit any comments. In no case did the citizen group participation exceed 11 percent. Neither NHTSA nor the EPA received a single comment from an individual citizen on any of the eight rules that were examined. There was modest participation by other government agencies . . . and by a few academic experts. (1998, 252–53)

The pattern of participation in the rulemaking process at HUD is significantly different.[11]

Golden (1998) also examines the geographical source of public comments. Contrary to what one might expect, she finds that rulemaking "is not the sole province of so-called Washington insiders" (1998, 256). Overall, all three agencies receive more comments from outside Washington DC than from inside. Her findings suggest that rulemaking participants are diverse and that studies of lobbyists should not be conducted exclusively in the nation's capitol. Previous research on interest groups (for example, Schlozman and Tierney 1986; Heinz et al. 1993) focuses entirely on lobbyists inside the beltway.

Finally, Golden (1998) studies interest group influence in the rulemaking process by investigating whether and, if so, to what extent differences occur between an agency's NOPR and its final rule. Since the *Federal Register* publishes the NOPR and the final rule as well as detailed explanations for any changes, it can be assumed with some confidence that the public comments submitted during the notice and comment period were responsible for these changes. She classifies the amount of change resulting from public comments into four categories, "none," "minimal," "some," and "a great deal." In the case of EPA, the agency changed its rules only to "some" extent. (Only once did the other two agencies change a rule "a great deal.") In general, she does not find "undue business influence" in the rules she examines. The primary bias she finds is the tendency among all the agencies to favor supporters of its rules over detractors.

This research builds on Golden's (1998) analysis of the source, nature, and impact of public comments in the rulemaking process. In contrast to her approach, the present study applies theories of issue definition, framing processes, and agenda building in investigating public comments on proposed rules. Such an approach should yield greater insight into the role of interest groups, especially business groups, in the rulemaking process, and how they seek to influence the contents of final rules. In addition, her study only considers rules promulgated by the EPA, and she does not include rules governing the management of natural resources. It is possible that different patterns might emerge in comments submitted to agencies involved in natural resource management. This study thus provides a fuller explanation of corporate involvement in rulemaking by applying theories of issue definition, framing processes, and agenda building and by incorporating natural resource rules in the investigation.

### Rule Selection and Data Collection

The author selected five proposed rules by the EPA in order to study the influence comments by business interests have on the contents of final environmental rules. The five rules address arsenic standards in drinking water, revision of criteria for solid waste disposal facilities and practices, revision of the extremely hazardous substance list, the adoption of regulations to establish a voluntary national low-emission vehicle program, and efforts to control emissions of hazardous air pollutants from mobile sources. Two rules concerning natural resources, a roadless area conservation plan and the reclassification of the gray wolf, are also included in the analysis. A complete description of each proposed rule (and final rule) appears in the *Federal Register*. In brief summary:

*National Primary Drinking Water Regulations; Arsenic and Clarifications to Compliance and New Source Contaminants Monitoring.* In 1942 the U.S. Public Health Service first established an arsenic drinking water standard at 0.05 mg arsenic per liter (or 50 parts per billion). No reason was given for selecting this standard, and its determination seemed arbitrary. Since then studies have been done on the potential health and environmental effects of arsenic, and results show that the present allowable level is too low. In other words, based on these findings, the federal government permits too much arsenic in drinking water. Both the European Union (EU) and the World Health Organization (WHO) have adhered to a higher standard of 10 parts per billion for many years.

The EPA proposes a maximum contaminant level (MCL) for arsenic at 5 parts per billion. The EPA also requests comments on the adoption of MCL standards of 3 parts per billion, 10 parts per billion, and 20 parts per billion. As part of the proposed rule, and in anticipation of opposition from small towns, the EPA lists technologies that will meet the MCL, including affordable compliance strategies for certain categories of small water systems serving fewer than ten thousand people.

*Criteria for Classification of Solid Waste Disposal Facilities and Practices; Identification and Listing of Hazardous Waste; Requirements for Authorization of State Hazard Waste Programs.* The EPA proposes revisions to the existing criteria for solid waste disposal facilities and practices. The recommended changes will establish specific standards for nonmunicipal solid waste disposal facilities that receive conditionally exempt small quantity generator wastes (CESQGs). The EPA also proposes revisions to regulations for hazardous wastes generated by CESQGs. These actions are recommended in order to clarify acceptable disposal options under RCRA. The intent is to give states maximum flexibility in formulating standards appropriate to facilities under their jurisdiction.

*Superfund Program; Extremely Hazardous Substance List.*   The EPA recommends deleting phosphorous pentoxide, dithlycarbamazine citrate, fenitrothion, and tellurium from the extremely hazardous substance list. The agency also recommends revision of the threshold planning quantity for isophorone diisocyanate from one hundred to one thousand pounds.

*Control of Air Pollution from New Motor Vehicles and New Motor Vehicle Engines: Voluntary Standards for Light-Duty Vehicles.*   The EPA proposes regulations to establish a national low-emission vehicle (LEV) program. Under these regulations, automobile makers will be able to volunteer to comply with more stringent tailpipe standards for automobiles and light-duty trucks. Once a company opts into the program, the standards will be enforced in the same way as any other federal motor vehicle pollution control requirement. This program will relieve the thirteen Ozone Transport Coalition (OTC) states in the northeastern part of the country (the Ozone Transport Region) of the December 1994 regulatory obligation to adopt their own motor vehicle programs. The EPA also wishes to harmonize federal and California motor vehicle standards and test procedures to enable manufacturers to design and test vehicles to one set of national standards.

*Control of Emissions of Hazardous Air Pollutants from Mobile Sources.* This rule lists twenty-one Mobile Source Air Toxics (MSATs) including various volatile organic compounds as well as metal compounds and diesel exhaust. The EPA proposes a gasoline benzene control program that requires refiners to maintain the current levels of overcompliance with federal reformulated gasoline and antidumping toxics requirements. The proposal outlines the EPA's program to address emissions of hazardous air pollutants from mobile sources and offers a framework to construct a national mobile source air toxics program. The agency proposes to continue its toxics-related research activities to determine whether additional air toxics controls should be adopted in the future.

*Special Areas; Roadless Area Conservation and Draft Environmental Impact Statement (EIS).*   The U.S. Forest Service proposes new regulations to protect certain roadless areas within the National Forest System. If adopted, the rule will prohibit road construction and reconstruction in most inventoried roadless areas of the national forest and require evaluation of roadless area characteristics in the context of overall multiple-use objectives during land and resource management plan revisions. The draft EIS on which the plan is based is included for review and comment.

*Endangered and Threatened Wildlife and Plants; Proposal to Reclassify and Remove the Gray Wolf from the List of Endangered and Threatened Wildlife in Portions of the Conterminous United States; Proposal to Establish Three Special Regulations for Threatened Gray Wolves.*   The U.S. Fish and Wildlife Service wishes to change the classification of the gray wolf (*Canis lupus*) under the Endangered Species Act (ESA) of 1973 as amended. This proposal will establish four Distinct Population Segments (DPSs) for the gray wolf in the United States and Mexico. Gray wolves in the western Great Lakes DPS, the western DPS, and the northeastern DPS will be reclassified from endangered to threatened, except where already classified as an experimental population or as threatened. Gray wolves in the southwestern (Mexican) DPS will retain their endangered classification. Gray wolves will be removed from the protections of the ESA in all other areas of the forty-eight conterminous states. Other proposed regulations address wolf-human conflicts in various parts of the country. The rule does not affect the endangered listing of the red wolf under the ESA.

Several criteria were used to select these rules. Most importantly, rules were chosen because they would provide the best tests of theories concerning issue definition, framing processes, and agenda building. An effort was also made to select rules that vary in breadth and address different facets of major environmental and natural resource issues, including air and water pollution, hazardous and solid waste, forest management, and wildlife protection. In addition, proposed regulations that address diverse industrial sectors (for example, automobile industry, chemical industry, and timber) were selected. Finally, the rules included in the analysis vary in terms of profile level and the number of comments submitted by interest groups and the public.

Readers should use some caution in generalizing the results. The seven rules examined in this research were not randomly selected.

Moreover, participants are self-selected; therefore, their comments do not necessarily represent the dispositions of the general population or the groups with which they are affiliated. Nonetheless, the investigation provides a fair representation of the wide range of views submitted for consideration by interested and affected parties and a chance to assess competing explanations for issue definition, framing, and agenda building. The proposed rules chosen for analysis offer an excellent opportunity to learn about the influence of business in rulemaking in the areas of environmental and natural resource policy.

Public comments on the proposed rules by the three federal agencies were collected and analyzed by different researchers. The author obtained comments on all the proposed environmental regulations from the EPA's docket room in Washington DC. The characteristics and contents of those comments were analyzed by the author. Comments on the roadless area conservation rule and the reclassification of the gray wolf, however, were collected and analyzed by the Content Analysis Enterprise Team (CAET) in the U.S. Forest Service. The CAET is a research arm of the Forest Service and is located in Salt Lake City, Utah. The CAET employs both qualitative and quantitative methods in their evaluation of the contents of the comments received. Like the author, the CAET strives to identify and classify all major issues contained in the comments. Breadth and depth of comment are considered in the analysis. In addition to noting relevant factual input, the author and the CAET took into account the relative emotion and strength of public sentiment behind different viewpoints. Both the author and CAET made a strong effort to evaluate the comments objectively by considering all aspects of diverse views. Although the characteristics of the participants and the content of their comments on the EPA and the natural resource rules are determined and analyzed by different individuals, the methodological approach is similar, thereby allowing contrasts and comparisons to be made in the data.

### Data Analysis

Table 5.1 reports the exact number of comments received on rules proposed by the EPA, the Forest Service, and the FWS. The number of comments on each rule varies considerably. The enormous number of comments received by the Forest Service and the FWS makes reliance on

TABLE 5.1

*Number of Comments on Selected Proposed Rules*

| Rules | Number of Comments | Date of NOPR | Date of FR[a] |
|---|---|---|---|
| U.S. Environmental Protection Agency: | | | |
| Revised arsenic standards in drinking water | 989 | 6/22/00 | 1/22/01 |
| Revisions to existing criteria for solid waste disposal facilities and practices | 23 | 6/12/95 | 7/1/96 |
| Revision of extremely hazardous substance list | 7 | 10/12/94 | 5/7/96 |
| Regulations to establish a voluntary national low-emission vehicle program | 104 | 8/10/95 | 1/7/98 |
| Control of emissions of hazardous air pollutants from mobile sources | 52 | 8/4/00 | 3/29/01 |
| U.S. Forest Service: | | | |
| Roadless area conservation rule | 1,156,308 | 5/10/00 | 1/12/01 |
| U.S. Fish and Wildlife Service: | | | |
| Amend classification of gray wolf | 15,554 | 7/13/00 | 4/1/03 |

[a]NOPR = Notice of Proposed Rule; FR = Final Rule.

SOURCES: The U.S. EPA and the Content Analysis Enterprise Team (2000, 2001) in the U.S. Forest Service, U.S. Department of Agriculture.

the services provided by the CAET necessary. All the regulations were formulated and proposed during the latter part of the Clinton presidency, and two (control of emissions of hazardous air pollutants from mobile sources and reclassification of the gray wolf) were formally adopted at the beginning of the Bush presidency.[12]

Comments were transmitted to the agencies in different ways. Between 20 and 33 percent of the comments on the three rules receiving the greatest input (the EPA's proposed revision of the arsenic standard in drinking water and both rules addressing natural resource issues) were sent by e-mail. Most interest groups and citizens submitted their comments in letter form by facsimile or through the postal system. Responses containing more than one signature were counted as a single comment.[13] Form letters were rarely used to express views on possible EPA regulations. In contrast, the vast majority of comments received on the two natural resource issues were conveyed in various types of form letters. Both the high level of salience of the natural resource issues and the superior

TABLE 5.2
*Geographical Location of Participants in Rulemaking*

| Rules | Washington DC | Other Location | Not Identified | Totals |
|---|---|---|---|---|
| U.S. EPA: | | | | |
| Arsenic standards | 2.63% | 89.58% | 7.79% | 100% (989) |
| Solid waste disposal | 26.09% | 65.22% | 8.69% | 100% (23) |
| Hazardous substance list | 0.0% | 100.00% | 0.0% | 100% (7) |
| National LEV program | 24.51% | 72.55% | 2.94% | 100% (104) |
| Emission of air pollutants | 28.85% | 67.31% | 3.85 % | 100.01% (52) |
| U.S. Forest Service: | | | | |
| Roadless areas | 2.86% | 91.08% | 6.06% | 100% (1,156,308) |
| U.S. Fish and Wildlife Service: | | | | |
| Gray wolf | 0.32% | 90.51% | 9.17% | 100% (15,554) |

SOURCES: The U.S. EPA and the Content Analysis Enterprise Team (2000, 2001) in the U.S. Forest Service, U.S. Department of Agriculture.

organizational skills of business interests and citizen groups operating in these policy arenas largely explain this result. To some extent, greater reliance on the Internet by federal agencies to post information and invite public input on proposed rules also helps account for the high number of comments received on the two natural resource measures. Of course, regulators do not view the comment process as a straight up and down vote on their proposals. Rather, they take into account a number of factors (for example, size and importance of organization, whether new facts, information, and data are being submitted, and so on) in their consideration of the comments they receive.

Table 5.2 shows the geographic location of participants in rulemaking. As Golden (1998) finds, a large percentage of participants are located outside of Washington DC. This is especially true for natural resource issues, which is understandable since the two proposed rules directly involve sectors of the population living primarily in the Midwest and the West. Thus, as Golden (1998) also observes, future researchers should study lobbyists in the environmental and natural resource policy spheres both inside and outside the beltway.

TABLE 5.3

*Type of Group of Participants in EPA Rulemaking**

| Category | Arsenic Standards | Solid Waste Disposal | Hazardous Substance List | National LEV Program | Emission of Air Pollutants |
|---|---|---|---|---|---|
| Business | 91 | 13 | 6 | 47 | 36 |
| Utilities | 260 | 1 | 0 | 4 | 0 |
| Unions | 0 | 0 | 0 | 0 | 0 |
| Government Congress | 7 | 0 | 0 | 0 | 0 |
| Federal agencies | 6 | 1 | 0 | 0 | 1 |
| State/local | 399 | 5 | 0 | 38 | 6 |
| Citizen groups | 13 | 3 | 0 | 12 | 5 |
| Unaffiliated individuals | 176 | 0 | 0 | 1 | 2 |
| Tribal | 6 | 0 | 0 | 0 | 0 |
| Academics | 17 | 0 | 1 | 0 | 2 |
| Not identified | 14 | 0 | 0 | 2 | 0 |
| Totals | 989 | 23 | 7 | 104 | 52 |

* Figures in the table represent the actual number of responses within each category for each rule.
SOURCE: The U.S. EPA.

### Types of Participants in Rulemaking

The public comments contain information that allows one to iden-tify the types of groups to which people who express views belong. Affili-ations were determined based on information on letterheads and in the text. In order to make comparisons possible, the author adopted the same categories used by the CAET in their analysis of the two natural resource issues.

Table 5.3 shows the numbers of those who commented on the five EPA rules and their affiliation. Businesses provide a majority of comments on three of the five rules, specifically, solid waste disposal, hazardous sub-stance list, and emission of air pollutants. Comments by companies com-prise just less than half (about 46 percent) of the total input on a proposed voluntary national LEV program. Ninety-one responses addressing a revi-sion of the arsenic standards originate from firms, and 260 comments come from utilities. Citizen groups and unaffiliated citizens provide a small frac-tion of the total comments received. Individuals representing utilities (primarily water providers), state and especially local governments, and unaffiliated citizens are most likely to comment on arsenic standards for water. No unions and very few members of Congress, federal agencies, tribal groups, and academic institutions offer views on the five proposed

TABLE 5.4

*Type of Group of Participants in Natural Resource Rulemaking\**

| Category | Roadless Areas | Gray Wolf |
|---|---|---|
| Business | 562 | 57 |
| Utilities | 19 | 1 |
| Unions | 0 | 0 |
| Government Congress | 60 | 2 |
| Federal agencies | 11 | 3 |
| State/local | 502 | 35 |
| Citizen groups | 756 | 210 |
| Tribal | 20 | 7 |
| Academics | 69 | 2 |
| Unaffiliated individuals/ unknown | 1,154,309 | 15,237 |
| Totals | 1,156,308 | 15,554 |

* Figures in the table represent the actual number of responses within each category for each rule.

SOURCE: The Content Analysis Enterprise Team (2000, 2001) in the U.S. Forest Service, U.S. Department of Agriculture.

EPA rules. Overall, these patterns in the data are similar to those Golden (1998) reports.

Table 5.4 presents data on the number of comments on proposed changes in natural resource regulations by organizational affiliation. In contrast to the results reported in Table 5.3, citizen groups tend to submit more comments than business groups and other organizations. This finding probably reflects the widespread interest within the environmental community across the country in the establishment of roadless areas in national forests and the reclassification of the gray wolf. In comparison, given the narrow economic focus of the two rules, fewer businesses are directly impacted by the proposed changes in regulation. Those that are affected, of course, have a significant stake as to whether the rules are eventually adopted and in what form (for example, the timber industry and ranchers). Similar to the responses concerning the environmental rules, a substantial number of comments on the natural resource proposals come from state and local officials. At the same time, a modest number of responses originate from congressional representatives and academics. As in the case of the proposed environmental regulations, unions do not express opinions on the natural resource rules. In general, the patterns in the data reported in Tables 5.3 and 5.4 are different and suggest that the types of organizations that respond to proposed environmental and natural resource rules depend on the particular social, economic, and political dynamics surrounding the rules.

The data in Table 5.4 appear to support the argument by the "neo-pluralists" that the dramatic rise of citizen groups has countered the lobbying activities of business groups. Of course, the data reflect the amount of business and citizen lobbying at one point in time, and one must examine patterns in the submission of comments on proposed natural resource rules over a period of time before reaching this conclusion. Still, the larger number of comments received from citizen groups versus business interests is impressive and clearly shows that numerous environmental organizations are concerned about natural resource issues. Whether business interests are still privileged in the rulemaking process, however, is examined shortly.

### Contents of the Public Comments

The contents of the comments on the proposed EPA rules were carefully reviewed for this study, and specific themes and concerns were noted. In addition, the CAET conducted an in-depth analysis of the comments received on the proposed natural resource rules. This makes it possible to present an overview of the positions of the various stakeholders on the environmental and natural resource proposals.

Overall, positions on whether to increase the minimum standard for arsenic in drinking water are somewhat varied. About 43 percent of the responses are clearly against taking any action and favor continuing the current standard of 50 parts per billion. Almost 25 percent of the responses support increasing the current standard between 20 and 50 parts per billion. Approximately 18 percent of the comments suggest increasing the acceptable level of arsenic in drinking water to at least 10 parts per billion. Another 11 percent of the responses back a higher standard but do not signify what the new standard should be. The author was unable to categorize 4 percent of the responses.

The comments on the proposed rule to increase standards for arsenic in drinking water tend to focus on the tradeoff between added health protection and high compliance costs. For the most part, those who feel the costs of compliance will be too burdensome oppose any change in the present standard, maintaining that the scientific evidence is not strong enough to justify the increased MCLs. William L. Kovacs, vice president of Environment and Regulatory Affairs for the U. S. Chamber of Commerce, for example, writes that "the U.S. Chamber recommends that the EPA abandon efforts to establish a 5 ug / l MCL unless a conclusive risk assessment demonstrates such a standard is justified" (2000, 1). He believes more research must be undertaken before the EPA takes any action. In general, small-town officials, representatives of small water systems, rural residents who depend on these systems, and business interests strongly argue in favor of continuing the present requirement of 50 parts per billion for arsenic in drinking water. Hence, business is unified in their position on this issue. Public health officials, environmental groups, pro-environment citizens, and academics are most likely to support the adoption of at least a 10 parts per billion standard. Those most concerned about public health and the environment feel existing scientific research does justify increased protection from arsenic. They also mention that the present standard is outdated, and they note how both the EU and WHO adhere to stricter MCLs. The final rule adopted by the EPA will be discussed in the next section.

As a result of a suit brought by the Sierra Club, the EPA was forced to develop new requirements governing nonmunicipal solid waste disposal facilities and practices. The federal court ordered the EPA to establish specific standards for nonmunicipal solid waste disposal facilities that receive CESQGs and adopt regulations for hazardous wastes generated by CESQGs under RCRA. For the most part, businesses affected by the proposed rule are aware of the court ruling and generally understand the need for the new regulations. Business interests are therefore sympathetic to the EPA's situation and, for the most part, appear to temper their opposition in their comments concerning the proposed rule. Several, such as the National Association of Demolition Contractors, express concern over the increased costs of rule compliance. Some of the waste management companies, such as Laidlaw Waste System, however, believe that the recommended standards for construction and demolition sites are not strict enough. Thus, business interests are divided on whether the rule should be adopted (that is, a conflictual issue). The Sierra Club argues, "EPA has not justified its decision to promulgate a weaker rule than that applicable to municipal facilities" and "urges the EPA to reject the option of a performance-based rule" (1995, 1).

The small handful of companies who submitted comments all support the EPA's proposed rule to delete from Superfund's extremely hazardous substance list phosphorous pentoxide, dithlycarbamazine citrate, fenitrothion, and tellurium and to revise the threshold planning quantity for isophorone diisocyanate from one hundred to one thousand pounds. The new rule reflects current science and, if adopted, will save a select few companies money. This regulation is a good example of a particularistic issue as described by Mark Smith (2000).

Most of those who commented on the EPA's proposal to establish a voluntary national LEV program support the agency's plan. Even large and small oil and gasoline companies and associations such as the Empire State Petroleum Association, Independent Oil Marketers Association of New England, Virginia Gasoline Marketers Council, Service Station Dealers of America and Allied Trades, Conoco Incorporated, Marathon Oil Company, and Amoco believe the program is viable. Texaco Oil Company withheld its support because the proposal does not specifically stipulate whether vehicles will have to use fuels other than gasoline or reformulated gasoline. James C. Pruitt, vice president of Federal Government Affairs for Texaco, states, "Texaco cannot support the national LEV program until it has been made clear in the final rule that the national LEV will not require or provide a basis for a change in existing fuel specifications. The EPA must make clear, in the final rule, that the national LEV program will not require, and cannot be relied upon to support, any modification in fuels currently available in the marketplace" (1995, 1). Other oil and gasoline companies voice this concern, too, but not as strongly as Texaco. Various chapters of the American Automobile Association (AAA) support the plan as do United Parcel Service (UPS) and motor vehicle manufacturing companies. In general, northeastern states favor the proposed rule. The American Lung Association, the Clean Air Council, and other pro-environment organizations, however, thought that the requirements of the program should be much stricter. The Clean Air Council argues, "EPA's national LEV program undermines the ability of the OTC states to implement Zero Emission Vehicle (ZEV) mandates" (1995, 2).

Public input on the EPA's effort to control emissions of hazardous air pollutants from mobile sources and regulate benzene and diesel exhaust are quite divided, with oil and gasoline companies and automobile manufacturers taking divergent stands on this issue. The Association of

International Automobile Manufacturers complements the EPA for proposing that additional research on air toxics must be done and for its efforts to regulate benzene. A similar view is expressed by the Alliance of Automobile Manufacturers. ExxonMobil, however, argues that the EPA's use of science to regulate benzene and diesel exhaust is "selective" in its application and that its implementation scheme for this proposal is too complex and impractical. The Phillips Petroleum Company agrees with most of ExxonMobil's views, while BP thinks the agency is generally headed in the right direction in its attempt to control air toxics emissions. Although Chevron has some quibbles, it also supports the EPA's proposed rule. As represented in comments by the U.S. Small Business Administration, small refiners complain that they will experience substantial increased costs if they are forced to comply with the rule.

Environmental groups and other organizations, such as the Consumer Policy Institute (Consumers Union), are disappointed with the EPA's delay in regulating air toxic emissions from mobile sources. Warren (2000), writing on behalf of the institute, criticizes the rule for, among other things, excluding a framework to construct a national mobile source air toxic program, lacking a clear and detailed research plan, placing public health at increased risk, and possibly violating President Clinton's executive order on environmental justice. The institute and other groups suggest that the scientific data on the health risks associated with air toxics are overwhelming and that the EPA is moving much too slowly to promulgate regulations on air toxics emissions.

As the public comments demonstrate, the roadless area conservation proposed rule and draft EIS has inspired intense public debate and has led to deep divisions between the stakeholders involved in the controversy (CAET 2000). Clearly, the rule touches on many complicated issues. According to the public comments, people disagree on whether roadless areas should be given more protection than they presently receive.[14] At the same time, both those who favor and those who oppose additional protection are at odds with the Forest Service over the proposed rule: those who favor protection believe it does not go far enough; those who oppose it feel it goes too far.

The debate over the proposed rule is driven for the most part by competing sets of values and perspectives (CAET 2000). People who favor the rule and those who oppose it fall roughly into two groups in terms of background and way of life, how they see the forest, and how they see the role of government in the management of natural resources. Those who express strong views on the regulation, which a majority of the participants do, are motivated by certain assumptions, values, and self-interest.

Although those who favor the proposed rule are not easily categorized in terms of background and lifestyle, opponents are involved in some way with forest resource industries. They also tend to be involved in motorized recreation on public lands or include people who, due to age or disability, are dependent on motorized access. People who are or have been associated with public land management also tend to oppose the rule (CAET 2000).

Opponents view the forests in terms of the resources they offer for human use. Their comments show they do care about the environment, and they favor natural resource conservation. They view the forests as an ecosystem capable, under effective management, of providing a variety of goods, including numerous recreational opportunities, for human well-being. For them, protection consists in managing forest lands as one would a farm for the purpose of maintaining sustained harvests. Roads are necessary to permit and facilitate management activities (for example, fuel thinning and treatment for insects and disease), allow responsible, sustainable resource extraction, and accommodate increasing recreational demands (CAET 2000).

Those who support the proposed rule are most likely to view forest lands as whole ecosystems that human activity disrupts. Thus, for these individuals, protecting roadless areas requires leaving the lands alone to evolve naturally through their own dynamic processes. (Some proponents condone some limited stewardship activity.) People who support the rule place a high priority on environmental protection and feel that roadless areas should be protected for their own intrinsic value as undisturbed wilderness, for the benefit of wildlife, and for the benefits these places offer to humans (CAET 2000). These areas are important, as comments by proponents note, as sources of clean drinking water and clean air, and as places of solitude and spiritual renewal. Thus, they argue that their value as places for passive recreation (for example, hiking and backpacking) far exceeds whatever value is attached to the commercial resources they contain.

The vast majority of responses the Forest Service received were form letters. Many people who sent such letters simply included their signature, while many others added personal comments. In addition to the original letters and communications, these form letters represent some of the strongest positions taken by participants. Form letters against the proposed rule almost always ask that continued access be maintained for forest management, resource extraction, and recreation (especially for motorized recreation). They also often highlight the negative effects respondents believe the rule will have on forest-dependent communities. Form letters in support of the proposed rule demand that the rule ban all extractive activities and motorized recreation from roadless areas one thousand acres or larger, that it accord such protection immediately on a case-by-case basis, and that it include the Tongass National Forest in southeastern Alaska. The CAET observes:

> The fact cannot be overemphasized that the debate over the proposed rule is—for many, many respondents—a highly emotional one; and it is only fair to acknowledge that while the majority of responses have been form letters, they are not thereby devoid of the same genuine, personal concerns and feelings expressed in original letters. (2000, xii)

CAET (2001) divides into two groups the public comments on the proposed rule to reclassify the gray wolf: remarks about the broad themes of FWS policy and management, and remarks either specific to the text of the proposed rule or specific to the DPSs. In terms of the first group, some of the participants question the position of the FWS that it did not have to develop an EIS to reclassify the gray wolf, while others allege that the agency did not follow "sound science" in the formulation of the plan. A number of the comments address agency-funding issues and the economic impacts of gray wolf recovery.

The most common response to the FWS-proposed rule is that the agency should not proceed with the reclassification of gray wolves (CAET 2001). Many voice concern about the precedent that down-listing gray wolves may set for other threatened and endangered species. Others argue that the proposed action will lead to a surge in both sanctioned and illegal killing of gray wolves. Numerous people demand that the FWS not delist the gray wolves outside of the identified DPSs. Citizens against the proposed delisting most often mention California and Nevada as areas in which the FWS should retain the endangered classification of gray wolves. Equally important, they say, is the need to include protections for gray wolves that migrate to states where delisting is proposed. A small number of individuals recommend that the FWS delist gray wolves because of the existence of large wolf populations in Canada and the gray wolf's depredation on domestic and wild animals (arguing that therefore the wolves deserve to be killed).

Many participants submitted comments on the recovery and reintroduction of gray wolves in the western United States. A large number of people commenting on the proposed rule maintain that the FWS should provide separate recovery plans for all states in the western DPS that have adequate potential for recovery, especially those with few or no established wolf populations (CAET 2001). Some participants claim that existing regulatory mechanisms are integral for guiding the gray wolf recovery in the West. Several people believe that western gray wolves face a serious threat from the FWS's own control program. Others argue that none of the states within the region have taken action to enforce gray wolf protective measures. The remaining comments address the designation of the northeastern DPS, the western Great Lakes DPS, and the southwestern DPS.

Similar to the proposed roadless area rule, most of the comments submitted to the FWS about the reclassification of the gray wolf were on form letters. Working Assets Long Distance Company generated more than three thousand citizen form letters requesting protection for gray wolves entering California. Most of the form letters request the establishment of viable populations of gray wolves in specific geographical regions.

### The Impact of Public Comments on Policy

By comparing the contents and requirements of proposed rules with the contents and requirements of final rules, as well as examining the reasons for changes outlined in the *Federal Register*, a determination can be made about the extent to which, if at all, public comments influence final rules. Table 5.5 summarizes the amount of change between the five EPA and two natural resource proposed and final rules. Golden's (1998) measure of the amount of change between proposed and final rules is used in the analysis. The amount of revision and the significance of the revision were evaluated simultaneously and were coded together as either "none," "minimal," "some," and "a great deal." As the table shows, four of the five EPA final rules are identical to the proposed rules. The proposed arsenic rule, which suggests an MCL of 5 parts per billion, is different from the final rule, which adopts an MCL of 10 parts per billion. The EPA took

TABLE 5.5
*Amount of Change between Proposed Rule and Final
Rule Resulting from Comments*

| Rules | None | Minimal | Some | A Great Deal |
|---|---|---|---|---|
| U.S. EPA: | | | | |
| Arsenic standards | | | X | |
| Solid waste disposal | X | | | |
| Hazardous substance list | X | | | |
| National LEV program | X | | | |
| Emission of air pollutants | X | | | |
| U.S. Forest Service: | | | | |
| Roadless areas | | X | | |
| U. S. Fish and Wildlife Service: | | | | |
| Gray wolf | | X | | |

this action in order to strike a balance between risk to public health and cost of compliance. These findings are similar to Golden's (1998) findings concerning the affect of public comments on recommended EPA regulations. Only "minimal" changes appear between the proposed and final rules involving roadless areas and the reclassification of the gray wolf. In both these cases, the final rules are slightly less strict than the proposed rule. None of the proposed rules examined in this study was changed "a great deal" in the final rule. Overall, public comments on environmental and natural resource proposed rules have little or no impact on the elements of final rules.

### Discussion

Interest groups have little influence over the structure and contents of proposed rules concerning environmental and natural resource issues. As Golden (1998) also finds, business interests do not exhibit excessive and unwarranted influence in the rulemaking process. Environmental organizations, too, fail to alter proposed rules to their liking. Hence, the ability of business to mobilize its forces and the tendency of environmental organizations to countermobilize have no major impact on final rules. Whether the regulatory issues are particularized, conflictual, or unifying does not matter either. The saliency of the controversy and the national-versus-regional orientation of the proposals fail to explain the final disposition of rules. For the most part, economic considerations play a minor role in environmental and natural resource rulemaking.

Although business interests have almost no influence over final rules concerning environmental and natural resource issues, they do make a strong effort to define the issues and frame the debate to their advantage. In cases where the proposed rules are most obviously intended to improve environmental quality or protect natural resources, companies and trade associations employ belief amplification when they argue that new regulations are too expensive, are not supported by science, and are unnecessary. In the present study, this is most evident in public comments on proposals regarding arsenic standards, emission of toxic air pollutants, and roadless areas in the national forests.

Theories of agenda building also help identify strategies pursued by firms in the rulemaking process. In cases where business interests most strongly oppose the adoption of a new rule (for example, timber companies against the roadless-area rule), they tend to engage in agenda blocking (Cobb and Ross 1997b). In other words, they try to persuade the agency to retract the rule entirely. Such strategies fail when the agency feels scientific consensus exists in support of the proposed action (for example, the arsenic rule).[15] Therefore, Haas's (1992) notion of "epistemic communities" applies here. In fact, it is remarkable just how much the EPA, the Forest Service, and the FWS rely on scientific studies to justify their recommendations and final decisions. This is evident in the large number of scientific studies cited in the justification of the rules printed in the *Federal Register*. As Renshaw of CAET observes:

> There are two main aspects to public comment. One is the indication of preferences and values provided; the other is new information, interpretation, or analysis. It is the latter that usually leads to changes between a draft and final proposal. It is the former that is more likely to influence political decisions over what proposals are actually made and implemented. Although we do often take note or even track preferences and values in various ways, our process focuses more on the information and analysis. In other words, even on highly contentious proposals we often do not track or report how many favor or oppose the action, we merely report what the concerns are. (Renshaw 2004, 1)

This observation and the findings reported in this analysis challenge Schneider and Ingram's (1993) and Litfin's (1994) views on the importance of language, symbols, and discourse in policymaking, at least in the rule-making process. Instead, Majone's (1989) argument that interests that are able to offer compelling and persuasive evidence will tend to influence policy is germane here.

The results of this study strongly suggest that future researchers ought to spend their time analyzing rulemaking across various presidential administrations. As far as rulemaking on environmental and natural resource issues is concerned, public input plays only a small role in shaping final policy. The kind of rules that are initially proposed is more critical and probably a better indicator of the amount of influence business has in the rulemaking process. Environmental protection and natural resource rule proposals are likely to vary substantially by the ideological and partisan makeup of Congress, the White House, and government agencies. In particular, the degree to which business has access to the executive branch will help determine the nature and contents of rules that are proposed under new and existing legislation. The more access business lobbyists have to important members of the administration, the more business is likely to get its way. Normally, it will have more access to officials in Republican administrations than in Democratic ones.

To a great extent, this has been the case in the administration of Republican president George W. Bush. In a survey of the scientific staff of the FWS conducted jointly by the Union of Concerned Scientists and Public Employees for Environmental Responsibility, more than two hundred scientists say they have been directed to alter official findings to lessen protections for plants and animals (Cart 2005).[16] More than 50 percent of the biologists and other researchers who responded to the survey said they knew of cases in which business interests, including timber, ranching, development, and energy companies, had applied political pressure to reverse scientific conclusions considered harmful to their enterprise.

Despite new scientific studies of possible health effects, the EPA approved an air pollution regulation addressing emissions of formaldehyde in 2004 that could save the wood products industry hundreds of millions of dollars. Research by the National Cancer Institute and the National Institute of Occupational Safety and Health shows that exposure to formaldehyde probably causes leukemia in humans. In drafting the regulation, the agency instead relied on a risk assessment generated by a chemical industry–funded think tank and a novel legal approach recommended by a timber industry attorney. The regulation was pushed through the agency by senior officials with previous ties to the timber and chemical industry. In essence, the rule was written by the industries that would benefit economically (Miller and Hamburger 2004). Environmental groups, led by the Natural Resources Defense Council and the Sierra Club, have petitioned the EPA to rescind the rule because it does not adequately protect public health. The case will be heard by a federal court of appeals if the agency, as most expect, rejects the petition (Hamburger and Miller 2004).

Similarly, in February 2005 the inspector general of the EPA, the agency's internal "watchdog," reported that the Bush administration had violated established scientific practices and regulatory requirements in drafting a controversial proposal to control mercury emissions from power plants (Miller and Hamburger 2005). According to Inspector General Nikki L. Tinsley, EPA officials failed to assess fully the health costs of mercury exposure and understated how much emissions could reasonably be reduced. Mercury is a toxic metal that pollutes water, contaminates fish, and accumulates in human tissue. Coal-fired utilities have been successful at persuading senior EPA officials appointed by the president to adopt standards for mercury emissions that risk the public's health for the benefit of this industry. In March 2005 the nonpartisan Government Accounting Office reported that the EPA distorted the analysis of its proposal to regulate mercury pollution from power plants, making it appear that the administration's market-based approach was superior to a competing approach endorsed by environmental groups (Vedantam 2005). The agency rebuked the EPA for a lack of "transparency." It said the EPA had failed to document completely the toxic impact of mercury on brain development, learning, and neurological functioning. Clearly, these and other examples of how commercial interests have successfully influenced the rulemaking process in the FWS and the EPA demonstrate the importance of who occupies the White House and the extent to which the president supports environmental protection and natural resource conservation.

### When Business Lobbies the Courts

Corporations often sue the EPA in federal court when they are not satisfied with the outcome of rulemaking (or other kinds of decisions) and believe they have compelling legal objections. Before taking legal action, business executives carefully weigh the cost of compliance against the amount of money required to pursue litigation. They are most likely to sue when compliance costs are estimated to be high relative to legal costs and when the chance of winning is real. Most large firms possess the resources necessary to hire experienced attorneys to represent them in court, and they include this expense in their annual budgets. The threat to sue can pressure the EPA to negotiate an agreement rather than engage in a lengthy and expensive legal battle it might lose.

As McSpadden (1995) explains, the judicial branch has long been considered as the third branch of government because its nonelective nature has relegated it to a position subordinate to the legislative and executive in the American political system. The power of judges to declare "what the law is" (based on *Marbury v. Madison*, 1803), however, permits courts to override legislative actions whenever they violate the Constitution and to negate administrative decisions whenever agencies abuse the power delegated by legal statute. The power of the courts to define law has long been a controversial issue (McSpadden 1995). Exactly how far courts can and should go in interpreting the law has been in dispute for some time.

In an administrative state, where scientific and technical expertise in policy spheres such as the environment is critical to understanding issues and reaching decisions, an increasingly large degree of policymaking has been delegated to government agencies not necessarily more responsive to direct political control than courts (McSpadden 1995). Judges are divided in their view as to how much oversight courts should exercise over agency discretion and how much freedom should be given to bureaucratic experts. Some judges argue that it is the responsibility of the courts to assure that agencies take a close look at all the factors that should be considered when making their decisions. Others tend to favor more agency autonomy and less interference from outside groups in administrative policymaking (McSpadden 1995).

The federal courts played a major role in the early evolution of social policy (Wenner 1982). In the 1980s, however, industry began mounting an aggressive defense against most government regulation (McSpadden 1995). This has been the situation, in particular, in the environmental arena. The property rights movement, for example, uses the wording of the Fifth Amendment to contend that government regulation that decreases the value of real property is unconstitutional because it "takes property without due process of law" (L. Epstein 1985; Rothenberg 2002). This line of reasoning has been used to challenge wilderness preservation and endangered species protection laws, as well as state zoning regulations.[17]

Exactly why interest groups choose the courts to pursue policy change and their level of success in this venue have been debated in the literature (Epstein and Rowland 1991). The political-disadvantage theory, initially developed by Cortner (1968), posits that disadvantaged groups elect to go to court because they are excluded from other points of access. Given their relatively limited resources, disadvantaged groups can achieve greater policy change in the courts even while risking judicial denial. Susan Olson (1990) finds limited support for the disadvantage theory at the federal district court level.[18] Richard Epstein (1985) shows that "advantaged" groups, especially conservative organizations, go to court more often because of the amount of resources they possess. Yet, Coglianese (1998) argues that it is not resources, per se, that determine when an organization pursues a litigation strategy, but the amount of real or perceived influence the organization has in the current political context that compels it to go to court. Thus, regardless whether they are civil rights organizations or business interests, groups that have had little or no success lobbying Congress or the executive branch will most likely turn to the courts for help.

The major opponents of the EPA in court are usually at opposite ends of the debate over pollution control policy (O'Leary 1993). Environmental groups (for example, the Environmental Defense Fund and the Natural Resources Defense Council) take the EPA to court on a regular basis. They complain that the agency's antipollution control measures are not stringent enough to protect the environment and public health. Major companies whose operations and products are regulated by the EPA (for example, Monsanto, Dow Chemical, ExxonMobil, and General Electric) and trade associations that represent groups of companies (for example, American Petroleum Institute and the National Solid Waste Management Association) frequently challenge EPA rules and administrative decisions in court. Industry often complains that EPA regulations cost jobs, restrict economic growth, and are unreasonably costly. It further argues that compliance can be cumbersome. In their analysis of agenda denial tactics, Cobb and Ross (1997a) consider legal action a high-cost strategy pursued when low- and medium-cost strategies do not work.

O'Leary (1993) explains the different ways disputes involving the EPA reach court. In cases where the EPA decides to assess a civil penalty against a party violating a statute or regulation, or where the agency proposes to deny, modify, or revoke a license or permit, most environmental laws require that it first grant the party a hearing on the issue. Most of these hearings are carried out according to the Consolidated Rules of Practice and are presided over by one of the EPA's administrative law judges. The administrative law judge issues an opinion following the hearing, which can be appealed to the agency administrator. This decision can then be appealed to federal district trial court. Challenges to agency rules, as well as alleged violations of the APA, are appealed to the courts of appeals (O'Leary 1993). Most of the laws the EPA oversees contain specific provisions for direct judicial review of other agency actions either in district courts or in courts of appeals.

Federal courts hear three types of environmental cases: (1) those national in scope and decided in the District of Columbia Appeals Court; (2) regulations or actions principally affecting localities or regions, which are heard in regional appeals courts; and (3) cases concerning violations of standards and administrative rules, which are considered in district courts (Wald 1992; Rothenberg 2002). Cases heard in district courts can be appealed to the appellate courts and later to the U.S. Supreme Court if necessary. In general, the courts can base their decisions on the constitutionality of given actions, whether agencies are properly using their delegated authority, and what interest can be heard in court (that is, judicial standing) (Rothenberg 2002).

O'Leary (2006) discusses the different and important ways in which the courts shape environment policy. Courts determine who does or does not have standing, or the right to sue, and they decide which cases are ripe, or ready for review. Courts also influence policy by their choice of standard or review, how they interpret environmental laws, and the remedies they choose. Finally, the U.S. Supreme Court, as the final arbiter of environmental cases, affects policy mostly through the cases it chooses to hear, the limits it places on other branches of government, and the restrictions it places on the states (O'Leary 2006). Among other things, the values, ideology, and policy preferences of judges influence the outcome of environmental disputes in court.

The vituperative debate over the nomination of William G. Myers to a seat on the Ninth Circuit Court of Appeals (covering nine western states) underscores the importance of the appellate courts in environmental policymaking. Myers was the chief legal officer in the Department of

Interior in the George W. Bush administration. Before that he was a mining industry lawyer and lobbyist and the director of federal lands for the National Cattleman's Beef Association. He has been a strong advocate for the interests of industries he represented and a harsh critic of environmental protection. He has argued in court that Congress does not have the power to protect wetlands and against federal management of the public lands. Based on his negative record on environmental issues, Democrats in the Senate vigorously opposed his nomination, citing his strong antienvironmental positions, his little courtroom experience, and his mixed rating from the American Bar Association committee that evaluates judicial nominees. Senate Democrats threatened to filibuster if a vote on his nomination was brought to the floor.

The federal courts have generally been viewed as a "friend" of environmental groups, particularly in the early days of the environmental movement. In more recent times, business interests have increasingly turned to the federal courts to challenge environmental legislation and rules promulgated by the EPA. The courts, therefore, represent another venue for corporations to protect and further their interests.

### Business Success Rate in Federal Court

A search was conducted of U.S. federal court database management statistics to determine which federal court of appeals tend to handle most of the suits filed against the EPA by business interests. The federal court of appeals was selected for analysis because of its ability to influence environmental policy on important issues. As previous research suggests (see, for example, Fiorino 1995), the District of Columbia Circuit handles most of the cases involving business and the EPA.[19] Jurisdictional requirements primarily explain why most appellate cases are brought to the District of Columbia Circuit.

The online database for the District of Columbia Circuit was used to identify all cases in which both business and the EPA were parties. These cases were located by using keyword searches as well as by reviewing the month-by-month case publication indexes for the years 1995–2002. This timeframe was selected because it spans two recent and different presidential administrations. In some instances information on case identification was supplemented by the results of searches of database sources

TABLE 5.6
*Business Success Rate in Court of Appeals,*
*District of Columbia Circuit, 1995–2002* *

| | WINNING PARTY | | |
|---|---|---|---|
| Controlling Environmental Statute | Business | Split | EPA |
| Clean Air Act | 11 | 9 | 14 |
| Clean Water Act | 2 | 0 | 2 |
| Comprehensive Environmental Response, Compensation, and Liability Act | 4 | 0 | 2 |
| Resource Conservation and Recovery Act | 2 | 3 | 3 |
| Toxic Substances Control Act | 3 | 0 | 1 |
| Safe Drinking Water Act | 1 | 0 | 0 |
| Emergency Planning and Community Right to Know Act | 0 | 0 | 1 |
| Totals | 23 | 12 | 23 |

* The figures in the table represent numbers of court cases.

maintained by the law schools at Emory and Georgetown universities. Cases involving business and the EPA that concerned issues beyond environmental policy (for example, contract disputes and so on) and cases dismissed for lack of jurisdiction were not included in the analysis. Settlements reached between business interests and the EPA prior to a decision by the Court of Appeals in the District of Columbia also were not examined. Information was collected on the parties, intervenors, issues on appeal, controlling environmental statute, case outcome / holding, winning party, judicial action, and legal basis for outcome. No formal effort was made to apply specific theories of issue definition, framing, and agenda building in the analysis; however, attempts to use the courts to change or block certain environmental policies are part of the agenda-setting process. Instead, the intent is to provide a general picture of the frequency with which business gets its way on environmental issues in the judicial system.

Table 5.6 shows how successful business interests have been in their appeals of EPA actions in the District of Columbia Circuit Court between 1995 and 2002.[20] As the data indicate, business groups appeal cases addressing a wide variety of environmental laws, though a majority of their appeals involve the Clean Air Act. Companies win more than they lose on legal challenges to regulations promulgated under CERCLA (Superfund) and the Toxic Substances Control Act. Business groups and the EPA are equally successful in cases involving the Clean Water Act. The EPA, however, wins more appeals concerning RCRA and the Clean Air Act than does business. Overall, as the totals at the bottom of the table reveal, between 1995 and 2002 business interests won as many cases as they lost on appeal to the District of Columbia Circuit Court. The data demonstrate that business has a moderate level of success in the federal court of appeals and that it gets its way in the judicial system a fair amount of the time.[21]

### Conclusion

As the findings show, public comments had little or no impact on the composition of final environmental and natural resource rules. Despite the best efforts of the private sector, four of five proposed EPA rules were adopted as final rules without changes by the agency. "Some" change occurred in the provisions of the final arsenic rule. Only "minimal" changes were made in the final rules on roadless areas and the reclassification of the gray wolf. All and all, business (and other) groups exerted no undue influence over the rulemaking process at the EPA, the Forest Service, and the FWS. This suggests that the kinds of rules that are initially proposed are more important than anything else. Thus, who serves as president has a major impact on determining the appointment of senior agency officials and exactly what kinds of rules are proposed by the EPA and natural resource agencies. In addition to the influence of firms in the rulemaking process, the level of success of business interests in the District of Columbia Circuit Court of Appeals was analyzed in this chapter. Between 1995 and 2002, companies and the EPA fought to a draw in the federal court of appeals. Although business does not always get its way in the judicial system, it tends to be more successful there than in the rulemaking process.

Environmental rules and regulations can have a major financial impact on corporations. Beginning with the passage of federal clean air and water laws in the early 1970s, businesses have complained loudly and often that environmental regulations place enormous financial burdens on their activities. Since 1970, utilities and factories have spent hundreds of millions of dollars upgrading their old equipment so that they emit significantly less pollution into the nation's air and water. Many industry leaders believe that they are doing all they can to obey current pollution control laws and that meeting additional restrictions will cost them too much money. Not surprisingly, therefore, utility and factory operators have fought hard against the adoption of increasingly tough, new environmental standards. The extent to which they have avoided complying with environmental laws or have effectively blocked or altered proposed environmental regulations—and thus have gotten their way—is the subject of this chapter.

This chapter examines the political role of industry in three major environmental regulatory conflicts, the dumping of polychlorinated biphenyls (PCBs) in the Hudson River in New York State by the General Electric Company (GE), the battle to control sulfur dioxide ($SO_2$) emissions and reduce acid rain, and the debate over climate change. As explained at the end of Chapter 3, the case studies analyzed in this and the next chapter were selected based on certain methodological objectives and previous research (on interest groups and environmental policy). Among the sampling criteria used were pollution control versus natural resource management; geographic dispersion; type and salience of the conflict; and the nature of the combatants. An effort was made to select at least one controversy that reflects each of Mark Smith's (2000) categories of unifying, particularistic, and conflictual policy issues. Following the advice of King, Keohane, and Verba (1994), Mahoney (2000), Gerring (2004), Ragin (2004), and George and Bennett (2005) the companies and policy issues vary across the case studies. As Prakash (2000) recommends, the companies are all large American businesses with considerable revenues and sales. All the cases encompass salient controversies (that is, they affected many people and they received media attention), and they represent interesting illustrations of several analytic issues raised earlier in the book (for example, bottom-up democratic mobilization, situations of inequality of the forces involved, evidence for or against beyond compliance, and neopluralist findings concerning the importance of citizen groups and public opinion). Conflicts were not selected, a priori, based on whether business won or lost. Most importantly, the analysis of the case studies will permit a thorough examination of the different theoretical concepts and perspectives introduced in Chapter 3. The analysis should provide valuable knowledge about, for example, the effect of certain political and economic variables on agenda building (for instance, partisanship and national versus regional economic conditions). The case studies will also shed light on critical aspects of theories pertaining to issue definition and framing processes and agenda building (proactive and denial). The theoretical concepts and principles discussed in Chapter 3 are applied following the presentation of each case.

It is difficult to measure political influence. Among other things, it is hard to know whether the actions of a particular individual, group, or coalition of groups were the direct cause of policy change (or no policy change), or whether policy change (or no policy change) occurred for other reasons. Also, how does one assess influence when business interests win at certain points in time but lose at others? In this and the next chapter, an attempt is made to gauge how much business interests influenced policy outcomes by carefully presenting the public positions of business groups, analyzing their lobbying activities and other related actions, noting how much effort (that is, time and money) these groups devoted to a conflict, analyzing the reactions of political actors to the demands of business groups, and determining the extent to which, if at all, government officials altered environmental or natural resource policy. This study considers how often business interests win and lose as well as the level of importance of each victory and defeat in an effort to arrive at an overall judgment of how influential business was in a given conflict. As is always the case regardless of the methodology used, it will be up to the reader to determine whether the author's conclusions are supported by the evidence and are compelling.

This chapter begins with an examination of the attempt by the federal government to force GE to remove PCBs from the bottom of the Hudson River. This is followed by an investigation of the role of business in the acid rain and climate change controversies. The major findings are reviewed at the conclusion of the chapter.

### The Pollution of the Hudson River

The scenic Hudson River is located in eastern New York State and runs approximately two hundred miles between Albany, the state capital, and New York City. The river has played a central role in the lives of nearby inhabitants for more than five centuries. Native American tribes and early Dutch and English settlers depended extensively on the river for fish, shellfish, commerce, and travel. Later, steamboats, ferries, houseboats, and white-sailed sloops were common sites on the river, transporting people and goods. Large companies, such as GE, built factories along the waterway in the 1930s and 1940s. The Hudson River contains a complex aquatic ecosystem, including various species of fish and shellfish. A wide variety of birds and wildlife also live along the river. Along with tourism and recreation, a thriving fishing industry existed in the region for many years. Today many people farm and reside near the river. Unfortunately, particularly since World War Two, the river has become increasingly polluted. The New York State Department of Environmental Conservation monitors the water quality and the general ecology of the waterway (New York State Department of Environmental Conservation 2004).

Between 1946 and 1977 two plants owned and operated by the GE company, one located in Hudson Falls, New York, and another in nearby

Fort Edward, New York, discharged approximately 1.3 million pounds of PCBs into the river (Perez-Pena 1999).[1] GE officials argue that, at the time, there were no environmental laws that prevented them from discharging chemicals into the Hudson; New York State officials and environmentalists dispute this claim. Understandably, the massive dumping of PCBs into the river has greatly alarmed local residents, business people, environmentalists, scientists, public health officials, and local, state, and national elected leaders and policymakers. In addition to the negative impact PCBs have on the ecological system, they are a dangerous threat to public health.

According to the EPA, PCBs are a group of chemicals consisting of 209 individual compounds (U.S. EPA 2004a). For many years PCBs were widely used as a fire preventive and insulator in the manufacture of transformer capacitors because of their ability to withstand extremely high temperatures. Widespread concern over the toxicity and persistence in the environment of PCBs led Congress to pass the Toxic Substances Control Act in 1976, which included, in addition to other regulations, prohibitions on the manufacture, processing, and distribution of PCBs (Crine 1988).

PCBs have been demonstrated to cause a number of adverse health effects in humans and different animal species. The EPA reports that PCBs cause cancer as well as a variety of noncancer health effects in both humans and animals, including effects on the immune, reproductive, nerve, and endocrine systems (U.S. EPA 2004a). Research on humans provides strong evidence for potential carcinogenic and noncarcinogenic effects of PCBs, including premature births and development disorders (Erickson 1993).

Studies also show that PCBs bioaccumulate in the environment, increasing in concentration as one moves up the food chain (U.S. EPA 2004a). This is of particular concern in localities where fish are exposed to PCB contamination—as in the Hudson River—and, where, in turn, they may be consumed by birds, wildlife, and humans. People who fish have been asked to reduce their risk of exposure to PCBs by following the most recent advisories by the New York State Department of Health regarding the consumption of different kinds of fish caught in the river. In early 2004 it was illegal to possess fish above Troy Dam located just north of Albany. Below this point women of childbearing age and children under age fifteen were urged not to eat fish from the river while others have been told not to eat more than one meal (one-half pound) a week of most aquatic species (New York State Department of Health 2004).

*Response by General Electric*

Since the early 1980s the EPA has considered whether it should force GE to remove the PCBs from the Hudson River under the authority of the Natural Resource Damages provisions of the Comprehensive Environmental Response, Compensation, and Liability Act of 1980 (Superfund).[2] Beginning in the mid-1990s and beyond the turn of the twentieth century the company waged a multimillion-dollar media campaign to convince political leaders and the public that removal of the PCBs was unwarranted and, in fact, dangerous. GE sponsored a large number of television "infomercials," radio spots, and full-page newspaper advertisements claiming that PCBs in the Hudson were down 90 percent and that a proposed massive dredging project was unnecessary and a waste of money. Advertisements by the company denied any connection between various cancer- and noncancer-related illnesses and PCBs. Scientists were brought in by GE to articulate and promote this view. In GE spokesman Mark Behan's view, "Twenty years of research has uncovered no credible evidence that PCBs are associated with any of 92 diseases that have been studied. The increased risk comes only if someone ate a half-ton of Upper Hudson fish over 40 years. What kind of person would do that to begin with?" (Glionna 2001, A17). He adds, "We don't believe that digging up the bottom of this river and killing everything that lives there is the right way to continue the natural recovery that's going on very well without the help of these government scientists" (Glionna 2001, A17). The GE advertisements argued that the dredging would disrupt river life for a generation. Moreover, disturbing the bottom of the Hudson River would result in PCB-laden sediment traveling downstream to as far as New York City. Television spots regularly showed huge clamshell dredges profusely dripping contaminated sediment onto a waiting fleet of trucks.

GE's aggressive and expensive campaign against cleaning up the Hudson River was not surprising given how much was at stake for the company. The PCB contamination of the Hudson represents the most extensive Superfund site in the nation, and it will cost hundreds of millions of dollars to abate it. In addition to the huge expense of dredging the forty "hot spots" of PCB-tainted silt and the potential cost of claims by the federal and state governments for damage to natural resources, the decision on the Superfund site on the Hudson could affect abatement efforts at many of the seventy-four other Superfund sites where GE is responsible for some pollution (Revkin 1998). GE, therefore, was intent on doing everything it could to avoid cleaning up the river. The fact that the company was one of the largest employers in New York State gave it considerable leverage.

During summer 1997 GE scientists reported results of extensive studies they had conducted on a six-mile stretch of the Hudson River below its factories at Hudson Falls and Fort Edward. Their data showed that the PCBs in the water were emanating from recent releases, not the old "hot spots" created more than two decades ago. They maintained that PCBs would soon stop leaching into the water now that the company had found and plugged almost all new releases of the chemicals from its two factories. Federal wildlife biologists and other scientists disagreed with the findings and conclusions of the GE scientists (Revkin 1997b).

During GE's media campaign to convince leaders and citizens that leaving the PCBs in the Hudson River was the prudent thing to do, emerging scientific research challenged its claims. In early 1997, for example, new studies by federal and New York State scientists found that PCBs on the shores and bottom of the river were not being cleaned away by natural means as GE claimed (Revkin 1997a). In addition, their research showed that toxic compounds were evaporating from mud flats and were traveling through the air, placing nearby residents and wildlife at risk. A separate federal study released about the same time found PCBs in high concentrations in several species of birds. GE criticized the new findings, contending that the research was flawed.

In spring 1997 EPA officials released a preliminary study of the river indicating that PCBs were not being naturally degraded as GE had claimed (Revkin 1997b). Based on their data, the stain of PCBs now stretched along nearly the entire length of the river bottom and had ruined commercial fisheries, harmed wildlife, and posed a risk to people. The PCB problem was especially troublesome, they said, because so many of the river's other pollution problems have been reduced over time.

However, in February 1998, under pressure from GE and Gerald B. H. Solomon, a powerful upstate Republican congressman, the EPA decided to slow down completion and release of a comprehensive and critical study of PCB contamination in the Hudson River (Dao 1998). EPA officials said they were postponing the final release of the report to allow for additional outside scientific and public review of its findings. They noted that whatever they eventually decide must be defensible in court. Several environmental organizations and a bipartisan group of five members of Congress representing districts along the Hudson from Westchester County to Albany informed EPA's administrator at the time, Carol Browner, that they strongly objected to the delay. As chairman of the powerful House Rules Committee, however, Mr. Solomon wielded a great deal of influence and, along with GE, was able to persuade the Clinton administration to agree to the delay.

Continuing to fight back, GE's public relations campaign intensified at the end of the 1990s. The company argued that the risk of leaving PCBs in the silt was very low, while the cost of dredging the contaminated bottom would be very high, possibly costing as much as several hundred million dollars. In May 1998, John Welch Jr., the Chairman of GE, asserted, "Living in a PCB-laden area is not dangerous" (Revkin 1998, B4). Steven Ramsey, vice president for environmental programs at GE, said in an interview that the company had compiled a long list of independent studies showing no link between PCBs and human cancer. He added that other studies questioned any connection to other health effects, like disruption of hormones (Revkin 1998).

Nevertheless, at the end of 2001 researchers from Mount Sinai School of Medicine in New York City released a study showing increased PCB levels and health problems in people who consumed fish from the Hudson River (Glionna 2001). The study examined forty-five fishermen / women who ate crabs, eels, and fish caught in the river. The researchers found that the more fish people ate, the higher were their levels of PCBs.

Environmentalists also placed considerable political pressure on GE to clean up the Hudson River. Local environmental groups along with chapters of national environmental organizations worked hard to convince Hudson River residents and state and federal officials of the need to remove the PCBs from the river's bottom. In addition to organizing protests and meetings, they helped bring scientific information to the attention of policymakers and citizens. Some of the groups that participated in the campaign against GE included Scenic Hudson, Friends of a Clean Hudson, New York Public Interest Research Group, The Riverkeepers (with the support of Robert Kennedy Jr.), and the local chapter of the Sierra Club.

Additional political pressure on the company came from state and federal officials. During the Clinton administration, Secretary of the Interior Bruce Babbitt, speaking from a hilltop overlooking the Hudson River, assailed GE as a corporate giant bent on delaying the restoration of the river (Revkin 1997b). He said that GE, which had built its business and reputation on science, was now using science to confuse, instead of clarify, the pollution problems in the Hudson through a deceptive media campaign. GE's Stephen Ramsey criticized Babbitt, calling his speech "pure politics" and arguing that the company had every right to lobby to protect its interests (Revkin 1997b).

Babbitt was not the only high-ranking federal official to question the truthfulness of GE's ongoing publicity campaign. Carol Browner, the administrator of the EPA during the Clinton presidency, accused the company of trying to confuse the public as part of a broad effort to delay or limit the cleanup of tons of PCBs (Revkin 1998). Testifying before the Environmental Conservation Committee of the New York State Assembly, Browner argued that the company's efforts were undermining state health advisories warning young women and children not to eat fish from the river. She said, "GE would have the people of the Hudson River believe, and I quote, 'Living in a PCB-laden area is not dangerous.' Well, you know something? The science tells us the opposite is true" (Revkin 1998, B4). One year later, to bolster Browner's point, the EPA released a comprehensive study revealing that PCBs pose an unacceptably high risk of cancer and other serious diseases in people who eat fish from the river's northern section (Perez-Pena 1999).

At the end of 1999 newly elected New York State Attorney General Eliot Spitzer, a Democrat, sued GE, not for environmental or health damages caused by the dumping of PCBs, but for interfering with the state's responsibility to maintain a shipping canal that links the Hudson River to Lake Champlain (Perez-Pena 1999). He invited local governments and private interests along the length of the river to join in his suit or file their own on similar grounds. The legal theory behind the suit made it easier for outside parties to join the court action. The suit was intended to put pressure on the company to reach a settlement with the EPA for large-scale dredging of the river. Governor George Pataki, a Republican, took issue with the action, feeling it was unnecessary and that it might interfere with other ongoing negotiations with GE. One year later, in a major blow to GE, Governor Pataki yielded to political pressure and called for dredging of the Hudson River to remove PCBs.

Just weeks prior to Clinton leaving office, EPA Administrator Browner ordered GE to spend nearly half a billion dollars to dredge toxic PCBs embedded in the Hudson River mud. In handing down the order, she noted that the decision followed the most intensive EPA review ever. GE immediately said it would fight the order because dredging would disperse toxins safely buried in the river's sediment. Richard Bopp, a geologist at Rensselaer Polytechnic Institution in Troy, New York, has studied PCB contamination of the Hudson River for more than two decades and, along with other experts, disputed this claim (Revkin 2000).

GE representatives hoped they might be able to reverse, or at least substantially alter, the EPA decision with the election of Republican George W. Bush to the White House. Their prospects appeared to brighten when President Bush selected Christie Todd Whitman, a former Republican governor of New Jersey, to head the EPA. They immediately began lobbying the new administration to reverse the EPA order to dredge. After reviewing the case, however, Whitman announced in August 2001 that her agency would proceed with the dredging plan formulated under the Clinton administration and would order GE to carry out the nearly half-billion-dollar cleanup. The company was surprised and disappointed when Whitman revealed that the new administration endorsed the Browner order; the company vowed to fight the proposal (Seelye 2001a). At the end of the year Whitman rejected GE's request to scale back the abatement of PCBs in the river and stated that the EPA would move forward with the nearly five-hundred-million-dollar dredging plan.

The Sisters of St. Dominic in Caldwell, New Jersey, and dozens of religious, public, and private owners of GE stock submitted a proposal to company shareholders requesting the board of directors to report its annual expenditures since 1990 on legal fees, expert fees, lobbying, public relations, and media use relating to the health and environmental consequences of PCB exposure from the Hudson River. The request that the company disclose the actual costs of its long-term resistance to the remediation of this and other contaminated sites was made in response to GE's continued persistence in its lawsuit challenging the constitutionality of Superfund legislation. The board of directors opposed the proposal because they felt they were doing everything possible to comply with current environmental regulations, including Superfund, and they were currently in negotiations with government agencies, including the EPA, on abating other toxic waste sites in addition to the Hudson River site. The board believed nothing would be gained by this action and advised shareholders to vote against the proposal. People holding 30.5 percent of shares in GE stock voted in favor of the proposal (General Electric Company 2004).

In April 2002, after exhausting nearly all avenues of appeal, GE changed its position and offered to clean up the Hudson River. The company filed notice with the EPA that it will negotiate with government in good faith about removing chemicals, including collecting sediment samples, designing a dredging strategy, and then performing dredging as required. The government was asked to find a disposal site for the contaminated mud that would be removed. In 2002 and 2003, GE collected more than twenty-six thousand samples from approximately five thousand cores of sediment in the Hudson. The samples were analyzed for PCBs, other chemicals, and engineering characteristics by independent laboratories approved by EPA and New York State (General Electric Company 2004).

The EPA was finally able to move ahead with its project plans and cleanup program. EPA officials announced in March 2003 that an additional year would be needed for planning and design beyond the three years already allotted. As a result, the dredging would not begin until spring 2006 at the earliest, making the projected completion date six years later. The complexity of the project, along with the need for good relations with anxious upstate residents whose communities would be affected, was the main cause for modifying the schedule. Local environmentalists, including Scenic Hudson, a conservation group based in Poughkeepsie, New York, expressed dismay at the one-year delay and accused the EPA of succumbing to GE pressure (Seelye 2001b). Company officials, however, said that the request for more time had not come from GE.

The EPA and GE reached agreement on the design of the Hudson River abatement plan in August 2003. At the end of 2003 the EPA released a draft of comprehensive quality of life performance standards intended to reduce the wide range of possible negative effects of dredging, sediment processing, transferring and dewatering, and support operations on people, businesses, recreation, and community activities in the project area (U.S. EPA 2003a). By taking this action, the EPA hoped to convince Hudson River communities and residents that every precaution was being taken to ensure the safety of the dredging project. Based on the sole involvement of GE throughout this dispute, one can define this controversy as a particularized conflict.

### Internal Company Management Dynamics

Theories of internal management dynamics and corporate strategies reviewed in Chapter 3 offer some insight into GE's failed effort to avoid abating the PCB contamination of the Hudson River. To a significant degree, rational choice theory explains why the company fought long and hard against forced removal of PCB-contaminated sediment from the river. The company was well aware of the exorbitant cost of dredging and the additional cost of cleaning up other Superfund sites for which it was a responsible party. Consequently, company executives conducted a cost-benefit analysis and chose to adopt a less costly but still rather expensive public relations campaign and to pay for research and legal fees to oppose the cleanup. Obviously, their main goal was to protect company assets.

Elements of organization theory and corporate culture theory also are applicable to this case to some extent. GE possesses a traditional hierarchical and centralized management structure. Judging by the company's handling of its PCB contamination of the Hudson River, the need to shield financial assets outweighed the firm's concern for protecting the environment and public health. This perspective dominated internal corporate discussions and reflected the values and culture of the company. Debate inside the organization was stifled, and no managers condemned GE for its actions. (Most stockholders also supported GE's decision to oppose government efforts to force the company to clean up the river.) The need to fight the EPA and New York State in order to protect profits was a position perpetuated by the board of directors and upper echelon of the company. Whether company executives truly believed that the PCB contamination had no or a minor negative impact on the environment and public health—despite good scientific research to the contrary—is unknown.

#### Political and Economic Variables

Political variables to some extent explain the evolution of the controversy regarding the abatement of PCBs in the Hudson River. Although no public opinion polling was conducted by the media, it is clear from newspaper accounts and personal interviews with various individuals involved in the controversy that New York State residents, especially those residing in proximity to the river, were extremely concerned about the serious negative effects the contamination was having on the environment and public health. In spite of the company's aggressive media campaign, it appears that most citizens never believed that the huge quantity of PCBs in the river was harmless and that dredging would only exacerbate the pollution problem as GE repeatedly claimed. It is noteworthy that, with the exception of Republican Congressman Solomon's actions, federal and state elected officials in both political parties publicly supported the dredging of the river by GE. This undoubtedly reflected their assessment of the problem and what the public believed should be done. Thus, partisanship played almost no role in this controversy.

Through their actions, environmental groups were successful in countering GE's media campaign against dredging. In addition to letter writing and protesting, they continuously challenged the company on its claims that the PCB sediment was harmless. Environmentalists were particularly effective in educating citizens about the effects PCBs have on fish, wildlife, and humans by citing research findings by neutral scientists and organizations. They also were successful in convincing elected leaders of the need to address the issue aggressively.

Somewhat surprisingly, economic conditions played only a minor role in this controversy. Like many Northeast and mid-Atlantic states, New York experienced tight budgets and considerable unemployment in the 1980s and 1990s. Nevertheless, the fact that GE was a large employer did little to dissuade federal and state officials from pursuing the cleanup of the river. Of course, knowledge of the PCB contamination and the widespread belief that it was harmful had a major negative economic impact on the fishing industry, recreation, and tourism in the area. Perhaps, as a consequence, neither side was able to use economic conditions to their advantage.

### Issue Definition and Framing Processes

The battle over how the PCB pollution issue was defined and the framing processes that were used help to explain how the controversy unfolded and the level of influence GE had throughout the dispute. GE, a world-class corporation highly respected for its application of science, was unable to use frame bridging (Snow et al. 1986) effectively in their media campaign to convince leaders and citizens that the PCB problem was not serious and that dredging would do much more harm than good. The EPA and New York State health and environmental officials, however, were successful in linking GE discharge of large amounts of PCBs into the Hudson River—something the company never disputed—to significant environmental degradation and harm to public health. Health advisories concerning the consumption of fish from the river by childbearing women and young children struck a chord with many leaders and the broad public. In this regard, frame amplification (Snow et al. 1986) involving both values and beliefs explains how the issue was portrayed and perceived and accounts for GE's failure to avoid dredging the river in the end. As much as it tried, GE was unable to transform the PCB contamination issue by employing frame transformation techniques (Snow et al. 1986) into widespread economic concern. Applying Riker's (1996) Dominance Principle, environmental interests were able to dominate the volume of rhetorical appeals on the theme of protecting the natural environment and public health, especially the health of the helpless (that is, young children) in society, to the point where the company finally acquiesced and agreed to dredge the river.

### Agenda Building

Agenda-building theory also accounts for the level of influence of GE and the outcome of the company's fight to avoid cleaning up the Hudson River. Hirschman's (1991) perversity thesis, futility thesis, and jeopardy thesis apply to this case. GE argued that any effort to introduce change (that is, dredge) will only make conditions worse, will cost too much, will do little to correct the problem, and will actually produce problems worse than the current one (that is, by spreading the PCB contamination over a wider area in the river). To some extent, this strategy delayed a final resolution of the dispute. Since stakeholders and scientists on both sides of the issue disagreed about what should be done, if anything, about the PCB contamination, neither Sabatier's (1993) advocacy coalition framework nor Haas's (1992) notion of epistemic communities applies here.

Explanations by Cobb and Ross (1997b) and Litfin (1994) also allow us to understand the level of influence of GE and the policy outcome. As Cobb and Ross (1997b) discuss, certain groups choose to follow particular strategies to keep issues off the formal (government) agenda, thereby preventing government from taking any action. GE employed a "medium-cost" strategy by trying to discredit environmentalists and even government scientists in their call for dredging the PCB-laden sediment at the bottom of the Hudson River. The company's effort failed because, as Litfin (1994) explains, "knowledge brokers" operating at low and middle levels of federal and state government were able to transform important scientific findings into a call for government to force GE to clean up the PCB contamination of the river. In contrast to GE's claims, the testimony and research results by government agencies and neutral third parties were widely perceived to be legitimate and the need to take action warranted. "Knowledge brokers," with the assistance of prominent government officials, were able to use language and symbols skillfully to make the need for dredging apparent. This clearly undermined the influence of GE in the dispute. As a consequence, the EPA administrators under both Clinton and Bush ordered the company to dredge the Hudson River and pay the high cost for removing the PCB-contaminated sediment. Following a lengthy battle, the company agreed to comply.

### The Acid Rain Problem

Acid rain is a by-product of fossil fuel combustion and metal smelting, which produce sulfur dioxide ($SO_2$) and nitrogen oxides ($NO_x$). These gases, transformed into sulfuric acid and nitric acid, normally remain in the atmosphere for weeks. They often are transported hundreds of miles by high-altitude winds before falling to earth as dry particles or precipitation. In the process, these gases become sulfate and nitrate aerosols and then join with other airborne chemical compounds, including the volatile organic compounds ozone and hydrogen peroxide, and water, to become the chemicals that return to earth dissolved in water or fixed in ice crystals (Rosenbaum 2005). Acid particles and gases can also be formed at ground level and can be absorbed directly by plants or oxidized into sulfate and nitrates and absorbed by the soil (Bryner 1995). Microscopic solids of heavy metals, referred to as microparticulates, can become acid precipitation, too. Rosenbaum (2005) reports that from 60 to 70 percent of acid precipitation found in rain or snow is sulfuric acid; the rest is predominately nitric acid.

The level of acidity of a substance is measured by its pH factor on a logarithmic scale that ranges from a low of 0 to a high of 14. Thus, a change of one point of pH indicates a tenfold change in acidity or alkalinity. Battery acid, for example, has a pH level of 1.0, lemon juice has a pH level of about 2.0, and milk has a level of 7.0, the neutral point on the scale. Values over 7.0 represent degrees of alkalinity. Rainfall containing no pollution has a pH factor between about 5.5 and 7.0. Precipitation with a pH factor below 5.6 is sufficiently acidic to have a negative impact on the environment (Bryner 1995).

Scientists have known about the effects of acid rain since the late 1800s. Robert Angus Smith, a nineteenth-century English chemist, was the first to identify acid rain (Layzer 2002). He conducted extensive research on its characteristics, but his studies were generally ignored. Scientific interest in acid precipitation was revived in the late 1960s when Swedish soil scientist Svante Oden, incorporating knowledge from the disciplines of limnology, agricultural science, and atmospheric chemistry, conducted a comprehensive analysis of the behavior of acid deposition over time and across regions (Layzer 2002). In the early 1970s Swedish scientists, extending Oden's work, found that hundreds of Swedish lakes had become too acidic to permit usual biological processes. They reported that the normal plant and animal life was absent or dying. These findings were reported at the 1972 United Nations Conference on the Human Environment in Stockholm. The scientists showed that acid precipitation was the result of $SO_2$ emissions from human-made sources, especially utilities and industrial processes, and that it was having harmful effects on the environment and human health (Layzer 2002). The emissions that resulted in increased levels of acidity in the Swedish lakes originated in Eastern and Western Europe and other parts of Scandinavia.

These findings led to further research in other countries on the causes of acid deposition and on its direct and indirect environmental effects. By the mid-1980s research demonstrated that lake acidification and other ecologically disruptive effects of acid rain were increasing at a rapid rate in Scandinavia, Eastern and Western Europe, Great Britain, and North America (Rosenbaum 2005). In the late 1980s scientists discovered

high amounts of acid precipitation over rain forests in Central Africa. Today, China is experiencing severe acid rain problems due to high rates of
$SO_2$ emissions. The Chinese government is working closely with the U.S.
government to devise new policies, including a cap-and-trade program, to
control acid precipitation (Wang et al. 2004).

### Acid Rain in the United States

As Layzer (2002) explains, scientific concern about acid rain began to grow in the mid- to late 1970s in the United States.[3] Scientists were
becoming increasingly alarmed about the problem, and they began calling for more funding for research and analysis. The Forest Service held an
international conference on acid rain in 1975, and, in 1977, the Council
on Environmental Quality under President Carter recommended that the
United States develop a comprehensive national program to address the
acid rain issue. As a consequence, in 1978, Carter asked Congress to increase funding for research and to examine possible regulatory strategies
under the Clean Air Act. In addition, he formed the Bilateral Research
Consultation Group on the Long-Range Transport of Air Pollution to
conduct joint research with Canada.

The International Joint Commission (IJC), which had been created
to address American and Canadian water quality problems in the Great
Lakes, issued a series of reports between 1978 and 1980 (Layzer 2002).
The IJC found that, if not controlled, acid rain could make fifty thousand
lakes in the United States and Canada lifeless by 1995, destroy the productivity of large areas of forest, and threaten the drinking-water supplies
of millions of people (Morriss 1988). At the same time the Bilateral Research Consultation Group, after reviewing the scientific evidence concerning acid rain and its probable impact on eastern North America, reported that at least half of Canada's acid precipitation came from the
United States, while only 15 percent of the U.S. acid precipitation originated in Canada (Wilcher 1986).

These findings generated concern among environmentalists and
Canadian leaders and placed pressure on the United States to take action
on acid rain (Layzer 2002). In 1980, President Carter signaled his intent to
negotiate an agreement with Canada on transboundary air pollution and
signed the Acid Precipitation Act. The new law established the Interagency

Task Force on Acid Precipitation and required it to develop the National Acid Precipitation Program (NAPAP), an extensive research program addressing the causes and effects of acid deposition.

The acid rain issue gained momentum in the early 1980s. Although few Americans knew about the acid rain problem in 1980, a Gallup poll showed that approximately two-thirds of Canadian adults were aware of acid rain as an environmental issue (Regens and Rycroft 1988). By 1983, however, a Harris poll found that 63 percent of Americans were aware of acid rain and about two-thirds of the public supported stricter controls on $SO_2$ emissions (Regens and Rycroft 1988). Acid rain had also emerged as a serious foreign-policy issue between the United States and Canada by this time, and there was growing pressure on Congress to act. President Reagan and several influential congressional leaders opposed addressing the problem and blocked efforts to control emissions responsible for the formation of acid deposition.

According to Bryner (1995), research conducted throughout the 1980s in the United States demonstrated that acid rain is a threat to watersheds, lakes, and streams in New England; forests and coastal plains in the mid-Atlantic states; and forests in northern Florida. Acid precipitation was also found to harm red spruce and pine trees in the eastern and southeastern regions of the country. In addition, the Office of Technology Assessment reported in 1984 that acidic aerosols (fine droplets containing sulfur, nitrogen, and chlorine compounds as well as other chemicals) seriously threaten people with respiratory problems and may be responsible for as many as fifty thousand deaths in the United States each year (U.S. EPA 1984).

Since the 1980s acid precipitation has become increasingly widespread and acidic. Acid precipitation now exists throughout much of the world, and it is believed to be ten to thirty times more acidic in many of America's industrialized regions than it would be naturally (Rosenbaum 2005). Research shows that most of this increase is attributable to the increased burning of fossil fuels, particularly by electric utilities and industry. The United States discharges about forty-one metric tons of $SO_2$ and $NO_x$ annually, more than any other nation in the world. Acid rain is a global problem because all industrialized nations and many developing ones discharge substantial amounts of $SO_2$ and $NO_x$ (Wang et al. 2004; Rosenbaum 2005).

### Skepticism and Acid Rain

A small number of policy analysts and natural scientists dispute the notion that acid rain is a serious environmental and public health problem. Wildavsky (1995), a political scientist, has analyzed the science involving acid rain and presents a summary and evaluation of the research in this area. Based on the scientific studies he reviews, acid rain has no impact on agriculture and public health, and the effects on forests are relatively minor. Lomborg (2001), a statistician and political scientist, echoes this view. Wildavsky also examines the effects of acid rain on lakes, streams, and swamps since "the impact on aquatic systems has received the most attention because the effects there appear to be dramatic" (1995, 281). After assessing the harm done, he concludes:

> The damage has turned out to be much less extensive and severe than it was believed to be a decade ago. Widespread acidification of lakes and streams in both North America and Europe has been reported and has been blamed for the deaths of many aquatic environments. Reports have also indicated that lakes and streams that once held an abundance of fish are now devoid of them. These reports have generally been blown way out of proportion. There have been some documented cases of acidification and fish deaths, but the vast majority of lakes in the United States (even the Northeast, which has the most acidic rain) have not been damaged by acid rain. (1995, 281)

He primarily blames the media for inaccurately reporting and exaggerating the claims made by certain scientists and environmentalists.

Bolch and Lyons (1993), an economist and chemist, respectively, likewise argue that there is scientific disagreement over whether acid rain is a serious problem. In their opinion, there is a "growing number of scientists and economists who question the payoff from large spending schemes designed to reduce acid rain, such as the Clean Air Act Amendments of 1990" (1993, 95). They contend that acid rain provides free fertilizer because it contains nitrogen, a nutrient for plants. In addition, they say that sulfur dioxide can reduce global warming because it helps cool the earth. They, too, blame "the media and professional environmental agitators" for distorting the "real truth" about acid rain (Bolch and Lyons 1993, 103). Despite these arguments, the vast majority of scientific evidence indicates that acid rain is a serious environmental and public health problem in the United States and abroad.

## Politics and Acid Rain

After taking office in 1981, President Reagan ignored growing scientific consensus regarding acid rain and made clear his opposition to related regulation (Layzer 2002). Some administration officials, such as David Stockman, director of the OMB during Reagan's first term, questioned the economic value of spending billions of dollars to control emissions. Most administration officials, however, were not as candid and, instead, questioned the science and cited scientific uncertainty as a reason for delaying the regulation of $SO_2$ and $NO_x$ emissions. In fact, as Layzer (2002) points out, the Reagan administration stuck to this position even after the respected National Academy of Sciences (NAS) released an in-depth study of the negative effects of acid rain (and other consequences of fossil-fuel burning) and even when its own EPA released a "Critical Assessment" of acid precipitation demonstrating cause and effect between $SO_2$ emissions and acid rain as well as damage to the environment and public health from acid rain. In 1983, similar findings were reported in the bilateral study initiated by President Carter in 1980. While the Canadians recommended reductions in acid rain, the United States downplayed the threat and did not see the need to control emissions. The Reagan administration convened a scientific panel to review the bilateral study; to the administration's disappointment, the panel urged that action must be taken to control pollutants. The administration ignored the panel's findings, refused to release the panel's report, and significantly altered key passages and statements regarding the seriousness of the acid rain problem and the need to take immediate action to control precursor emissions in reports by the EPA and the NAS. The Reagan White House did everything it could to protect utilities, industrial polluters, and the coal industry by opposing regulation, even in the face of strong scientific evidence that pointed to the deleterious effects of acid rain on the environment and human health. Instead, political appointees evoked the mantra of "scientific uncertainty" in response to calls from scientists and environmentalists to take action.

While the Reagan administration dragged its feet, environmentalists urged members of Congress to pass comprehensive revisions to the Clean Air Act, including measures to control acid rain (Layzer 2002). Richard Ayres, cofounder of the Natural Resources Defense Council (NRDC), was the leading advocate for the Clean Air Coalition (CAC), an organization consisting of environmental and other groups attempting to link $SO_2$ and $NO_x$ emissions to the acid rain problem. The Canadian Coalition on Acid Rain was a major ally of CAC and an active participant in the U.S. policy debate. Lobbyists representing recreation interests in New York and New England, along with the Canadian government, also favored sharp reductions in acid precipitation. In the other corner of the ring stood a powerful coalition of utilities, industrial polluters, the eastern and midwestern high-sulfur coal industry, the United Mine Workers, and government officials representing eastern and midwestern coal-producing states. Members of the coalition argued that the harm posed by acid rain was questionable and that the huge cost of controlling emissions responsible for acid rain was not justified.

As Layzer (2002) explains, congressional legislators in both houses were divided over three important questions:

1. Exactly how should polluters decrease sulfur dioxide emissions?
2. By how much and how quickly must polluters have to reduce sulfur dioxide emissions?
3. Who should pay for the reduction in sulfur dioxide emissions?

Not surprisingly, the last question was the most contentious. All three questions concerned the allocation of costs and benefits by region and created significant political divisions between environmentalists, industry, and elected leaders.

In the Senate, Democratic Majority Leader Robert Byrd from West Virginia, a high-sulfur coal-producing state, played an enormous role in blocking consideration of Clean Air Act legislation in general, and acid rain bills in particular. Democrat George Mitchell of Maine and Republican Robert Stafford of Vermont both represented states adversely impacted by acid rain. As members of the Senate Environment and Public Works Committee, they introduced legislation to reduce emissions of acid rain precursors containing different financing provisions. The committee repeatedly endorsed these bills; however, Byrd was able to block consideration of the legislation on the Senate floor in each session of Congress.

Similar regional and political differences thwarted efforts in the House. John Dingell, a Democrat from Michigan, served as chairman of the powerful Energy and Commerce Committee and was able to prevent clean air legislation from reaching the House floor. As a representative from a state in which the automobile industry wielded considerable influence, he feared such legislation would contain stringent automobile emissions standards. In 1984, Democrats Henry Waxman from California and Gerry Sikorski of Minnesota sponsored a major acid rain bill. The Waxman-Sikorski legislation sought a ten-million-ton reduction in $SO_2$ and a four-million-ton reduction in $NO_x$. It distributed the cost nationally by establishing a fund financed by a one-tenth-of-a-cent federal tax per kilowatt hour of electricity used. Sharp political divisions existed between the members of the Energy Committee's Health and Environment Subcommittee, which Waxman chaired, and constituencies on both sides killed the bill.

Bryner (1995) explains how the free flow of money helped stiffen opposition of some members of Congress, especially in the House, to strict clean air legislation. Members of the House Energy and Commerce Committee, for instance, received in the nonelection year of 1989 almost $612,000 from PACs established by industries affected by air pollution controls. The most generous contributors, Bryner (1995) reports, were the electric utilities, which gave more than $150,000 to representatives on the committee. Also contributing heavily to committee members were oil, natural gas, automobile, and chemical industries; gas utilities; coal and steel companies; diversified energy firms; construction firms; and farm equipment manufacturers. The extent of lobbying within this issue area was understandable given how much was at stake for industry. In Bryner's view, "For industry, PAC contributions have become a cost of doing business, a prerequisite for ensuring that its voice will be heard in committee decision making" (1995, 113).

### The Final Push for Acid Rain Controls

As Bryner (1995) and Layzer (2002) discuss, prospects for adopting new clean air regulations and controls on acid rain brightened considerably in the late 1980s. First, Representative Dingell failed in his attempts to extend clean air deadlines into 1989, thereby keeping the pressure on Congress to pass a major overhaul of the Clean Air Act. Second, in the Senate, longtime foe of clean air legislation Robert Byrd stepped down as majority leader and was replaced by George Mitchell of Maine, who was a strong supporter of acid rain controls. Finally, George Bush, who hoped to take advantage of a pro-environment backlash against the Reagan administration, promised to reauthorize and update the Clean Air Act during his campaign for the presidency. After taking office, Bush followed through on his campaign pledge by assembling a team of advisers (from the White House, OMB, the Department of Energy [DOE], and the EPA) to draft legislative proposals that eventually would become the Clean Air Act Amendments of 1990.

Bryner accurately describes the politically sensitive position in which the Bush administration found itself:

> If its bill was to have any legitimacy in Congress, it had to be as aggressive in attacking air pollution as other bills proposed by members of Congress. But if it was too aggressive, it would alienate important business constituencies. On the other hand, if it was too weak, it would be dismissed as irrelevant to what the president had repeatedly promised to do. Some members of Congress and representatives of environmental groups had argued that the president's bill would have to propose a reduction in sulfur dioxide emissions of at least 10 million tons in order to be taken seriously. Whichever bill he introduced would likely become the minimum position for the bill that Congress would finally enact. (1995, 114–15)

Clearly, the White House would have to walk a tightrope to get its clean air program through Congress.

Once crafted, the president's bill contained key measures addressing the nonattainment of national ambient air quality standards, air toxics, and acid rain. The bill also included additional measures regarding permit requirements for sources of pollution and enforcement by the EPA and the states. The most innovative and aggressive initiative of the proposed law dealt with acid rain, and it became the centerpiece of the overall effort to improve the nation's air quality. Designed by Dan Dudek of the Environmental Defense Fund, President Bush proposed a system of allowance trading combined with a nationwide cap on total $SO_2$ emissions. This market-based approach sought to reduce $SO_2$ emissions by ten million tons by the year 2000. Nevertheless, after the president's bill was introduced, it was immediately attacked by environmentalists as too weak and by industry as too expensive and inflexible.

Those who stood to lose the most under the president's plan quickly mobilized to oppose it. The opposition included the United Mine Workers (UMW), many of whom labored in high-sulfur coal mines, and the midwestern utilities that heavily relied on high-sulfur coal. The UMW contended that the Bush bill would require major coal purchasers to switch to low-sulfur coal, costing thousands of coal-mining jobs in the end. Midwestern interests argued that the bill would force nine states responsible for 51 percent of the nation's $SO_2$ emissions to achieve 90 percent of the reduction and shoulder about three-quarters of the cost in the form of high electricity bills in the first phase of the plan (Layzer 2002). Industry groups opposed to the legislation included the Business Roundtable, the National Association of Manufacturers, and several trade associations in the coal, electric utilities, steel, chemicals, and automobile industries. These organizations formed the Clean Air Working Group (Bryner 1995).

The CAC pressured Congress and President Bush for stricter, national clean air standards. Among the environmental groups playing a key role in the lobbying effort were the Sierra Club, the NRDC, the Environmental Defense Fund, the National Wildlife Federation, and the Audubon Society (Byrner 1995). These organizations were joined by the U.S. Public Interest Research Group, the American Lung Association, the United Steel Workers Union, and the National Council of Churches in their attempt to push clean air legislation through Congress. With public opinion perceived to be on their side, these groups helped shape the clean air debate, especially on the acid rain issue.

The Senate took ten weeks in early 1989 to pass its version of the Clean Air Act Amendments. Senator Mitchell, in his role as the new majority leader, devoted nearly all of his time to persuade his colleagues to support the legislation (Layzer 2002). His main challenge was to soften the opposition to the Bush bill by those in the Senate representing high-sulfur states and industrial interests, including utilities and, at the same time, maintain the support of pro-environment senators. Mitchell and other Democratic proponents of the Bush clean air plan were in a difficult position since the new regulations would hit already economically depressed areas in the country. Senator Byrd and Republican Senator Christopher Bond of Missouri proposed giving the biggest polluters extra credits at the start to help them buy their way out of the abatement effort (Layzer 2002).

Mitchell and his supporters agreed to accept the Byrd-Bond amendment in exchange for their support on the acid rain initiatives in the bill. Largely due to Mitchell's hard work and diplomatic skills, the Senate passed its version of the Clean Air Act Amendments by a vote of 89–11.

Clean air bills in the House of Representatives generally fell within the jurisdiction of the Energy and Commerce Committee's Subcommittee on Health and the Environment. Dingell, who had chaired the full committee since 1979, worked closely with Democrat House Speaker Jim Wright of Texas to appoint members who supported his attempts to block stringent clean air legislation, especially bills that sought to reduce automobile emissions. In order to undercut Waxman's influence, Dingell placed his allies on the subcommittee (Bryner 1995; Layzer 2002). When President Bush presented his proposal, however, Dingell was told by several of his key supporters in the House (for example, Majority Whip Tony Coehlo) that stalling tactics would no longer succeed and might even damage him politically.

Although Dingell gave Waxman's Subcommittee on Health and the Environment responsibility for marking up most of the clean air legislation, he referred the acid rain and alternative fuels measures, the two most controversial portions of the bill, to the Subcommittee on Energy and Power, chaired by Philip Sharp of Indiana (Layzer 2002). Sharp sought to protect Indiana's old, polluting utilities and threatened to block the administration's clean air legislation by stalling the acid rain provisions in his subcommittee. He and other midwestern representatives tried to generate support for the position that cleanup costs should be shared broadly beyond utilities and rate payers in their districts (Bryner 1995). They complained that nothing was being done to address their concerns and announced they would back whatever faction would best help minimize the cost of acid rain regulations. In the end, however, the midwestern legislators were unable to convince House members from other states to accept their cost-sharing program. Negotiations were further complicated by legislators from "clean" western states who felt that limits on $SO_2$ emissions would hurt local economic growth (Bryner 1995).

Several conditions tended to weaken the position of those fighting against the new clean air legislation. The continued stubborn opposition by the utility interests and their backers left them vulnerable during the debate over acid rain controls (Layzer 2002). Throughout the 1980s they insisted that there was no acid rain problem, and they refused to provide congressional representatives with information on their operations. This proved frustrating to many members of Congress. In addition, debate over Bush's legislation drove a wedge between the antiregulation midwestern contingent. Within this block, some members were concerned about the utilities and wanted flexibility in lowering their emissions while others wanted to protect high-sulfur coal miners and therefore supported a scrubber mandate. Furthermore, as Layzer points out, "The utilities themselves were deeply divided depending on their energy source and the extent to which they had already engaged in pollution control" (2002, 276–77).

In an effort to resolve deep differences among the members of the House Energy and Commerce Committee, Dingell held almost all of the meetings behind closed doors and frequently at night. As a result, compromises were reached whereby midwestern utilities received more time to curtail emissions, greater flexibility on emissions credits, and money to accelerate development of technology to reduce coal emissions. At the same time, members from the "clean" states obtained greater flexibility under the trading system for their utilities and all the permits the midwestern representatives initially opposed to give them. The House finally passed its version of the bill by a 401–21 vote.

A conference committee was established to reconcile the different House and Senate versions of the clean air bill. A number of concessions were made on both sides of the debate. Although extra allowances were granted to some midwestern utilities, the final acid rain measures represented a major defeat for the Midwest and the old, dirty utilities located there. In the end, the Senate was able to get its way on most of the acid rain issues.[4]

### Acid Rain Controls in the 1990 Clean Air Act Amendments

Title IV is the cornerstone of the acid rain program as outlined in the Clean Air Act Amendments of 1990 (U.S. EPA 2002). It requires a nationwide reduction in $SO_2$ emissions by ten million tons, about 40 percent from 1980 levels, by the year 2000. In order to meet this goal, a two-phase $SO_2$ allowance trading system was adopted. Under the rules of the trading system, the EPA provided each utility with a particular number of allowances, each of which permits its holder to release one ton of $SO_2$ in a given year or any subsequent year. Utilities whose emissions exceed their allowances can reduce their emissions through pollution control measures or by purchasing allowances from other utilities. Utilities whose allowances exceed their emissions may trade, bank, or sell their extra allowances (Kamieniecki, Shafie, and Silvers 1999).[5] Utilities, brokers, environmental organizations, private citizens, and anyone else are permitted to hold allowances. In addition, Title IV requires a two-million-ton reduction in $NO_x$ emissions by 2000. In order to meet this goal, Congress required the EPA to formulate emissions limitations for two types of utility boilers by mid-1992 and for other types by 1997. All regulated utilities are required to install equipment to measure $SO_2$ and $NO_x$ emissions on a continuous basis to guarantee compliance. Finally, the new clean air bill contained clear guidelines and strict penalties for noncompliance and for failure by the EPA to establish $SO_2$ regulations.

The implementation of the 1990 Clean Air Act Amendments has put a substantial dent in the acid rain problem (U.S. EPA 2003b). According to the EPA, $SO_2$ emissions from power plants were 10.2 million tons in 2002, 9 percent less than in 2000 and 41 percent lower than in 1980 (U.S. EPA 2003b). $NO_x$ emissions from utilities continued to decrease as well; they declined 4.5 million tons in 2002, a 13 percent drop from 2000 and a 33 percent reduction from 1990 emissions levels. The agency believes that the acid rain program is making good progress toward achieving its goal of a 50 percent reduction from 1980 $SO_2$ emissions. The $SO_2$ cap-and-trade approach has effectively created economic incentives for utilities to seek new and low-cost measures to reduce emissions and improve the effectiveness of pollution control equipment. The EPA reports that the level of compliance with the acid rain provisions continues to be over 99 percent (U.S. EPA 2003b). Even with this success, the EPA proposed new reductions for $SO_2$ and $NO_x$ for thirty states at the end of 2003 (Lee 2003a).

Despite these gains, however, new research suggests that a great deal more needs to be done to reduce emissions and curtail the negative effects of acid rain. A study by Gregory Lawrence of the U.S. Geological Survey concluded that nineteen of twenty-two streams in the western part of Adirondack Park in New York State exceeded the acidity threshold for wildlife and that acid rain continues to harm aquatic life in these streams (Reeves 2002). Research on the health impacts of $SO_2$ and $NO_x$ emissions increasingly show that these pollutants can cause lung cancer and other respiratory illnesses. A study conducted for the Rockefeller Family Fund by the technical consulting firm Abt Associates, Incorporated, estimates that $SO_2$ and $NO_x$ emissions from more than eighty power plants owned by eight electric utilities will cause six thousand premature deaths in the year 2007 (Seelye 2002a). These and other findings suggest that the federal government will have to increase emissions standards for power plants in order to protect the public health. This will likely revive the same regional and political conflicts as before.

### Explaining the Evolution of Acid Rain Regulation

Whereas environmentalists were united in their call for strict controls on $SO_2$ and $NO_x$ emissions, the acid rain issue drove a wedge between certain energy interests (for example, low-sulfur versus high-sulfur coal producers) and, by doing so, reduced their influence. This controversy, therefore, is most accurately categorized as a conflictual issue (M. Smith 2000). Given the diverse set of stakeholders involved, the number of powerful politicians lined up on both sides of the debate, and the numerous obstacles that needed to be overcome, it is quite remarkable that an effective acid rain policy was ever adopted. Although new scientific evidence points to the need for additional controls, the overall success of the cap-and-trade program must be considered one of the major accomplishments in the environmental policy arena.

Different theories help explain the development of acid rain regulation in the United States and the influence of business interests in this debate. Most of the political variables thought to be important in accounting for agenda building and corporate influence over environmental policymaking, for example, played a critical role in this issue area. As citizens became increasingly aware of the potential harm acid rain can cause to the natural environment and public health, public support for regulation grew dramatically, thereby placing pressure on elected leaders to act. Partisanship seemed to be a significant variable during the two terms Reagan occupied the White House; however, Republicans and Democrats later joined together to formulate acid rain regulation during the Bush administration. No doubt, as Bryner (1995) suggests, campaign contributions and intense lobbying by affected firms, especially high-sulfur coal producers and many fossil-fuel interests, helped convince a number of congressional members to oppose clean air legislation. These tactics proved highly effective at delaying the final adoption of the acid rain program. Environmental groups, bolstered by growing scientific evidence of the negative effects of air pollutants on the environment and public health, managed to engage rather successfully in countermobilization and finally force the passage of acid rain policy despite their early misgivings about Bush's cap-and-trade proposal. Although the overall cost of implementing clean air legislation was a concern, business tended to accept the cap-and-trade approach as a flexible, cost-effective way to control $SO_2$ and $NO_x$ emissions. In the end, regional and national economic conditions failed to derail the effort.

To a large extent, the ebb and flow of the debate over acid rain reflected attempts on the part of protagonists on both sides to define the issue, frame the debate, and influence the policy outcome. The fossil-fuel industry, especially coal producers, relied on frame bridging (Snow et al. 1986) to make appeals to other industries to join their side. Business leaders, influential members of Congress, and key officials in the Reagan administration repeatedly argued that acid rain was not a large enough problem to justify the enormous cost to reduce it and that additional scientific research was necessary. Yet, the effort by polluters to draw attention to the plight of economically struggling coal miners as well as electric consumers in the Midwest represented value amplification (Snow et al. 1986). Environmentalists, however, engaged in belief amplification (Snow et al. 1986) by drawing attention to the scientific evidence pointing to the negative effects of acid rain on aquatic ecosystems, forests, and humans, particularly in the Northeast and Canada. The perceived legitimacy and compelling nature of the scientific findings allowed them to persuade many neutral observers through the media to support new controls on $SO_2$ and $NO_x$ emissions. Finally, the change from the Reagan administration to the Bush administration and the replacement of Byrd with Mitchell as majority leader of the Senate dramatically altered the political landscape and how the choice process was structured. Riker's (1996) notion of the heresthetic, therefore, applies here.

Theories of agenda building probably best explain the evolution of the acid rain issue and the level of influence of both sides in the dispute. Kingdon's (1995) discussion of how streams of problems, proposed policies, and politics help account for the early history of the acid rain issue. The problems, policies, and politics concerning $SO_2$ and $NO_x$ emissions appeared to exist independently during the Reagan administration; as a consequence, little was accomplished. Business interests successfully pressured key members of Congress to block clean air legislation of any kind (Cobb and Ross 1997b) by continuously invoking the futility thesis with scientific uncertainty as the basis (Hirschman 1991). The election of Bush as president and the selection of Mitchell as Senate majority leader opened a policy window of opportunity, thereby allowing policy entrepreneurs to gain the attention of critical legislators, couple solutions to problems, and connect both problems and solutions to politics. At the same time, an epistemic community appeared to form around the acid rain issue (Haas 1992) and significant policy learning took place, leading to the establishment of an advocacy coalition for reducing pollution precursors of acid rain (Sabatier 1993). Once this happened, it became possible for the national government to formulate, adopt, and implement a highly successful $SO_2$ cap-and-trade program to reduce acid rain.

### The Climate Change Debate

During Memorial Day weekend in 2004 Twentieth Century Fox studios released a $125 million Hollywood science-fiction film, *The Day After Tomorrow*. The film grossly exaggerates the possible effects of climate change on the planet by showing scenes of tornadoes in Los Angeles and New York City under water. The Northern Hemisphere succumbs to an ice age at the end of the movie, and Americans (including the president) are forced to flee to Mexico to seek refuge. The controversy regarding the film generated a great deal of publicity, and the movie grossed nearly half a billion dollars worldwide in the first month of its release (Leiserowitz 2004). Despite the obvious fantasy nature of the movie, it has drawn attention to climate change. In fact, a survey conducted before and after the release of the movie indicates that the film had a significant impact on the climate change risk perceptions, conceptual frameworks, behavioral intentions, policy positions, and voting intentions of those who saw the movie (Leiserowitz 2004).

The debate over climate change involves a broad range of interests with a divergent set of concerns (J. Browne 2004; Pizer 2004).[6] Many U.S.

and international environmental groups have allocated considerable time and resources to lobbying political leaders to address the need to control "greenhouse gas" (GHG) emissions (Carmin, Darnall, and Mil-Homens 2003; Carey 2004). Most of their policy proposals, if adopted, will require huge expenditures by business (Pizer 2004; Toman 2004). Both fossil-fuel producers and fossil-fuel consumers, including average citizens and a wide variety of small and large companies, will be forced to pay a large sum of money for even a moderately aggressive program to curtail GHG emissions (Shogren and Toman 2001). Also, insurance companies are worried about the possible high cost of claims due to the impacts of increasingly severe weather (Gelbspan 1998). In fact, 2004 was the most expensive for the insurance industry in coping worldwide with damage from hurricanes, typhoons, and other weather-related disasters. Scientists are under pressure to produce research findings that clearly show the exact sources of the problem, the extent of the problem, how much must be done, and how quickly action must be taken. Additional research on climate change will require significant government funding and will likely take considerable time because of the complexity of the issue (J. Browne 2004). Meanwhile, American politicians and policymakers are caught in the middle of the contentious debate and must keep a vigilant eye on the results of scientific studies and public opinion. The public is likely to reject required and costly lifestyle changes unless the danger is perceived to be real and immediate action is warranted.

The roots of the controversy over climate change can be traced back to the mid-nineteenth century with the development of climatology. As a science, climatology evolved from theories and research of scientists in many disparate fields. During this time scientists became fascinated by the discovery that the Northern Hemisphere had been buried under one mile of ice during an "ice age." As research continued, it became clear that there had been several ice ages and that temperatures had alternated between extremes for millennia. According to Weart (2003), many of the earliest climate change theories represented attempts to explain how the earth could have gone through an ice age and then warmed so much in a relatively short amount of time geologically.

As Fleming (1998) points out, the idea that climate could change was not altogether new. It long had been believed that human settlement and the clearing of forests for farmland improved the weather, and a conscious effort was made to achieve climate change in the settlement of North America. The notion that climate could vary so much, however, was inconceivable. For the most part, scientists assumed that nature was a closed, self-maintaining system that did not change much even over long passages of time (Weart 2003). Initially, the suggestion that ice ages occurred was greeted with skepticism. As the evidence mounted, however, scientists began turning their attention to explaining how the variations in weather were possible.

At the time, climate change posed a challenging scientific puzzle. Except for the fear among a few scientists that glaciations could occur again someday, there was no potential catastrophe seen looming on the horizon, and the issue was a century away from becoming a highly politically charged controversy. Most of the earliest writings were based on questionable assumptions, and numerous theories of climate change were discounted with new research. While many of the basic scientific tenets of climate change theory are now widely accepted, certain facets of climate variation remain a mystery (Carey 2004; U.S. EPA 2004b, 2004c).

### The Greenhouse Effect

Today, scientists studying climate change link it to a phenomenon referred to as "the greenhouse effect" (Bryner 1992). Researchers have discovered that, of the solar radiation (sunlight) that makes it to earth, approximately 25 percent is reflected back into space by the atmosphere and about another 25 percent is absorbed by it. Of the remaining 50 percent of the solar radiation, 5 percent is reflected by the earth's surface and the rest is absorbed into the planet as infrared (heat) radiation. Almost 30 percent of the absorbed radiation is lost to evaporation and thermals. The remainder is radiated from the surface, at which point certain gases in the atmosphere (that is, GHGs) trap most of the infrared radiation and reradiate it back to earth, thereby maintaining surface temperature (U.S. EPA 2004b).

Although the exact extent to which human activities influence the greenhouse effect is still disputed, the existence of a naturally occurring greenhouse effect is widely agreed upon (Carey 2004; Monastersky 2005). In fact, the greenhouse effect is necessary for the existence of life on earth. Satellite measurements of the atmosphere record an average temperature radiating from the earth's surface at $-18°$ C ($0°$ F), not nearly warm enough to sustain life. Accumulated measurements of surface heat, however, indicate an average temperature of $15°$ C ($59°$ F) (Wolfson and Schneider 2002). This more than $30°$ C disparity in readings is the result of the greenhouse effect and is the difference between a frozen planet and one warm enough to sustain life.

Interestingly, nitrogen and oxygen, the atmosphere's two most abundant gases, have almost no impact on the climate of the earth (Soroos 2004). Instead, it is much smaller concentrations of various other gases, specifically carbon dioxide ($CO_2$), methane, ozone, and nitrous oxides, in addition to water vapor and chlorofluorocarbons (CFCs), that affect the earth's climate. These GHGs warm the climate by retaining the long-wave infrared energy radiated back from the planet that would otherwise escape to outer space (U.S. EPA 2004b). $CO_2$, which accounts for less than 1 percent of the atmosphere's volume, is responsible for more than 25 percent of the greenhouse effect. Water vapor, which comprises less than 5 percent of the atmosphere, is also a critical GHG, accounting for about 60 percent of the warming effect of the atmosphere. The impact of microscopic liquid and solid particles known as aerosols (for example, pollen, dust, soot, and sulfates) on climate is brief compared with those of the predominant GHGs, such as $CO_2$, which can remain in the atmosphere for a century (Trenberth 2001).[7] The earth's oceans also influence weather, although the dynamics of the relationship between oceans and climate change are not completely understood.

In 1988, the World Meteorological Organization (WMO) and the United Nations Environmental Programme (UNEP) established the important Intergovernmental Panel on Climate Change (IPCC) to evaluate and summarize available scientific studies that provide knowledge about climate variation (Betsill 2005). The top scientists in the field have served on the IPCC. Since its creation the IPCC has issued several assessment reports intended to educate policymakers about the state of climate change science and to inform negotiations on international agreements to address the issue (Pittock 2002).

Concern over climate change arises because human activities have added to the naturally occurring concentrations of GHGs (Carey 2004; U.S EPA 2004b; Monastersky 2005). Since the 1890s the fossil fuel-driven industrial revolution and the reduction of carbon sinks due to deforestation have been primarily responsible for an increase in atmospheric concentrations of $CO_2$ from about 280 to 367 parts per million (ppm), an increase of more than 30 percent. According to a 2001 report by the IPCC, today's concentrations of $CO_2$ are substantially higher than the natural levels that have occurred at any time during the last 420,000 years, and perhaps during the last 20 million years (IPCC 2001). In March 2004 U.S. scientists at Mauna Loa, Hawaii, reported measurements of carbon dioxide at an alarming 379 ppm (*Los Angeles Times* 2004). The amount of methane in the atmosphere has increased more than 150 percent since 1750 as a result of emissions from fossil fuels, cattle, rice fields, and landfills. Concentrations of nitrous oxides, which are emitted from agricultural soils and cattle feed lots, have increased 17 percent since 1750 (IPCC 2001).

The precise impacts of increasing concentrations of GHGs in the atmosphere are likely to differ from region to region, and modeling them is quite complicated. Nonetheless, reliable weather data, which exist since 1861, show that the earth's surface has warmed about 0.6° C overall (Soroos 2004). This rise has not been steadily upward as one might expect given the increasingly higher concentrations of GHGs in the atmosphere. The warmest periods have occurred between the 1920s and 1940s and since the late 1970s, while somewhat cooler average temperatures existed between these two periods. Since 1976 warming has occurred three times faster than during the last century, and for twenty-three consecutive years the average temperature has been above the annual average between 1960 and 1990 (World Meteorological Organization 2001). In fact, the 1990s may have been the warmest decade in the past thousand years. Nine of the ten warmest years have been recorded between 1990 and 2001, with 1998 and 2001 being the warmest and second warmest years, respectively. Blistering heat throughout Europe caused more than nineteen thousand deaths (fifteen thousand in France alone) in 2003, the third warmest year on record. The year 2004, punctuated by four strong hurricanes in the Caribbean and deadly typhoons in Asia, was the fourth warmest on record. Because of the recent dramatic rise in temperatures in different parts of the world, the term "global warming" is often used in discussions of climate change.

Until recently scientists were cautious about directly linking some or all of these increases in average temperatures to human factors, including increases in GHG emissions (Revkin 2003a). Nevertheless, a number

of environmental conditions have changed, coinciding with higher concentrations of GHGs in the atmosphere and the marked increase in earth
temperatures over the past two decades. Among other things, scientists report a retreat of mountain glaciers in most places outside of the polar regions during the last century (for example, in parts of Africa, Alaska, Asia,
Montana, and Greenland), a rise in sea levels of 0.1 to 0.2 meters, changes
in ocean temperatures, an increase of 2 to 4 percent in the frequency of
heavy precipitation events during the latter half of the previous century,
and a large drop in the amount of long-wave radiation escaping from
the atmosphere since 1970 (Mayell 2001; *Los Angeles Times* 2002a;
Revkin 2004).[8]

In November 2004 a coalition of eight nations that have Arctic
territories (Canada, Denmark, Finland, Iceland, Norway, Russia, Sweden,
and the United States) released a comprehensive report containing the
most extensive international assessment of Arctic climate change (Arctic
Council 2004; Eilperin and Weiss 2004). Based on four years of study involving hundreds of scientists, the report concludes that earth's upper lat-
itudes are experiencing unprecedented increases in temperature, glacial
melting, and weather-pattern changes, with most of those changes attributable to the human generation of GHGs from automobiles, power plants,
and other sources. Average temperatures in the Arctic have risen nearly
2 degrees Fahrenheit in the last century (twice the global average), while
winter temperatures have risen nearly 4 degrees. Parts of Alaska and Russia have seen average winter temperatures increase 11 degrees since the
1970s and are at their highest levels in four hundred years. The amount of
ocean covered by ice over the last three years has been the smallest ever
recorded. The melting of the massive Greenland ice cap and other Arctic
glaciers and the destruction of northern forests by foreign insect invasions
are among the most pronounced changes. Coastal villages inhabited by in-
digenous people in Alaska and elsewhere are threatened by erosion and
rising sea levels. Caribou and reindeer that feed on tundra vegetation are
in decline, and seals and polar bears that depend on sea ice will probably
decline. At the same time a warmer Arctic could increase the numbers of
some species, extend the growing season for wheat in Canada, and open
up treacherous sea routes for shipping and resource exploration. Overall,
however, the reduction of snow and ice cover in the Arctic is likely to accelerate warming across the globe and have a dramatic, negative impact

on the earth's ecosystem. For months the Bush administration fought hard to keep policy proposals to curb global warming from being included in the Arctic Council's report (Eilperin 2004b). Despite the rigorous nature of the study, administration officials questioned the science underlying the report and opposed specific policy recommendations to counter global warming (Eilperin 2004c). Today, the vast majority of scientists argue that climate change is occurring and believe that human activities are mostly responsible for this phenomenon (Monastersky 2005).

If global warming continues to accelerate, it might have a multiplicity of impacts on other aspects of climate and the ecosystem, as well as on humans (Carey 2004). For example, more severe droughts, an increased incidence of extreme precipitation events and tropical storms, rising sea levels, the premature disappearance of species of flora and fauna that are unable to adapt, and the creation and spread of old and new diseases all may occur. Although some agricultural regions may benefit, other agricultural areas may be negatively affected. In fact, certain consequences could be highly disruptive and possibly catastrophic and permanent. Given the intricacies and complexities of the climate change issue, more research must be done on how and to what extent human activities influence the earth's climate and the negative effects continued global warming might have on the environment and future generations (Bryner 1992; Holdren 2001, 2002; Pittock 2002; Revkin 2003a).[9]

### Criticisms of Climate Change Research

A few researchers dispute the overall importance and potential environmental impact of climate change. Some analysts question studies, for instance, regarding how much the earth has warmed and how much more it can be expected to warm (for example, Lomborg 2001; Burnett 2004). They believe present studies greatly exaggerate variations in the earth's climate, and they charge that most scientists studying climate change portray the issue as being much more complex than it really is (see, for example, Balling 1992, 1994; T. Moore 1998; Michaels and Balling 2000; Goklany 2001; Schlesinger 2004). Other skeptics reject claims that recent global warming is linked to human activities (Balling 1994; T. Moore 1998; Michaels and Balling 2000; Lomborg 2001; Schlesinger 2004). A few even argue that the effects of warming may not be negative at all and could benefit humanity in the long run. Thomas Gale Moore, an economist and leading proponent of this view, contends that service industries can operate equally well in warm climate (with air conditioning) as in cold climate (with heating) (T. Moore 1995, 1998). Furthermore, he argues that warmer weather and additional $CO_2$ in the atmosphere will increase plant and crop growth and production, thus providing more food for the expanding global population over time.[10]

As Layzer (2002) observes, opponents of climate change science have successfully taken advantage of the media's principle of presenting both sides of an issue regardless of the merits of each side's claims. In 1994, for instance, Frederick Seitz, director of the conservative Marshall Institute and member of the NAS, accused the authors of the IPCC scientific summaries of distorting the findings of scientific studies on climate change and creating the impression of a consensus where none existed. His criticisms were widely reported in the media. Two years later he charged Benjamin Santer, an eminent climate modeler at the Lawrence Livermore Laboratory, of excluding references to gaps in scientific research from the 1995 IPCC report. This allegation was reported in the *Wall Street Journal* and the *New York Times* without investigation of its accuracy. No IPCC scientist supported Seitz's charge against Santer, and forty-two IPCC scientists published a letter in the *Wall Street Journal* in his defense (Stevens 1996).

Seitz's active opposition against proponents of climate change did not end there. In 1998 he circulated a petition among thousands of scientists opposing efforts to control GHG emissions. A letter on stationery that closely resembled NAS letterhead accompanied the survey in the mail. The letter cited a scientific study that found $CO_2$ emissions did not pose a threat to the earth's climate (Stevens 1998). The NAS immediately disavowed and condemned the deceptive letter.

### International Efforts

Although this study focuses primarily on American business and environmental politics and policies, it is worth briefly reviewing recent international attempts to address climate change.[11] International efforts to analyze changes in the global climate have been reflected in conferences organized by concerned scientists (for example, the First World Climate

Conference in Geneva in 1979), the creation of the World Climate Program in partnership with the WMO, UNEP, and the International Council of Scientific Unions (ICSU), and the inauguration by the ICSU of the Stockholm-based International Geosphere-Biosphere Program. Formal negotiations that began in 1991 have led to the development of two major agreements, the Framework Convention on Climate Change (FCCC) in 1992 and the Kyoto Protocol in 1997 (Betsill 2005). The FCCC was formally adopted in 1994 after ratification by fifty nations. The first of a series of annual Conference of the Parties (COP) was held in Berlin to consider additional policies to address climate change.

The Kyoto Protocol was drafted by delegates to COP 3 and was discussed at the Kyoto conference in December 1997. With 120 countries represented and global media coverage, Kyoto became one of the most important international environmental meetings ever held (Victor 2001, 2004; Rosenbaum 2005; Betsill 2005). In contrast to expectations entering the meeting, the U.S. delegation agreed to a fairly rigorous schedule of reductions in GHGs. The U.S. supported the draft treaty and agreed to:

- Along with other developed nations, set emission targets for GHGs, whereby the United States would reduce emissions by 7 percent overall;
- Meet emission goals over a set of five-year periods beginning with the years 2008–2012;
- Allow nations to receive credit toward their emission targets by participating in joint projects to reduce GHG emissions with other nations;
- Establish an emissions trading regime where nations could buy and sell emission allowances for GHGs; and
- Invite developing nations to join voluntarily in the emissions trading scheme and encourage these nations to set timetables and goals for their own emission reductions.

The Kyoto Protocol is supposed to become law when at least fifty-five nations, accounting for at least 55 percent of the total 1990 $CO_2$ emissions of Annex I countries (developed nations), formally ratify the agreement. Since the United States accounts for about 25 percent of these emissions, its continued rejection (along with Australia) of the Protocol means that ratification by all of the other significant emitters is needed (Victor 2001,

2004). In July 2001, 180 countries adopted the treaty at a session of the United Nations Convention on Climate Change in Bonn, Germany. Additional international meetings to revise and further clarify the Protocol, however, have had limited success (Victor 2001, 2004). In November 2004 the 55 percent emissions objective was reached when President Vladimir V. Putin of Russia (which accounts for 17 percentof $CO_2$ emissions) signed legislation ratifying the treaty. The 1997 pact, which took effect on February 16, 2005, has been ratified by 141 nations. Yet, without participation by the United States and Australia, it is unclear whether the agreement will lead to a significant reduction in GHGs.

The EU has taken an aggressive stand on climate change by agreeing to strict GHG emissions targets (J. Browne 2004). Most European nations and Japan have signed the Kyoto Protocol and have actively lobbied other nations, including the United States and Russia, to reduce GHG emissions. American and Japanese automobile manufacturers have voluntarily agreed to reduce GHG emissions by 25 percent in Europe by 2008 using existing technologies. They are doing so, however, in order to head off tough regulations threatened by the EU (Bustillo 2004a, 2004b, 2004c). Overall, many European nations, as well as Japan, have fallen significantly behind their reductions targets set by the Kyoto Protocol (Daly 2003; *Japan Times* 2004).[12]

Slow progress on reaching international agreement on effective measures to reduce GHG emissions has led a number of economists to recommend the adoption of economic tools to control climate change (for example, Shogren and Toman 2000; Toman 2001, 2004; Pizer 2004). In general, they call for a clear commitment to broad, market-based controls on GHGs. Such an approach might be modeled after the successful U.S. $SO_2$ program. A tax on carbon and other tax systems have also been proposed (Shogren and Toman 2000). In early 2005 Europe will launch a cap-and-trade program for GHGs (the European Union Emissions Trading System) that is considerably larger and more complex than the $SO_2$ trading program in the United States (Kruger and Pizer 2004). The implementation of a market strategy on a massive scale at the international level will require world leaders and policymakers to resolve numerous issues, obstacles, and problems so that a fair and effective market system could be established. Monitoring and enforcement strategies, for example, will need agreement. The huge disparity in wealth and technology between developed and developing nations will have to be factored in as well. These concerns aside, economic instruments will have to play a central role in any future climate change policy. Due to a high level of uncertainty, American business interests have thus far been cool to the idea of implementing economic measures to regulate global warming.

### Interest Groups, American Politics, and Climate Change

Within the United States, a wide range of business interests are involved in the regulatory fight over the control of GHG emissions (Carey 2004; Rosenbaum 2005). The major combatants include the electric utilities, which account for 80 percent of all domestic coal combustion; petroleum producers and automobile manufacturers, whose products emit significant amounts of $CO_2$; agricultural crop and livestock producers; and almost all other fossil-fuel dependent industries, of which there are many. At the same time scientists, environmentalists, and segments of the national media publicly support efforts to adopt controls on GHG emissions.

As Rosenbaum (2005) observes, potentially regulated sectors of the U.S. economy, led by the utilities, the automobile industry, and the producers of fossil fuel, were joined by organized labor in early opposition to any national or international initiatives establishing compulsory timetables and targets for cutbacks in GHG emissions. Developing nations, which collectively account for 30 to 40 percent of current global GHG emissions, also oppose such reductions. Most leaders of developing nations are fearful that controls on GHG emissions would stifle their economic growth.

The estimated initial costs to the United States to cut back its $CO_2$ emissions would be enormous, and these costs would fall most heavily on automobile manufacturers and coal users and producers, especially electric utilities. The capital cost of installing equipment to control $CO_2$ emissions is estimated to be 70 to 150 percent of the total cost of a new electric-generating facility (Rosenbaum 2005). In Rosenbaum's view, "Every American would feel some impact of abatement policies on his or her lifestyle and pocketbook" (2005, 352–53). Of course, if no action is taken and the earth experiences severe weather conditions as a result of climate variation, the cost to the United States and other nations will be even higher, and the results might be disastrous in certain parts of the world.

A number of environmental and scientific groups have attempted to persuade leaders and citizens of the immediate need to control GHG emissions. Greenpeace, the Sierra Club, the World Conservation Union, the World Wildlife Federation, the Worldwatch Institute, the Union of Concerned Scientists, and other groups have sought to inform Americans about the potentially serious effects of climate change and to mobilize public opinion in favor of U.S. and international policies that would substantially decrease GHG emissions. They argue, often through the media, that the scientific evidence for linking human activities with climate change is strong and underscores the need to take action now. Postponing the adoption of required solutions will only cause more damage, take that much longer to reduce the concentration of GHGs in the atmosphere, and cost a great deal more in the long run.

These arguments as well as the call for the reduction of GHG emissions have been strongly attacked by other wealthy and powerful organizations and industry groups. The Cato Institute, the Western Fuels Association, and the Global Climate Coalition (GCC) have questioned the validity of scientific research on climate change and the need to decrease the U.S. reliance on fossil fuels. The GCC, which was spun off from the National Association of Manufacturers in 1989, initially boasted fifty-four corporate members, principally from the oil, coal, and automobile industries. At the beginning of the 1990s, a coalition of utility and coal companies established the Information Council on the Environment (ICE) to promote positions questioning climate change science. Through its clever use of the media, the ICE created public confusion about climate change. The council was forced to disband, however, when environmentalists alerted the media about its funding source.

In addition to focusing on scientific uncertainty, the corporate sector has successfully blocked the adoption of climate change policies by addressing—and often times exaggerating—the potential costs of such policies (Victor 2001, 2004; Layzer 2002). A 1990 study by President Bush's Council of Economic Advisors projected the cost of reducing GHG emissions by 20 percent by the year 2100 at between $800 billion and $3.6 trillion (U.S. Council of Economic Advisers 1990). The study strongly recommended against imposing such costs on the economy until more scientific research on climate change has been conducted. Political and corporate opponents seized on the report to derail government efforts to cutback GHG emissions. At the Rio Earth Summit in 1992, the GCC argued that certain proposals under consideration could cost the U.S. $95 billion and 550,000 jobs (Rowlands 1995). The Coalition for Vehicle Choice, funded by the American automobile industry and other interests, attempted for a long time to persuade small business, labor, and civic groups that proposed climate change policies would irreparably harm the U.S. economy. Two months prior to the Kyoto meeting, the group published a statement in the *Washington Post* with the endorsement of thirteen hundred groups promoting this position (Rowlands 1995).[13]

Proponents of GHG emissions reductions responded with their own studies. The Alliance to Save Energy, an environmental group, conducted an analysis that showed U.S. carbon emissions could be cut by 25 percent by 2005 and 70 percent by 2030 at a net savings of $2.3 trillion over forty years (Rowlands 1995). Similarly, in a 1991 report the NAS argued that the United States could cut GHG emissions between 10 and 40 percent of 1990 levels at minimum cost, or even net savings, if the correct policies were adopted (National Academy of Sciences 1992). The Institute for International Economics echoed this view in a 1992 study. William Cline (1992), the author of the report, argued that opponents of reductions in GHG emissions fail to consider the use and net beneficial impact of cost-effective energy efficiency approaches and technological innovation.

Certain interest groups also attack climate change proposals, such as the ones contained in the Kyoto Protocol, as inequitable (Victor 2001, 2004; Layzer 2002). They argue it would be unfair for developing nations to be exempted from achieving GHG emission reductions while developed nations would be forced to meet specific target reductions over time. While the percentage of emissions by developed nations would decline substantially, developing nations would become major emitters. Indeed, several large developing nations (for example, China, India, South Korea, and Mexico) already account for 44 percent of GHG emissions and are likely to exceed the emission levels of the developed world between 2020 and 2030 (Layzer 2002). Furthermore, opponents contend that many developing nations are responsible for much of the deforestation and other unwise land use practices that have reduced carbon sinks (Victor 2001, 2004).

Proponents counter these arguments by pointing out major inequities between developed and developing nations. The United States, for example, has only 4 percent of the world's population, yet it emits about 36 percent of the world's total $CO_2$ emissions. Moreover, developed countries are responsible for 70 percent of GHGs already in the atmosphere. Yet, developing countries would probably suffer the most serious negative impacts of climate change. At the same time they lack the money and technology to mitigate, adapt to, or recover from those impacts (Layzer 2002).

According to Gelbspan (1998), corporate opponents of climate change policy have spent tens of millions of dollars to present evidence that contradicts most climate change science and to lobby Congress against the adoption of legislation to reduce GHG emissions. In 1994 and 1995, for example, the GCC spent more than one million dollars on lobbying and the media. The organization spent another $1 million for these purposes again in 1996. In 1992 and 1993 the National Coal Association budgeted more than $700,000 on Washington lobbyists and the media. Likewise, in 1993 the American Automobile Manufacturers' Association spent almost $100,000 for lobbying. In 1993 alone, the American Petroleum Institute (API), only one member of the GCC, paid $1.8 million to the public relations firm of Burson-Marstellar to defeat legislation to place a tax on fossil fuels and reduce $CO_2$ as a result. In 1997 and 1998 the GCC conducted a $13 million media campaign to foment public opposition to the Kyoto Protocol (Gelbspan 1998). The Western Fuels Association, a coal industry lobbying group, funded a quarterly publication entitled *World Climate Review* and spent $250,000 on producing a video entitled, *The Greening of Planet Earth*. The video contends that the warming of the planet will have many benefits and will especially be a boon for the United States (Layzer 2002). In contrast, total spending by all environmental groups in support of climate change legislation during the early to mid-1990s was $2.1 million (Gelbspan 1998).[14] Overall, business interests have been quite successful at blocking policy efforts to control climate change.

Recently, a handful of Fortune 500 companies have changed their positions on climate change and now support the adoption of controls on GHG emissions (Carey 2004). For example, several major companies including Ford, General Motors, Daimler Chrysler, DuPont, Texaco, and Royal Dutch / Shell have left the GCC. In addition, the Pew Center for Global Climate Change has successfully solicited a number of large corporations such as Boeing, IBM, DuPont, Royal Dutch / Shell, BP, Alcoa, Intel, PG&E, Cynergy, Georgia-Pacific, Weyerhauser, Whirlpool, and

Toyota to join its Business Environmental Leadership Council (Pew Center on Global Climate Change 2004). The council promotes responsible corporate leadership in attempts to address critical climate change issues.[15]

### The Bush, Clinton, and Bush Administrations

A series of severe droughts and other weather events during the 1970s, along with the "energy crisis" of 1973, convinced American scientists, journalists, and government leaders that climate change may pose a real threat to the environment and humans and requires research and analysis. In 1978 Congress passed the National Climate Act establishing the National Climate Program Office within the National Oceanic and Atmospheric Administration (NOAA, created in 1970). The new unit had little authority and a small budget. Soon thereafter, the cabinet-level DOE was established, and the National Aeronautics and Space Administration (NASA) created the Earth Systems Science Committee. About the same time NAS undertook a series of studies to determine the level of scientific understanding of the relationship between $CO_2$ and climate, all of which called for more research but also pointed to the potentially severe impacts of climate variation (Layzer 2002).

In 1988 James E. Hansen, director of the NASA Goddard Institute for Space Studies, testified to members of the U.S. Senate Energy and Natural Resources Committee that it was "99 percent certain" that the unusually hot summer that year was proof that global warming had already begun. In his view, humans were responsible for the warming trend and the phenomenon was sufficiently well understood that policymakers should take action to address the problem. Hansen's testimony caught the attention of Congress. The media widely reported his remarks and linked them to stories about the record-setting warm weather, hurricanes, and other extreme weather conditions in the United States and around the world. Although scientists at the time were hesitant to draw direct links between the high temperatures and global warming, the atypical weather in the United States and elsewhere provided the media with seemingly credible evidence that the earth was warming. Thus, climate change was given legitimacy by NASA science (and unusual weather events) and was no longer speculation. The media's coverage of the issue clearly raised public awareness. In 1981 only 38 percent of Americans had heard of global warming. By 1989, 79 percent of the population was aware of the problem (Weart 2003).

Despite heightened domestic and international concern, President George H. W. Bush refused to propose or support policies designed to reduce GHG emissions. When discussing climate change, President Bush focused on scientific uncertainties and called for further research on the issue. He downplayed the scientific consensus on climate change and believed it was premature to implement policies to control GHG emissions. He virtually ignored a petition by forty-nine Nobel Prize winners and seven hundred members of the NAS indicating that climate change is a real problem resulting from human activity and that action must be taken now so that future generations will be protected.

Why did President Bush oppose the adoption of climate change policy but strongly support efforts to improve air quality and control acid precipitation in the United States? For the most part, the causes and effects of air pollution and acid rain are concentrated within the United States, whereas the causes and effects of climate change are dispersed throughout the world (Hempel 2006). Thus, climate change is generally viewed as an international problem, not solely a domestic one. Perhaps because of this American scientists and environmental groups directed their energies toward improving air quality and reducing acid rain within the United States, thereby making it difficult for President Bush (who said he wanted to be the "environmental president") to ignore air pollution. Also, clean air had matured as an issue since the passage of the Clean Air Act in 1970 and had been on the radar of the American public for two decades already. In contrast, leaders and citizens were only just learning about the climate change issue. In addition, President Bush may have spent most of his political capital championing the passage of the Clean Air Act of 1990. As a former oil man and with the 1992 presidential election looming on the horizon, he no doubt wanted to avoid further alienating powerful fossil-fuel producers who had supported his election in 1988.

In May 1992, at the Earth Summit in Rio de Janeiro, 154 nations signed the FCCC (mentioned earlier). The primary goal of the agreement was to stabilize GHG concentrations in the atmosphere at a level that would not impede the earth's climate system. In particular, the FCCC specifies that policies should be consistent with the "precautionary principle," which requires "playing it safe" and acting prudently when scientific certainty is absent. President Bush signed the FCCC reluctantly, with the understanding that it intended to encourage, but not require, reductions in GHG emissions (Layzer 2002). The Senate ratified the agreement in October 1992.

The election of President Bill Clinton raised expectations among advocates of climate change policies that the United States would now take a leadership role in international negotiations. He supported the FCCC and strongly favored setting aggressive targets for the reduction of GHG emissions for both developed and developing countries. He desired to achieve the reductions "not through regulations and taxes but through market incentives to promote energy conservation and the use of clean energy technology" (Clinton 2004a, 767). Congress failed to pass his proposed national energy tax, however, and he quickly retreated (Layzer 2002). Clinton probably believed that the political climate in Congress would not permit the adoption of emissions reductions legislation. The 1993 White House Climate Change Action plan, therefore, did not address GHG emissions directly and, instead, contained about fifty voluntary federal programs to promote energy conservation.

Throughout much of the 1990s, senators from both political parties expressed strong opposition to committing America to international agreements that would require substantial reductions in GHG emissions. In July 1997, several months prior to the development of the Kyoto Protocol, the Senate adopted Resolution 98 by a vote of 95 to 0. The Byrd-Hagel Amendment, a nonbinding resolution, requested the Clinton administration not to agree to a treaty requiring reductions in GHG emissions that would hurt the American economy and would not mandate a clear schedule of emission reductions or limits by all nations, including developing ones. Soroos correctly observes:

> The opposition of some senators can be explained in part by the lobbying efforts of key industries in their states, such as coal and petroleum producers or automobile manufacturers, whose profits could be adversely affected by policies that would discourage consumption of fossil fuels. Senators also fear a backlash from voters if unpopular policies or taxes are needed to achieve emission-reduction targets. (Clinton 2004a, 93)

Thus, despite growing scientific consensus, senators experienced intense pressure from powerful business interests not to support climate change legislation.[16]

As a consequence, President Clinton chose not to submit the Kyoto Protocol for ratification (Victor 2001). Instead, he submitted a five-year, $6.3 billion package of tax breaks and research funding to help reach the Protocol's emissions reduction levels. By executive order, Clinton also required the federal government to reduce petroleum use in federally owned automobiles to 20 percent below 1990 levels by 2005 and cut GHG emissions from federal buildings by 30 percent by 2010. At the same time, he continued to try to convince the public that the science underlying the Protocol was valid.

Despite the unanimous vote in support of the Byrd-Hagel Amendment, opponents of climate change policies were taking no chances. Cognizant of the persuasiveness of the scientific consensus generated by the IPCC reports, in early 1998 a powerful coalition including the API, Chevron, and ExxonMobil began a multimillion-dollar campaign to challenge that consensus (Layzer 2002). In an effort to shape public opinion, the coalition recruited a number of skeptical scientists and trained them to convey their positions convincingly to science writers, editors, columnists, newspaper correspondents, and reporters in the electronic media.

During his 2000 campaign for the presidency against Vice President Al Gore, George W. Bush promised to support $CO_2$ emissions trading as a way to reduce the concentration of the gas in the atmosphere. After taking office, however, President Bush stated that more research on climate was necessary before any actions could be taken. Soon thereafter, in March 2001, he broke his campaign promise and announced that he would not seek $CO_2$ emissions reductions. In fact, Bush's energy plan, crafted under the direction of Vice President Dick Cheney, included initiatives to relax environmental regulations and develop new fossil-fuel supplies, including drilling in the Arctic National Wildlife Refuge. The White House also ordered EPA officials to reduce a long section about the serious nature of the climate change problem to a few noncommittal paragraphs in a major report on the state of the environment (Revkin and Seelye 2003; Glanz 2004; Shogren 2004). In addition, the EPA under Bush concluded that, under its present legal authority, it is unable to regulate carbon dioxide because the greenhouse gas is not a pollutant (Lee 2003b). Although he finally accepted the major finding of his own expert panel that the earth's atmosphere is becoming warmer and that human activity is largely responsible, he angered Europeans by continuing to oppose the Kyoto

Protocol and emissions limits as a way to address the problem (Andrews 2001a; *Los Angeles Times* 2001; Williams 2001). President Bush did support voluntary measures by industry to reduce GHG emissions (the Global Climate Change Initiative) and appropriated a modest sum for fuel cell research (Revkin 2003b). Analyses of the president's climate policy, however, show that it will do little to reduce GHG emissions in the United States during the next decade (Ellison 2002; Gardiner and Jacobsen 2002; Feder 2003; Hempel 2006). Likewise, the massive energy bill signed into law in August 2005 does nothing to control GHG emissions.

Given the lack of meaningful action on the part of the Bush administration, there is little doubt that powerful business interests have been highly successful in thwarting development of climate change policies, despite the willingness now of some large companies to support such policies. For the most part, the growing scientific evidence concerning the serious nature of the problem and calls for immediate action from both inside and outside the United States have fallen on deaf ears (Shogren 2004; Monastersky 2005).[17]

### Public and Congressional Concern Grows

At the turn of the century, national surveys showed considerable public support for action on climate change. A 2001 Gallup Poll indicated that 40 percent of the public worried about global warming "a great deal," much higher than the level of concern reported in a 1997 Gallup Poll (27 percent) (Carlson 2001). As many previous surveys had reported, a July 2001 *New York Times*/CBS News Poll revealed that almost three-quarters of Americans thought it was necessary to take immediate action to address global warming. More than half of those interviewed felt the United States should abide by the Kyoto agreement (Andrews 2001b).

Amid growing concerns about climate change, Senators John McCain (Republican, Arizona) and Joseph Lieberman (Democrat, Connecticut) introduced the Climate Stewardship Act in 2003. Defeated by a 55 to 43 vote in the Senate, the bill would have set a national limit on carbon dioxide and other GHGs, requiring large companies to cut emissions to their 2000 level by 2010 and to 1990 levels by 2020. The legislation would permit companies to trade pollution rights to cover plants that exceed their limits. Specifically, the law would affect utilities, refineries, and commercial transportation but not automobile manufacturers, farms, or residences. Senator James M. Inhofe (Republican, Oklahoma, an oil-producing state), chairman of the Environment and Public Works Committee, led the opposition against the measure and called climate change "a hoax" (Shogren 2003). He warned that new constraints on industry would needlessly devastate the American economy, slashing production and forcing jobs overseas. In the senator's view, "The science just flat is not there. Not only is carbon dioxide not a pollutant, but it would be beneficial to have more of it because it promotes plant growth" (Shogren 2003, A32). Thirty-seven Democrats and six Republicans voted in favor of the bill.

Senator Inhofe was not the only senator concerned about the economic impact of the legislation. Senator George Voinovich (Republican, Ohio), another opponent, similarly argued, "The legislation would devastate my state, shut down manufacturing, and send thousands of jobs overseas" (Shogren 2003, A32). A study by scientists at the Massachusetts Institute of Technology on the economic consequences of the bill found no negative effects on employment, a small impact on economic growth, and a cost to consumers of approximately fifteen to twenty dollars per household per month by 2020. The fossil-fuel industry, a variety of manufacturing interests, certain labor unions, and President Bush lobbied hard against the proposed act. Although environmentalists desired deeper reductions in GHG emissions than those contained in the bill, they were very surprised and pleased by the closeness of the vote given the unanimous support of the Senate for the Byrd-Hagel Amendment only six years before.

In June 2004 the Program on International Policy Attitudes (PIPA 2004) at the University of Maryland released the results of a national survey showing that 81 percent of Americans supported the targets outlined in the Climate Stewardship Act. When informed that annual costs to the average American household would immediately increase by about fifteen dollars, 67 percent still said they supported the act. A majority (62 percent) opposed the idea of permitting companies to trade GHG emission allowances, although about the same percentage did find the arguments in support of the idea convincing. This suggests that public opposition to a cap-and-trade approach to climate change is not deeply rooted. Most people, however, supported giving companies tax incentives (75 percent) and cash incentives (80 percent) to reduce GHG emissions. Continued public and scientific alarm over climate variation may eventually neutralize the opposition and force the federal government to enact climate change policy.

### States and Localities Enter the Fray

Due to the recalcitrance of the federal government on the issue of climate change, a number of states and localities have adopted policies designed to control GHG emissions (Revkin and Lee 2003). Rabe (2004) presents an excellent, in-depth analysis of innovative state programs developed to reduce GHG emissions. In July 2002, for example, former Democratic governor Gray Davis of California signed a law requiring reduced tailpipe emissions of GHGs for automobiles and light-duty trucks by an average of 29 percent. The new law forces automobile manufacturers to meet tailpipe standards by 2009 (Polakovic and Bustillo 2002). The requirements grow increasingly tougher, peaking in 2016. Despite opposition from the Bush administration, Governor Arnold Schwarzenegger, a Republican, has vowed to defend the new regulations from legal attacks and to ensure that it goes into effect (Bustillo 2004a, 2004b; Sahagun 2005). A recent study by the NAS (2004) finds that California will suffer enormous negative impacts from climate change if effective action is not taken soon. CARB approved the final rules and guidelines for reducing GHS tailpipe emissions in September 2004 (Bustillo 2004c).

Other subnational governments have taken different approaches to addressing the climate change issue. Oregon and Washington are working on a plan to reduce smokestack emissions of GHGs. In 2003, on the initiative of Republican governor George E. Pataki of New York, ten northeastern states agreed to limit emissions of $CO_2$ from power plants (Shogren 2003). A number of states (for example, Arizona, Minnesota, and Wisconsin) have adopted renewable energy policies intended to reduce GHG emissions (Rabe 2004). In addition, the City Councils of Oakland, California, and of Boulder, Colorado, voted in December 2002 to join Friends of the Earth and Greenpeace in a lawsuit charging two federal agencies with failing to conduct environmental reviews before financing projects that contribute to climate change (Seelye 2002). Nearly 140

U.S. cities and counties participate in the International Council for Local Environmental Initiatives' Cities for Climate Protection Campaign (Kates and Wilbanks 2003).[18]

Legal and other obstacles threaten the ability of state and local governments to implement effective climate change policy (Lee 2003c; Revkin 2003; Bustillo 2004b). A major potential barrier concerns whether states and localities can formulate policies in areas that may be under federal jurisdiction.[19] Automobile-industry officials suggest that a recent ruling by the U.S. Supreme Court concluding that officials in Southern California overstepped their authority in approving vehicle fleet rules concerning air pollutants bolsters their case that California's GHG control policy goes too far. Nearly all requirements to reduce tailpipe emissions of GHGs will force automobile companies to increase the fuel economy of their vehicles, something the federal government is already authorized to do. As a result, automobile companies filed suit against California's attempts to regulate GHG emissions in December 2004. More generally, Kates and Wilbanks (2003) question whether climate change policies at the local level can be effective given the national and international causes of the problem.

### Accounting for the Lack of U.S. Climate Change Policy

Climate change has been the most contentious issue within the U.S. environmental policy arena. Pressure from American business interests largely explains why the United States has failed to take a leadership role at the international level and has not adopted a mandatory program to reduce GHG emissions of its own. Not only is the United States out of step with nearly the entire international community, but also its lack of action directly contradicts the scientific evidence on global warming. American fossil-fuel producers and industrial consumers, in particular, are extremely fearful of the huge costs they will incur if they are forced to reduce GHG emissions.[20] As a consequence, they have waged a fierce battle against climate change proposals by devoting substantial resources to lobby Congress and the executive branch and to influence public opinion through the media. To a large extent, business benefited from early scientific uncertainty regarding climate change as well as a Republican-controlled Congress and two Bush presidencies sympathetic to their view. Whether increasing alarm within the scientific community and growing public concern will be able to counterbalance the wealth and political influence of interest groups opposed to climate change policy remains to be seen. Rather than focus on the reasons why the federal government should not adopt GHG emission controls, a number of large companies are now concerned about what might happen if nothing is done to address the problem. Whether the climate change problem will eventually evolve from, using Mark Smith's (2000) terminology, a unifying issue to a mostly conflictual one within the business community is uncertain at this point.[21]

The theoretical principles and concepts discussed in Chapter 3 explain how business has thus far gotten its way by successfully blocking climate change policy at the federal level. Specifically, certain political variables help account for corporate influence and agenda setting within this issue area. Although public awareness and concern about global warming has increased in a short time, the intensity of opinion necessary to drive the issue is apparently absent. In terms of partisanship, Republicans have represented fossil-fuel producers and industrial consumers and have opposed climate change policy, while Democrats have generally supported proposals to reduce GHG emissions. Republicans and a handful of Democrats have received substantial campaign contributions from opponents of climate change legislation. Constituency interests have also shaped the attitudes of Republicans and Democrats in Congress. Representatives from fossil-fuel–producing states and states with large fossil-fuel–dependent industries have tended to oppose climate change legislation. Although the political winds appear to be shifting, opponents of climate change policy have presented a united front in their lobbying campaign and have been quite effective in blocking and defeating legislation. Most American environmental groups, however, have primarily focused their efforts on domestic issues and have not mounted an aggressive countermobilization effort. National economic conditions, per se, appear not to have played a role in the controversy.

Theories of issue definition and framing processes contribute a great deal to our understanding of agenda setting concerning climate change. Frame bridging (Snow et al. 1986) helps explain how the fossil-fuel industry has successfully expanded its scope of influence over policymakers. Through the media, they have managed to gain the strong support of agricultural interests, a wide variety of fossil-fuel consumers, and labor unions by arguing that climate change policy will cost American jobs and will permanently hurt the economy. Opponents also have successfully employed belief amplification (Snow et al. 1986) through their continued focus on the scientific uncertainties in climate change science. Their ability to enlist fairly prominent experts to criticize existing studies and question the scientific basis of global warming through the media has been generally effective in placing doubt in the minds of citizens and some government officials about the need for immediate action to reduce GHG emissions. As Entman (1993) might explain, frames presented by industry have called attention to some elements of reality while obscuring other facets. From Zaller's (1992) perspective, this is a case where industry leaders have taken advantage of a generally uninformed public by strategically framing the climate change issue in a way favorable to their interests. Riker's (1996) Dominance Principle applies to the climate change debate because opponents have dominated the volume of rhetorical appeals on global warming. In summary, the ability of the fossil-fuel industry and their supporters to define climate change proposals as scientifically unwarranted, unfair to the United States, and a threat to the American economy has effectively shaped the agenda-setting process within this issue sphere.[22]

Certain theories of agenda building also explain why the federal government has not adopted climate change policy. Cobb and Elder's (1983) set of issue characteristics, for example, sheds light on why the scope of conflict involving climate change hardly expanded, thereby preventing policy from being adopted. Although the issue is now on the public or issue agenda, it has not been placed on the government or formal agenda because of its abstractness and complexity, lack of categorical precedence, and the slow time it has taken to attract the public's attention. As Kingdon (1995) might argue, the windows of opportunity have not opened wide enough to permit the streams of problems, policies, and politics within this issue area to coalesce. Policy entrepreneurs, despite their best efforts, have failed in their attempts to join these three streams. Moreover, effective advocacy coalitions (Sabatier 1993) have failed to form in the United States despite the apparent presence of a global epistemic community that supports reductions in GHG emissions (Haas 1992). The ability of opponents to shape the discourse through the use of language (for example, scientific uncertainty) and symbols (for example, unemployment) helps explain how they have been able to define the climate change issue and prevent it from gaining access to the government agenda (Litfin 1994).

The conceptual frameworks suggested by Hirschman (1991) and Cobb and Ross (1997b) concerning agenda denial especially apply in the case of climate change politics. In line with Hirschman's (1991) jeopardy thesis, opponents of climate change proposals argue that the adoption of these proposals would devastate the economy. By inserting this fear in the debate, opposing interests have been able to block mandates for GHG emissions reductions from reaching the formal agenda. Furthermore, as Cobb and Ross (1997b) suggest, those against climate change policy have evoked the culturally rooted symbol of the Great Depression in their discussions of the likely catastrophic economic consequences of mandating the reductions of GHGs in the atmosphere. They have pursued a mixture of low- and medium-cost blocking strategies by denying that a problem exists and by actively discrediting the emerging scientific consensus on this issue, respectively.

### Conclusion

This chapter analyzed the political role of business in three major environmental disputes, GE's pollution of the Hudson River with PCBs, the battle to control $SO_2$ emissions and reduce acid precipitation, and the debate over climate change. All three cases involve regulatory issues; however, in addition to other things, they differ in the extent to which business has been able to get its way and the outcome of the controversy. Theories concerning internal company management dynamics, political and economic variables, issue definition and framing processes, and agenda building were used to explain the level of corporate influence in the policymaking process. Table 6.1 summarizes which theoretical concepts and principles played a major or minor role within each dispute. (Theoretical concepts and principles not included in the table failed to have a bearing on the level of success of business in the conflicts.) Different factors explain the level of influence of business interests in the three environmental regulatory cases analyzed in this chapter. This suggests that explanations for the influence of business tend to vary depending on the nature of the conflict. The implications of the findings reported in this chapter are examined at the conclusion of the study.

TABLE 6.1
*Summary of Theoretical Explanations for Business Influence
and Policy Outcomes in Three Environmental Regulatory Conflicts*

| Environmental Regulatory Conflicts | Theoretical Explanations / Importance |
|---|---|
| General Electric and the Pollution of the Hudson River (particularistic issue) | Internal Company Management Dynamics: rational choice theory / major organization theory / minor corporate culture / minor Political and Economic Variables: public opinion / major countermobilization / major state economic conditions / minor Issue Definition and Framing Processes: frame amplification, values and beliefs / major Dominance Principle / major Agenda Building: perversity, futility, jeopardy theses / major knowledge brokers / major language and symbols / major agenda denial / major |
| Acid Rain Regulation (conflictual issue) | Political and Economic Variables: public opinion / major partisanship / minor business mobilization / major countermobilization / major regional and national economic conditions / minor Issue Definition and Frame Processes: frame bridging / major frame amplification, values and beliefs / major heresthetic / major Agenda Building: streams of problems, proposed policies, politics and policy window / major futility thesis / major epistemic community / major advocacy coalition / major agenda denial / minor |
| Climate Change Debate (unifying issue) | Political and Economic Variables: public opinion / minor business mobilization / major partisanship / major regional and national economic conditions / major Issue Definition and Frame Processes: frame bridging / major belief amplification / major Dominance Principle / major Agenda Building: specific issue characteristics / major language and symbols / major jeopardy thesis / major agenda denial / major |

At the beginning of this study there was considerable discussion about the role interest groups, especially business, play in democratic societies. Clearly, business and other interest groups must be allowed to participate actively and to voice their concerns using all legal methods available to them. Often, companies provide policymakers with valuable information about the issues under consideration. Democratic theory suggests that government must not only be responsive to corporate stakeholders, but it also must listen to and consider the views of citizens. In doing so, legislators and policymakers are supposed to sort out and balance needs and demands among interest groups and the public. Of course, sometimes this can be very difficult given the complex nature of American politics, economics, and society. Above all, government is expected to protect the safety and security of its citizens. Most would agree that it is immoral and undemocratic for public officials to place profit and economic gain of the private sector above the well-being of society.

In two of the three cases examined in this chapter, the federal government carefully analyzed views on both sides of the issue and weighed the various alternatives prior to deciding on a course of action. By forcing GE to abate the PCB contamination in the Hudson River and adopting an acid rain control strategy, the federal government placed the environment and public health above corporate profit. Thus, in these two cases business did not get its way. The battle over climate change, however, presents a completely different story and, at least at this point, demonstrates that business profits have been weighted more heavily than the well-being of this and future generations. In this case, business has gotten its way, and American democracy, in the process, has been undermined.

The climate change issue is characterized by a tension between economic concerns and scientific knowledge (Hempel 2006). Business leaders are extremely worried about the potential economic impact climate change policy might have on their companies. As a consequence, the producers and principal consumers of fossil fuels have consistently blocked all climate change proposals strongly recommended by the scientific community. They have managed to prevent the matter from reaching the formal (or government) agenda by demanding that scientists have more knowledge about the issue than is normally required to formulate public policy. According to most scientists, the costs to society will be enormous if government fails to address the problem.

The next chapter focuses on the role of business in the management of natural resources. Specifically, it analyzes the influence of business in the restoration of the Florida Everglades, logging in old-growth forests and the protection of the northern spotted owl, and the attempt to amend the General Mining Law of 1872. Once again, the study examines the extent that certain political and economic variables and theories of issue definition and framing processes and agenda building explain the influence of business in natural resource policymaking.

# 7  Corporate Involvement in Natural Resource Policy

The investigation now turns to examining corporate involvement in natural resource policy. Specifically, this chapter explores corporate involvement in attempts to amend the General Mining Law of 1872, the battle to restore the Florida Everglades, and the effort to protect the northern spotted owl and old-growth forests in the Pacific Northwest. Political and economic variables and theories of issue definition and framing processes and agenda building are used to explain how often business gets its way in natural resource politics and policy.

## Background

Almost immediately following the birth of the nation, the United States began acquiring large amounts of public lands and selling millions of acres to private individuals. The Ordinance of 1785 granted the federal government the authority to sell parcels of land to the highest bidder at a minimum price of one dollar per acre, with a 640-acre minimum. Numerous parcels of public land were sold to private interests under this law.

Beginning with the establishment of Yellowstone National Park in 1872, the federal government changed its policy from selling land to preserving it (Lowry 2006). Under growing pressure from the conservation movement and leaders of the Progressive Era, Congress passed the 1891

Forest Reserve Act (later repealed in 1907) to set aside forested land to protect future timber reserves (Switzer 2004). Congress also passed the American Antiquities Act of 1906, which gave the president the authority to withdraw certain federal lands from settlement and development if they had national or historic importance. In 1934 President Franklin Roosevelt signed the Taylor Grazing Act, which terminated private sales and created grazing districts on the remaining federal lands. By then more than 1 billion acres of public land had been bought by private interests, with 170 million acres remaining under federal control (Switzer 2004).

Of the total 2.3 billion acres comprising the United States today, the federal government manages more than 650 million acres of public lands. The Bureau of Land Management (BLM) oversees nearly half this amount (about 262 million acres), of which more than 88 million acres are in Alaska. The Forest Service is responsible for an additional 192 million acres. The remainder of the public lands is under the authority of the FWS (93 million acres) and the National Park Service (77 million acres). Other agencies, such as the Department of Defense, manage the remaining public domain.

During the early 1960s, the federal government demonstrated its already established commitment to the concept of "multiple use" by passing the Multiple-Use Sustained-Yield Act (1960) and the Classification and Multiple Use Act (1964) (Lowry 2006). The two laws recognized that public land might be used for activities other than logging and grazing (for example, recreation). The Federal Land Policy and Management Act of 1976 required full stakeholder participation in land management decisions and mandated that all federal lands were to continue under federal ownership unless their sale was in the national interest (Switzer 2004). The policy of multiple use has led to intense conflict between economic interests and government agencies because agencies have their own constituencies (which sometimes overlap) and their own mission. Critics of the approach contend that it is simply an excuse to allow the federal government to justify the exploitation and development of public land and resources by certain privileged commodity interests (Switzer 2004).

States, too, have participated in the contentious debate over the use and ownership of the public lands. Angered by the Carter administration's "hit list" of water projects and decisions concerning the public lands, western states and certain interest groups, such as the League for the

Advancement of States' Equal Rights and the Public Lands Council, initiated the Sagebrush Rebellion and lobbied hard to secure the transfer of federal land to state ownership (Dowie 1995; S. Davis 2001). Although the future looked promising for the Sagebrush rebels with the election of President Ronald Reagan (that is, he promised "to get the federal government off everyone's back" and return power to the states during his campaign), they were unable to convince administration officials to support their cause, probably because many of them wanted to privatize public lands.

The United States is blessed with an abundance of natural resources. Although the exact amount of mineral, timber, and energy reserves on the public lands is unknown, estimates suggest that the potential economic value of the reserves is enormous. The following figures, reported by Rosenbaum, help explain why the public lands have assumed such importance to major U.S. logging, mining, and energy corporations:

- About 30 percent of the nation's remaining oil and gas reserves, 40 percent of its coal reserves, and 80 percent of its shale oil may be in the public domain.
- About 60 percent of low-sulfur U.S. coal resides on federal lands west of the Mississippi River.
- About 56 percent of undiscovered U.S. petroleum reserves and 47 percent of natural gas reserves are estimated to reside on federal outer continental shelf lands.
- About 30 percent of the nation's forests remain uncut on federal wilderness land or in national forest areas. (2005, 292)

These estimates are conservative, and there is a good chance that the public lands contain greater quantities of natural resources with even more economic potential (Tilton 2003).

In summary, the battle over the public lands has a long history in this country. As Rosenbaum observes, "Fierce political contention over the use of the public domain runs like a dark and tangled thread throughout the fabric of U.S. history, reaching to the republic's inception" (2005, 289). Whether wilderness should be set aside and protected or should be exploited for economic gain is a question this country will debate throughout this century. It is within this context that this study examines the influence of business over natural resource policy. The discussion begins with an overview of the General Mining Law of 1872.

### General Mining Law of 1872

California belonged to Mexico but had been occupied by U.S. troops for two years when gold was discovered in 1848. The discovery of gold prompted many people to travel west and seek their fortune. As Klyza (1996, 2001) explains, the discovery also sparked a debate over federal mining policy. At the time, and even after California was granted statehood, there was no federal policy for the transfer of mineral lands to private citizens and companies. As a result, miners created mining districts with codes governing how minerals would be collected. These districts and codes formed systems of property rights that were enforced and respected by other miners in the absence of governmental authority (Klyza 1996, 2001). Soon, miners in other western states adopted the same legal approach and established mining districts and codes (Leshy 1987). Those from the West supported continuing the status quo in order to help settle the region and mine minerals the country needed. Others believed that the gold and silver belonged to the public domain and the federal government should receive money for the extraction of these metals (Klyza 1996, 2001). This disagreement over mining rights continues today.

During the 1860s the major method of mining changed from placer mining, which was normally done in and along riverbeds and streambeds, to quartz or lode mining, which required the removal of minerals from hard rock. The latter method was more capital intensive, and investors demanded more secure property rights. At the insistence of western senators, Congress passed the Lode Law in 1866 addressing only quartz mining. Amendments passed in 1870 focused on placer mining. According to Klyza (1996, 2001), the 1866 law basically adopted and legitimized the extralegal property rights system that already existed. Miners were allowed to file claims and had the option to purchase (or patent) mineral lands for $5 per acre if they spent $1,000 in labor and improvements to develop the land. Under the 1870 law, claims could be made for 160 acres, and patents could be bought for $2.50 per acre. Thus, free and open access to minerals on the public lands continued with the blessing of the federal government and in accordance with local customs.

The General Mining Law of 1872 incorporated the bills passed in 1866 and 1870. A number of important changes were included, however, in the 1872 legislation. Only valuable (in 1872 terms) mineral deposits on the public lands were covered by the act. In addition, the law reduced maximum placer claims from 160 to 20 acres, it increased quartz claims from 200 to 1,500 feet in length, and it dropped the $1,000 development expenditure requirement and substituted a $100 work requirement to maintain a claim. Subsequent laws have made only minor changes in the General Mining Law of 1872. For the most part, the federal government has rarely intervened in the activities and business of the mining industry; few bills have been adopted and relatively few rules have been promulgated by government agencies.

Two mining laws that have been enacted are worth noting, however. The Mineral Leasing Act of 1920 removed oil, natural gas, and other minerals that could be used for fuel from the 1872 act. Instead, the government decided to lease these rights. Miners of coal, oil, and natural gas on public land were required to pay a royalty of 8 to 12.5 percent. This represented a significant change in mining policy that continues through today. During the 1990s the federal government collected $11.08 billion from companies extracting coal, oil, and natural gas, plus $35.8 billion in rents, bonuses, royalties, and escrow payments for offshore oil and gas reserves. In contrast, hardrock mines pay nothing for the gold, silver, platinum, copper, and other minerals they extract. Also, in 1977 Congress enacted the Surface Mining Control and Reclamation Act, which established environmental controls over strip mining, limited mining on farmland, alluvial valleys, and slopes, and required restoration of land to its original contours.

Congress came very close to changing the 1872 mining law in 1993 and 1994. The House passed legislation that contained an 8 percent royalty on the gross revenue of miners (minus smelting costs), the elimination of patenting of land, environmental guidelines for mining operations, the establishment of an Abandoned Locatable Minerals Mine Reclamation Fund to pay for cleanups, and a provision permitting the secretary of the interior to declare public lands unsuitable for mining. The bill that passed in the Senate was considerably weaker. It sought a 2 percent royalty on net value of the minerals and retention of patenting but required market value for the surface land. It only forced miners to satisfy very different state environmental and reclamation standards. A Conference Committee was convened to resolve the major differences in the two bills. House and Senate members serving on the committee, however, were unable to compromise the extent necessary to reach an agreement (Klyza 2001). Efforts to change the 1872 act died with the election of a new Republican-controlled U.S. House of Representatives in 1994.

An NAS panel closely examined the implementation of the 1872 mining law and found regulatory gaps and uneven enforcement by federal land managers who lack the authority to fine miners for violations (National Academy of Sciences 1999). As a consequence, all alleged violations must be negotiated. The panel called for substantial revision of the mining law.

The Clinton administration tried to alter the law through administrative rules it could enact without obtaining congressional approval (Clinton 2004a). At the very end of the Clinton administration, the U.S. Department of Interior adopted a regulation that gave the BLM the authority to veto proposed mining projects that would do "significant irreparable harm" to public lands. Immediately after President Bush took office in 2001, his newly appointed secretary of the interior, Gale Norton, suspended the rule. In October 2001 she officially rescinded the BLM's authority. The Bush administration also reversed prior policies that protected tribal lands from mining and granted permits for mining in wilderness areas. These actions were criticized by environmental groups and signified that the mining industry had regained its influence in the executive branch (Switzer 2004).

Since 1964, more than 289,000 acres of public land have been privatized or patented for mines (McClure and Schneider 2001a). Congress has temporarily prevented additional public land from being privatized, but applications already submitted prior to congressional action are eligible to continue the process. Approximately 73,000 acres could eventually be privatized this way (McClure and Schneider 2001a).

### Impact on Taxpayers

Since the 1970s the General Mining Act of 1872 has been the object of serious reform efforts, all of them unsuccessful. A major criticism of the law is that it allows miners to patent large parcels of federal land for an extremely low fee. Although legislators and members of the executive branch have proposed reforms over the years, the powerful mining industry has effectively lobbied western representatives in Congress and has defeated every attempt to adopt a major revision of the act (Charles Davis 1998; Klyza 2001; Switzer 2004; Lowry 2006).

In his discussion of the federal government's ability to manage natural resources, Lowry (2006) specifically identifies the 1872 law as a prime example of government inefficiency. He points out how mining fees and royalties paid on the use of public lands continue to be determined by the more than 130-year-old legislation. Lowry says that "mining companies enjoy incredibly sweet deals. In 1995, for example, ASARCO (originally known as the American Smelting and Refining Company) patented 347 acres of national forest containing an estimated $2.9 billion worth of minerals for just $1,735" (2006, 317).

There are many other examples where mining companies have paid very little money for the rights to extract valuable minerals from the public lands. Klyza (2001), for instance, recounts how in 1994 then Interior Secretary Bruce Babbitt was forced by a federal judge to sign patents transferring more than 1,800 acres of public lands containing valuable mineral deposits in Nevada to Barrick Goldstrike Mines for less than $10,000. In order to demonstrate the inequity of the 1872 mining law, Babbitt stood in front of an oversized check for $10 billion and called the transfer "the biggest gold heist since the days of Butch Cassidy" (McClure and Schneider 2001c). Like Lowry (2006), Klyza (2001) argues that the mining law is grossly inefficient and significantly shortchanges the American taxpayer.

In 1996 Crowne Butte Mines proposed to purchase twenty-seven acres of public land near Yellowstone National Park. Located on the lands was a closed mine that had been used occasionally during the last one hundred years. Under the terms of the legislation, Crowne Butte Mines could purchase the land, and the minerals beneath it, for about $135. The mineral deposits, including large gold, silver, and copper reserves, however, were estimated to be worth about $650 million, revenues on which the company would not have to pay royalties (Switzer 2004). Environmental organizations (for example, the NRDC) voiced concern over the possible negative impact renewed mining will have on Yellowstone National Park. Rather than allow the deal to go through, the Clinton administration negotiated an agreement to purchase the land in exchange for Crowne Butte's mining rights. The company also paid a cleanup fee of more than $22 million and received federal land worth $65 million.

Cambior, a Canadian company, has proposed to mine copper in Top of the World, Arizona, a town located seventy miles outside of Phoenix. Cambior and its subsidiary, Carlotta Copper Company, will pay no more than $1,700 for the public section of the land it will mine. The company expects to mine about 478,000 tons of copper worth about $728 million. Once again, the federal government will receive no royalties from mining of the copper (McClure and Schneider 2001a).

Mining-company officials are quick to point out that their industry provides many benefits to society and that it is misleading to consider only the five dollars per acre companies pay the government (Tilton 2003). They argue that they normally spend millions of dollars prospecting, obtaining permits, and paying legal fees. For instance, Cambior reports spending $61 million on these activities involving the Top of the World project. In addition, mining firms employ tens of thousands of employees across the country, many of them in western communities, who pay taxes and support many small businesses in their areas. Finally, mining-industry officials and some members of Congress contend that the 1872 law helps protect national security by providing strong economic incentives for mining companies to extract minerals here in the United States. As a result, the United States does not have to depend on other nations to supply its minerals (McClure and Schneider 2001a).

### Impact on the Environment

The mining industry also has been strongly criticized for the serious negative impact it has on the natural environment (Tilton 2003; Kelly 2004). Critics point out that there is a big difference between mines envisioned by Congress in 1872 and those operating today. Modern mines are much larger, and many use poisonous cyanide to leach precious metals from rock. The leaching technique was employed to a smaller degree by miners in the early 1900s to draw gold and copper out of ore so low in metal content that large-scale operators would have discarded it as waste (McClure and Schneider 2001b). Leaching used to be done by misting cyanide over a barrel or large vat filled with crushed ore. The cyanide dissolved tiny particles of gold from the rock. When gold reached $850 an ounce in the early 1980s, mining firms aggressively applied the leaching technique, extracting gold from mines that had been closed for a long time and developing new mines where the ore had been thought too poor to be worth the cost of extraction. Miners still mix cyanide and water and slowly pour it over piles of ore; however, the piles are now much larger than in previous decades. Today they blast away entire mountains of rock, place the ore in high stacks covering the size of a football field, and apply a river of cyanide, leaving behind hills of tailings and waste rock (Mc-Clure and Schneider 2001a, 2001b).[1]

Not surprisingly, environmentalists oppose the employment of this technique, not only because of the hazard of an accidental cyanide release, but also because of the long-term risk related to exposure of rock to the weather. Cyanide is a deadly toxin, and its dispersion must be contained. Moreover, the ore is usually high in sulfides, and water passing through the rock and soil creates sulfuric acid, which then leaches poisonous heavy metals into runoff water. The iron rock turns lakes and streams an orange-red color and harms the aquatic life (McClure and Schneider 2001a; Kelly 2004). Arsenic, mercury, and heavy metals are other dangerous pollutants discharged by mines, especially those that are old and abandoned (Kelly 2004).

The EPA's Superfund National Priority List includes more than twenty-five mines, several of which are still active. The contamination at these sites is extremely serious and widespread, and it will cost billions of dollars to clean up these sites (Kelly 2004). Although much of the damage done by mining in the West took place many years ago, environmental problems still persist. According to McClure and Schneider (2001a), entire towns in Montana and Idaho have been transformed into Superfund sites, their stream banks and hillsides denuded of plant growth. Coeur d'Alene Lake in Idaho contains about seventy million tons of mining waste, enough to cover a football field 4.7 miles high. The Spokane River runs from the lake, and the Spokane Regional Health District has posted signs along the river in Washington state warning the public, particularly infants, small children, and pregnant women, about the presence of elevated levels of lead and arsenic in the soils along the shorelines and beaches.

Cyanide pollution has affected animals and wildlife in several western states. More than seventy-six hundred animals, for example, were killed by cyanide at gold mines in Arizona, California, and Nevada in the 1980s (McClure and Schneider 2001b). Most were birds, although approximately five hundred mammals also died. Countless fish have been killed by cyanide poisoning, too. Even in very low concentrations, cyanide can seriously interfere with the reproduction of fish and other aquatic life.

Mining is a financially risky business, and numerous companies have gone bankrupt over the years, leaving small communities with huge cleanup bills. For example, a Canadian firm managed a failed mine near Deadwood, South Dakota, and went out of business, leaving taxpayers a $40 million cleanup bill. Another bankrupt Canadian firm operated a mine on Montana's Fort Belknap Indian Reservation. The public will now have to spend $33 million to abate the contamination left behind. Overall, more than five hundred thousand mines have been deserted since the 1800s, costing taxpayers more than $30 billion in abatement costs (Kelly 2004; Switzer 2004). The General Mining Law of 1872 does not address the huge financial problems mining companies have experienced nor the major negative impact their operations have had on the environment.

### Failure to Reform the General Mining Law of 1872

Although there is widespread agreement on the need to reform the General Mining Law of 1872 and for environmental safeguards to be placed on the public lands (National Academy of Sciences 1999), attempts to do so have been consistently thwarted for over a century. For the most part, mining policy and practices have not attracted the public's attention, and a strong lobbying effort by mining companies has put pressure on Congress to leave the law unchanged. Most environmental organizations have focused on other issues and have not lobbied hard to amend the law. This has made it easier for mining interests and influential western congressmen to keep the law intact (Footer and VonLunen 1999). Varying demographic, economic, and political conditions and trends in the West have complicated reform efforts.

Since 1960 the demographic characteristics of the West have dramatically changed (C. Davis 2001). The population of the thirteen western states has more than doubled and now accounts for nearly one-quarter of the nation's population. At the same time the West has become more urbanized. Most relevant to mining and natural resource politics is the growth in second-home residences throughout the West, exemplified by such towns as Aspen, Jackson, Bend, Moab, Santa Fe, Taos, and Telluride (Klyza 2001). As these communities have grown, the type of people who live in them has changed, reflecting new orientations toward mining in particular, and politics in general (C. Davis 2001). In addition, Californians unhappy with increasing population density and traffic have migrated to the Pacific Northwest and other less-populated areas in the West (for example, Arizona, Nevada, and New Mexico) seeking a better quality of life.

In Klyza's (2001) view, these demographic changes in the West have had three important effects. First, as population and urbanization have increased, there has been less reliance on mining and other natural resource-related industries to support the local and state economy. Second, the influx of new people into the West has translated into greater support for environmental protection and natural resource conservation. Lastly, these two changes have resulted in the election of politicians who are more protective of the environment, even if it means angering mining and natural resource-based industries.[2]

Two trends in economic conditions are worth noting (Klyza 2001). First, the relative economic contribution of mining, logging, and ranching has declined. Second, the growth of the tourism and recreation industries in the West and related outdoor businesses has led to greater concern about the natural environment. Simultaneously, there has been a decrease in the number of hardrock mining employees, though some of the decline is due to increased mechanization and technological developments. Although mineral production remains an important regional and local industry, it has been subject to numerous boons and busts, leading to the disappearance of many communities as a consequence. These noticeable demographic, economic, and political changes in the West, however, have not been sufficient thus far to induce Congress to amend the 1872 mining law.

One reason why federal hardrock mining policy has not changed is because the executive branch is fragmented in this policy arena. Klyza (2001) points out that between 1982 and 1996 there were five agencies in the U.S. Department of Interior with substantial mining responsibilities (the BLM, the Bureau of Mines, the Minerals Management Service, the Office of Surface Mining and Reclamation, and the U.S. Geological Survey). Today, two different assistant secretaries oversee minerals mining, the assistant secretary of land and minerals management and the assistant secretary of water and science. The lack of a coordinated administrative capacity for mining policy was a source of considerable policy debate in the 1970s and 1980s. Little was done to improve the situation, thus contributing to the maintenance of the status quo with respect to mining regulation.

Since the passage of the 1872 law, there have been more than two hundred Supreme Court decisions concerning mining policy (Leshy 1987). The most significant cases have involved the determination on what a valuable mineral is and when a claim can be made (prior to or following a discovery). Despite the attention the Supreme Court has paid to mining issues, no recent decisions have substantially altered the law (Klyza 2001).

Congressional politics concerning the 1872 act during the last forty years have been complex. Due to the increase in population growth and diversity in the West, there has been an increase in the number of members from western states serving in the House of Representatives and its Interior and Insular Affairs / Natural Resources Committee. In addition to representatives with mining interests serving on the committee, however, other western members have strong and often opposing environmental interests. Conservative Republicans representing the rural West hold values similar to supporters of the Sagebrush Rebellion and the Wise Use Movement and are there to fight increases in mining and grazing fees and reduced logging (Dowie 1995; S. Davis 2001). They bring with them an ideological, pro-industry, states'-rights perspective and view policy proposals governing natural resource management through these lens.

In the Senate, the Committee on Interior and Insular Affairs became the Committee on Energy and Natural Resources. The new focus attracted representatives of energy-producing (and -consuming) states. The committee has had various chairpersons with very different interests over the years, though mining concerns have been well represented since the Republicans took control of the Senate most of the time after 1996. Even if the House overwhelmingly passes significant reform of the law (as it did in 1999 when it supported a waste-dumping provision), and even if most senators support such reform, a small contingent of western Republicans and Democrats can block the amendment by threatening to filibuster (Klyza 2001). As former Democratic senator Dale Bumpers from Arkansas observes, "The senators in those states live and die on this issue. They lobby furiously" (McClure, Olsen, and Schneider 2001, A1). At this point, a stalemate exists in the Senate, and it is unlikely that the 1872 act will be amended in the near future.

The mining industry has hired high-powered Washington lobbyists to represent and protect its interests on Capitol Hill. From mid-1997 through mid-2000, mining companies spent $20.8 million on lobbyists

(McClure, Olsen, and Schneider 2001). One of their best-known lobbyists is James McClure, a former three-term senator from Idaho. In 1997 and 1998, his firm earned more than $1 million in fees representing the National Mining Association (NMA), ASARCO, Battle Mountain Gold, and other companies. McClure's partner, Jack Gerard, eventually became president of the NMA. The NMA spent $3.3 million on lobbyists between 1997 and 2000. Among the mining firms that spent heavily on lobbyists during the same four-year period are Cyprus Amax (more than $2 million), Newmont Mining ($1.1 million), Battle Mountain Gold ($260,000), and Barrick Gold Corporation—also known as Barrick Goldstrike Mines—($1.5 million) (McClure, Olsen, and Schneider 2001).

Mining companies have also contributed heavily to the political campaigns of candidates who most strongly represent their views. Overall, these companies made contributions at the rate of more than $1,800 a day during the 1990s (McClure, Olsen, and Schneider 2001). As efforts to reform the 1872 mining law gained momentum in the Clinton administration, campaign contributions from metal-mining firms more than tripled during the 1990s (from $621,500 in 1991–1992 to $1.9 million in 1999–2000) (McClure, Olsen, and Schneider 2001). Some of the biggest beneficiaries were members of the Senate Appropriations and Energy and Natural Resources committees, which deliberate policy and budget issues concerning mining regulation. Fifty-two current and former members of those committees received a total of more than $750,000 from metal-mining firms in the 1990s (McClure, Olsen, and Schneider 2001). Twelve senators on those committees, nearly all from the West and nearly all Republican, attracted most of the funding (McClure, Olsen, and Schneider 2001).

According to a joint study by Earthjustice and Public Campaign, the Bush presidential campaign and the Republican National Committee (RNC) received a total of $3.1 million from mining interests during the 2000 and 2002 election cycles. Based on Weidner and Watzman's (2002) report, the companies that contributed the most money were Freeport McMoran Copper and Gold ($176,500), Barrick Gold Corporation ($36,350), and Coeur D'Alene Mines ($17,800). In Nevada alone, thirty of the eighty-eight registered lobbyists represent mining firms (planevada. org/cash 2004). Nevada state legislators received a total of $318,150 during the 1994 and 1996 elections (planevada.org/cash 2004). The national and Nevada state Democratic parties received little money from mining companies.

In addition, mining interests have supported the Wise Use Movement as a way to counter increasing environmentalism in the West and elsewhere in the country. The Wise Use Movement supports federal ownership but believes that public lands should be managed to maximize commodity production (Dowie 1995; Klyza 2001; S. Davis 2001). So far as mining is concerned, the movement argues for opening all federal lands, including wilderness areas and national parks, to the rules and regulations of the 1872 mining law. Members of the movement also want recognition of private possessory rights to mining claims on public lands (Klyza 2001). People for the West! is a Wise Use group funded by the mining industry that works hard to retain the basic provisions of the 1872 act.

Other groups are also very involved in mining politics. The NMA was established in 1995 by the merger of the American Mining Congress, the principal trade group of the hardrock mining industry, and the National Coal Association (Klyza 2001). The NMA opposes all leasing systems, royalty provisions, and environmental amendments to the 1872 legislation. In 1988 former interior secretary Stewart Udall and others established the Mineral Policy Center, whose primary purpose is to change significantly the General Mining Law of 1872. Compared to other environmental groups, total membership in the organization is small. Today, it is the major group lobbying to reform mining practices and to protect the natural environment.

### Why Federal Mining Law Has Not Changed

Certain political and economic variables help explain why the General Mining Law of 1872 has not been substantially amended since its inception even though most politicians and experts agree it needs to be reformed. Issues concerning the equitable use of the public lands and the environmental damage that results from mining operations have not attracted the attention of the media or the public. Indeed, only a small number of Americans are probably aware of the negative environmental effects of mining and the high price of cleaning up pollution generated by mining operations. Perhaps even fewer people are cognizant of the low fees the federal government charges mining firms for the use of public lands. The battle over reforming the 1872 law can best be labeled as a particularistic conflict.

Although western Republicans have received the bulk of campaign contributions from mining companies, certain Democrats representing rural western states in Congress have also received campaign money from mining interests. Democrat Harry Reid from Nevada, the minority leader of the Senate, for example, has been given substantial campaign contributions from mining corporations and has been a strong defender of mining interests in Congress. The impressive ability of the mining industry to mobilize political support throughout the West and in Congress, along with a lack of effective countermobilization by environmental groups, helps explain why the federal government has failed to change mining policy. Clearly, Mancur Olson's (1965) theory of collective action and reasons why certain private interests are most successful at organizing and lobbying government is relevant here.

Changing national and regional economic conditions do not appear to have affected the political influence of mining interests. For many years mining was a major source of employment in western states, and tens of thousands of people still work in the industry today. Even though the economies of western states have become more diverse and connected to the quality of the natural environment, mining still remains influential in Congress and other branches of government.

The mining industry has been quite successful in defining the issues at stake in debates over reforming the 1872 mining law. Through value amplification (Snow et al. 1986), it has effectively tied together its economic welfare with the welfare of the states and communities in which it operates. At the same time there has been a lack of opposition to its industrial activities in the western states. Thus, Riker's (1996) Dominance Principle applies in this case.

Agenda denial theory (Cobb and Ross 1997b) best accounts for why the 1872 mining law has not been substantially altered. The mining industry symbolizes many positive aspects of the western culture and ethos in the United States. Blazing new frontiers through exploration, independence from federal government intervention, and the romance associated with risk taking are all embodied in the vocation of mining. Citizens who have resided in the West for a long time identify and support this type of business and want to see it continue unfettered. These views and sentiments have effectively translated into regional public support and political power at the federal level. Using a mixture of low-cost strategies (Cobb and Ross 1997b), mining companies have helped recruit and elect candidates to the Senate and House of Representatives who are fiercely loyal to their cause. Although outnumbered in the House, the filibuster rule in the Senate provides ample means for a handful of western representatives to block reform legislation. In summary, the inability of the federal government to change the 1872 mining act is a consequence of constituency representation, regional politics, corporate influence, and strategic application of Senate debate rules.

### The Florida Everglades

For Marjory Stoneman Douglas, the author and environmentalist who died at the age of 108 in 1998, the Florida Everglades were the shimmering "river of grass," a unique, fragile region to be preserved and cherished by all Americans (Douglas 1988). According to biologists and wildlife experts, no other region in North America is like it. The Everglades comprise one of the most extensive wetland ecosystems in the world, containing an astonishing variety of insects, plants, wildlife, and marine life (Lodge 1998).

Since the 1880s, much of this once seemingly boundless freshwater marsh has been lost to agriculture, housing, shopping centers, roads, golf courses, and development. Today, about half the original Everglades remain. At 2.4 million acres, however, the expanses of sawgrass prairies, sloughs, and tree islands still encompass an area larger than the state of Delaware.

The Everglades include the land from Lake Okeechobee south to the tip of Florida. Southward from Lake Okeechobee, it is a slow-moving river about fifty miles wide and no more than two or three feet deep. The Atlantic Coastal Ridge, now a highway, borders the wetland on the east, and the Big Cypress Swamp borders the river on the west.

The Everglades have been aggressively replumbed with one thousand miles of canals, seven hundred twenty miles of levees, and sixteen huge pumping stations as a way to meet the demands of flood control, drainage, navigation, irrigation, and the local population's increasing need for water. This construction has had a devastating effect on the once lazy flowing "river of grass." Now, areas that receive among the heaviest rainfall in the United States are subject to drought as large amounts of water are redirected and dumped into the ocean to prevent flooding in populated areas. Water flows to the Everglades have declined by nearly 75 percent, and the numbers of herons, storks, egrets, and other large birds have decreased by as much as 90 percent (Dahlburg 2003). Damage to the ecosystem has been compounded, too, by the increasing amounts of phosphorous in the water. Runoff from peat-rich soils in the 700,000-acre agricultural region to the north has polluted the once pristine waters of the Everglades. Due to the control structures that have been built, the water flows quickly, reducing the time sawgrass and other plants have to filter phosphorous and other pollutants. The phosphorous content has been measured as high as 200 parts per billion (ppb), many times higher than the minimum EPA standard. Nonnative cattails thrive as a result, depleting the waters of oxygen, blocking sunlight, and hindering the growth of fish, crayfish, and wading birds.[3] Food for large birds has decreased as a consequence. Today, sixty-eight species of animals in the Everglades are threatened or endangered (Cushman 1998; McKinley 1999b; Dahlburg 2003).

### Transforming the Florida Everglades

The assault on the Florida Everglades can be traced back more than 155 years. In the 1840s, Florida's first state legislature considered the Everglades an unproductive, worthless area and asked the federal government to drain it. Following a series of dry spells between 1931 and 1945, two major hurricanes hit the Everglades in 1947, dropping one hundred inches of rain and flooding 90 percent of southeastern Florida (Layzer 2002). Congress acted quickly and approved the Central and South Florida (C&SF) Flood Control Project, a huge billion-dollar hydrologic development plan formulated by the U.S. Army Corps of Engineers. In 1949 the state legislature created the Central and Southern Florida Flood Control District to act as the federal government's local partner on flood control. At about the same time Congress authorized the creation of the Everglades National Park in the southwestern part of the Everglades. The nation's most ambitious hydrologic project began in 1950 under the direction of the Corps and continued for the next twenty years.

Nearly all of the thousand-square-mile area south of Lake Okeechobee and north of the Everglades National Park was cleared for farmland, most of which was eventually used to grow sugarcane. This region became known as the Everglades Agricultural Area (EAA). Three additional sections located between the park and the EAA were designated Water Conservation Areas (WCAs). WCA 1 later became the Arthur R. Marshall Loxahatchee National Wildlife Refuge managed by the FWS.

As McCally (1999) explains, the combination of effective water control, improved soil fertility, and abundant labor allowed commercial agriculture to thrive in the Everglades. By the 1950s the EAA permitted growers to produce an abundance of winter vegetables and sugarcane, and ranchers were able to graze their cattle in the area. In 1961 relations between the governments of the United States and Cuba broke down, terminating a prime source of sugar for America. Shortly thereafter, sugarcane came to dominate the EAA in terms of acreage planted and profits earned. Government subsidies and sugar-import quotas helped fuel the expansion of sugarcane growing in the EAA (Lowry 2003; Weisskoff 2004). Today, sugarcane growing is a $500 million industry and employs more than twenty-five thousand people, mostly in rural areas where job opportunities are limited.

Cattle ranchers and landowners were successful in persuading public officials to have the C&SF Project include plans to channel the hundred-mile-long Kissimee River (Layzer 2002). Both the FWS and the Florida Game and Fresh Fish Commission opposed this project, arguing that it would have a major negative impact on the region's ecosystem. Despite their protests, the project began in the early 1960s. In the end the construction of the fifty-mile-long channel proved their concerns were warranted; 80 percent of the surrounding marshes and 90 percent of the duck population were destroyed, water levels in the acquifer were substantially reduced, and the amount of nutrients flowing into Lake Okeechobee increased, leading to severe eutrophication (Layzer 2002).

Additional construction in the early 1960s had a negative impact on the region's ecosystem. The Corps built more canals and levees, decreasing even further what little water was flowing from the north. Two major new highways, Alligator Alley and the Tamiami Trail, significantly slowed the southward flow of water as well. Moreover, developers dug 183 miles of canals outside the Big Cypress Preserve to allow for the building of homes and new development, reducing the water table even further.

By the late 1960s, Everglades National Park was in serious trouble. Despite pleas by park officials, the Corps and the district refused to provide more water, maintaining that water was for people and not for plants and wildlife (McCally 1999). By the early 1970s, 90 percent of wading birds had disappeared and alligators, panthers, and other plant and animal species were endangered. Other environmental problems included occasional muck fires, substantial soil erosion, and the intrusion of salt water into freshwater areas (Layzer 2002).

### Environmentalists Respond

Environmentalists and a small number of scientists quickly mobilized to oppose additional development efforts. In 1969 they were successful in blocking the Cross-Florida Barge Canal and the Big Cypress jetport proposal (Blake 1980). According to Layzer (2002), these victories represented a significant turning point and signaled the demise of the exclusive, development-controlled South Florida water government network—a cohesive association of government agencies, congressional committees, and business interests that favored further economic growth. In 1970 environmentalists successfully lobbied Congress for legislation requiring the Corps to release a minimum of 315,000 acre-feet of water annually into the dry Everglades National Park.

Emboldened by increased public concern over the state's declining environmental quality, environmentalists lobbied the Florida state government for the adoption of a new land and water management approach. Floridians were becoming alarmed about the negative effects of uncontrolled development, overpopulation, pollution, and water shortages. Following a legislative overhaul, the election of two conservationist governors (first, Claude Kirk and later, Reuben Askew), and the adoption of a new constitution, the legislature enacted the Water Resources Act of 1972. The act ended the existence of the Central and South Florida Flood Control District and created the South Florida Water Management District (SFWMD). Critical for the Everglades, the new agency was responsible for water supply and quality. In the same year the legislature passed the Florida Environmental Land and Water Management Act to improve water quality, provide effective utilization of water resources, and give the governor the authority to identify areas of vital state concern. In 1975 the legislature placed control over water quantity and quality and drinking water standards under the newly formed Department of Environmental Regulation. The agency was also required to oversee the state's five water management districts and water quality planning efforts. Yet, in spite of these actions, business interests continued to be reflected in the C&SF Project's intricate water distribution system, and the Everglades suffered as a result (Layzer 2002).

Following a series of environmental disasters, including large algae blooms in Lake Okeechobee and serious flooding brought on by torrential rains in 1983, a coalition of sixty environmental organizations, commissions, and local municipalities mobilized and began a political campaign to make reviving the Everglades a major priority. At one point participation in the coalition topped about two hundred fifty thousand and included the Florida Wildlife Federation, the Friends of the Everglades, the Florida Audubon Society, the Coalition to Repair the Everglades, the Defenders of the Environment, and the Everglades Protection Association (Layzer 2002).

### "Save Our Everglades"

In 1983 Governor Bob Graham introduced his "Save Our Everglades" initiative. The initiative represented an attempt by the governor and his supporters to reframe the Everglades issue and place greater importance on ecology over urban water supply. In addition to other actions, he appointed a new executive director of the SFWMD and five new board members sympathetic to environmental concerns.

Despite hard work by environmentalists and Governor Graham's strong support, the "Save Our Everglades" initiative ran into several obstacles as well as formidable political opposition. First, proponents of the initiative experienced difficulty raising the salience of environmental problems in the Everglades within the broad public; it was hard to convince citizens about the importance of a vast, mosquito-infested swamp. Second, the National Park Service, a strong ally of environmentalists in their fight to gain support for improving the ecological conditions of the Everglades, lacked the capability to collect the scientific data necessary to document and dramatize the plight of the Everglades. Third, the South Florida Research Center, established by Congress in 1976 and located within the Everglades National Park, suppressed scientific studies about the ecological problems in the park. Last, and perhaps most significantly, the initiative was strongly opposed by the sugar industry, a wealthy and influential lobbying force. Layzer explains, "Throughout this period, the Florida legislature was . . . deferential to sugar despite its exploitative labor practices and environmental abuses, in part because of the legislature's traditional rural bias and its recognition of the economic potency of the industry, but also because sugar executives provided allies with generous campaign contributions" (2002, 297).

### The Sugar Industry, SFWMD, and the Army Corps of Engineers

Sugar interests had close ties to the SFWMD. By the 1980s the SFWMD was a well-financed, powerful, and highly professional agency with considerable policymaking authority. Initially, the agency's purpose was flood control; however, the Florida Water Resources Act of 1972 made Everglades management part of its mandate. Despite Governor Graham's replacement of the SFWMD's board, the district continued to privilege short-term economic growth over long-term environmental needs. Officials running the daily operations of the agency tended to be development-oriented engineers, and the district's internal culture supported economic expansion in the region. Clearly, the goals of sugarcane growers and the SFWMD coincided.

Furthermore, the sugar industry was an important client of the U.S. Army Corps of Engineers, which, in partnership with the SFWMD, managed South Florida's water supply (Layzer 2002). The Corps' activities have always been oriented toward economic growth. Since 1850 it has been required to manage flood control and other water development projects to promote farming and real estate development. After Congress formulated a national flood control policy and gave the Corps more responsibility over this issue area, it expanded the Corps' authority in 1936, making it the engineer consultants and contractors of Congress. Although the Corps began to consider the environmental consequences of its work following the adoption of the National Environmental Policy Act in 1969, in the mid-1980s the Corps was still regularly denying the SFWMD the permits it needed to restore the Everglades and was widely thought to be impeding such efforts (Layzer 2002).[4] Overall, attempts by environmentalists and

Governor Graham to repair the Everglades were largely unsuccessful due to the intransigence of the Corps and the influence of business interests.

A small victory was achieved, however, in 1987 when the Florida legislature passed the Surface Water Improvement and Management Act, requiring the state's water districts to formulate water quality protection and improvement plans. The legislation established parameters for the amount of phosphorous entering Lake Okeechobee and created a technical advisory council to research the effects of phosphorous on the WCAs and other areas located south of the lake. In addition, water management districts were ordered not to divert polluted water to the Everglades National Park.

### Pursuing Legal Actions

By the late 1980s scientists had a comprehensive understanding of how land use and water management practices in South Florida had seriously harmed the Everglades ecosystem (Layzer 2002). Numerous species of plants and animals were categorized as threatened or endangered, including tropical trees, rare orchids, the West Indian manatee, the southern bald eagle, and the brown pelican. The number of alligators decreased because too much water flooded their nests at the beginning of the wet season. Declining fish and shellfish populations led to a ban on commercial fishing in 1985.

The acting U.S. attorney for South Florida sued the state in federal court for not enforcing its own water quality laws by allowing the EAA to direct water into the Loxahatchee National Wildlife Refuge without obtaining a permit from the district, consequently harming the refuge and the Everglades National Park. Environmentalists took advantage of the media's coverage of the lawsuit to demonstrate how the sugar industry and other businesses had made huge profits at the expense of the taxpayer and the Everglades. Much of the debate centered on whether increased levels of phosphorous had endangered the Everglades. Both sides hired their own technical experts and distinguished scientists as part of an effort to control the discourse and frame the controversy. Environmentalists appealed to hotel and dive-shop operators in the Keys and sport and commercial fishermen from the Florida Bay on economic grounds in an effort to expand the scope of conflict and gain additional political support.

Following a number of meetings, scientists representing the sugar indus-try and the government agreed that, in order to protect the Everglades, phosphorous levels should not exceed about 10 ppb.

After three years the lawsuit was settled when newly elected gover-nor Lawton Chiles admitted in court that the water flowing into the Ever-glades was indeed polluted and said the state was ready to "surrender" (Dahlburg 2003). Scientists agreed that at least 34,700 acres of artificial wetlands, at a cost of approximately $400 million to build, would be nec-essary to improve the quality of the water flowing into the park (Layzer 2002). Over numerous objections and appeals by the sugar industry, the federal district judge handling the case, William M. Hoeveler, issued a Consent Decree in 1992 whereby the state agreed to implement a water quality restoration plan by constructing artificial filtration marshes, re-quiring best management practices (BMPs) on farms to control runoff, and establishing an interim phosphorous limit of 50 ppb and long-term (about fifteen years) limit of 10 ppb. The Consent Decree was based on a settlement agreement that had been reached by federal and state officials; the sugar industry did not participate in negotiations concerning the agreement. Following the announcement of the Consent Decree, sugar companies said they were willing to adopt BMPs in their operations. However, they strongly opposed the more expensive solution of con-structing artificial wetlands, and they threatened to spend millions of dol-lars to fight the proposal in court. As a result, Florida officials and the U.S. Department of Justice were forced to begin another round of negotiations, this time including both environmentalists and representatives of the sugar industry in the discussions.

During the second round of negotiations sugarcane growers con-tinued to criticize the mounting scientific evidence that phosphorous was a serious problem. They also argued that their agricultural practices were not the reason for the elevated phosphorous levels and that flooding was responsible for the widespread growth of cattails in the region. Further-more, sugar-industry firms maintained that provisions included in the first agreement would destroy the economic base of South Florida, costing thousands of jobs. They contended that the Corps should finance and cor-rect the pollution problem since it built the C&SF Project system (Layzer 2002). Environmentalists argued that sugar companies had received ex-tremely generous financial assistance from the federal government and had reaped huge profits over the years. They insisted that sugar companies are responsible for the pollution and, therefore, should pay for the cleanup of the Everglades.

Pressure on the sugar industry to participate and help finance the restoration of the Everglades quickly grew despite its protestations. The group of scientists and technicians formed to assist in the second round of negotiations reached agreement on desirable phosphorous levels similar to those chosen during the first round of negotiations. Additionally, the group formulated a plan to develop artificial wetlands and improve the hydroperiod at the same time. Moreover, the SFWMD and the Corps finally agreed that restoration is required, and they began to take effective actions to revive the Everglades.

In July 1993 Interior Secretary Babbit announced that the parties had reached a tentative agreement to divide the costs of implementing the Mediated Technical Plan, which had been developed by the scientific and technical group. Sugar companies agreed to pay 50 percent (between $233 and $322 million over twenty years), the state government would pay 42 percent, and the federal government would be responsible for the remaining costs. Among other things, the plan called for the adoption of a combination of BMPs and the establishment of approximately forty thousand acres of Stormwater Treatment Areas (STAs). Flo-Sun, U.S. Sugar, and other companies promised to halt their legal actions so that the details of the proposal could be ironed out.

Not all environmental groups cheered the agreement. Some environmental groups questioned whether the proposal obligated the sugar industry to a long-term commitment to reduce pollution. Nineteen national and state organizations petitioned Babbitt to set aside between seventy and one hundred and twenty thousand acres of EAA land for wetlands and for additional treatment of any polluted water flowing into the Everglades to correct the hydroperiod (Layzer 2002).

Efforts to restore the Everglades proceeded immediately on various fronts. Secretary Babbitt created the South Florida Ecosystem Restoration Task Force consisting of assistant secretaries from a variety of federal agencies and bureaus to formulate an ecosystem-based science plan. The task force formed the South Florida Management and Coordination Working Group to collect and assess relevant scientific and technical data. At the same time the Corps' C&SF Project Comprehensive Review Study (or Restudy), established by Congress as part of the Water Resources

Development Act of 1992, pursued a multiagency, cooperative approach to designing a restoration program.

In addition, a Science Subgroup was formed to develop the technical framework for a restoration plan. A report released by the subgroup stated that a hydrologic restoration program was required in order to reclaim the ecosystem of the Everglades. Specifically, the report recommended flooding 195,000 of the 450,000 acres under cultivation in the EAA and placing the remainder of the EAA under water 60 percent of the time. The sugar industry was incensed by the report's recommendations and withdrew from the agreement to split the costs for implementing the Mediated Technical Plan. Sugar interests filed thirty-six lawsuits to block the state's plan to adopt and implement the technical proposal.

In 1994 the Florida legislature attempted to put an end to the sugar industry's legal actions by passing the Everglades Forever Act. The new law established the need for Everglades cleanup and hydroperiod remediation, stated the abatement program was suitable, and supported the Statement of Principles previously negotiated by Secretary Babbitt as a framework for remediation. It included recommendations from environmental groups to improve the Mediated Technical Plan. The act authorized the state to administer (but did not allocate) a $700 million abatement plan for the Everglades. Finally, the Everglades Forever Act required agriculture to make a substantial financial contribution toward supporting the restoration.

In 1996 Floridians were asked to vote on three ballot initiatives concerning the abatement and restoration of the Everglades. Voters endorsed a constitutional amendment to require those who polluted the Everglades to pay for its cleanup and a second amendment to create a trust fund for Everglades reclamation. The third constitutional amendment would have placed a penny-a-pound tax on sugar to finance the $700 million cleanup (as stipulated under the Everglades Forever Act). Sugar firms targeted the tax amendment and spent $23 million on a television campaign to persuade voters to oppose the tax. Their campaign was successful, and they were able to defeat the measure by a 54 to 46 percent vote.[5]

### Financing Pollution Control and Restoration

Prospects for the restoration of the Everglades improved after the federal government took several steps to support and help finance the effort. Congress appropriated $5 million annually between 1994 and 1996 to buy land for buffer areas around the Everglades National Park and in 1996 approved $200 million to restore the Everglades. The Clinton administration publicly endorsed the restoration project and recommended spending $500 million over the next several years in addition to the $100 million the federal government had already allocated to the Department of Interior's Everglades Restoration Fund (Cushman 1996). Congress encouraged planning efforts by including Section 528, the Everglades and South Florida Ecosystem Restoration, in the Water Resources Development Act of 1996. The legislation provided $75 million between 1997 and 1999 to fund research and planning projects by the Corps. Congress added $269 million for fiscal year 1998 and another $221 million for fiscal year 1999 to continue research, planning, and abatement. In 1999 Secretary Babbitt unveiled the South Florida Multi-Species Recovery Plan to restore the ecosystem in the Everglades in order to protect the many endangered and threatened species located there. The plan was developed in collaboration with federal and state wildlife officials, environmentalists, sugar-industry representatives, and other local stakeholders (Cushman 1998; McKinley 1999a, 1999b; Kraft 2004).

In October 1998 the Corps released a draft of its ambitious Comprehensive Everglades Restoration Plan. Implementation of the plan would cost $7.8 billion and would redirect water flow to benefit the ecology of the Everglades. The plan also called for the treatment of urban and agricultural runoff before discharge into the Everglades by creating tens of thousands of acres of new wetlands.

Opponents of restoration were quick to criticize the Corps' draft plan. Angry business and agricultural leaders argued that the technology required to achieve the plan's goals was too new and untested. The Florida Citizens for a Sound Economy, representing opponents of the plan, contended that the proposal would cost the state nearly three thousand jobs and add $120 per household per year in taxes and water charges (King 1998). The Corps, however, projected the plan would create between thirty-nine hundred and sixty-eight hundred new jobs. State legislative opponents attempted to sabotage the proposal by pushing through two bills, one giving the legislature oversight authority over the activities of the Corps and the other making it more costly for the federal government to acquire land for the restoration. Governor Chiles believed the two bills would damage the federal-state partnership and vetoed them in 1998.

Park officials and environmentalists also voiced reservations about the Corps' proposal (Layzer 2002). Park officials questioned whether enough water would be redirected and treated to result in the recovery of a healthy, sustainable ecosystem. The Sierra Club broke with the Everglades Coalition, which endorsed the plan, and criticized the plan's emphasis on engineering strategies rather than solutions employing natural environmental conditions and approaches. The organization recommended that the approach be evaluated by an independent group of prominent scientists prior to final adoption. This was done in February 1999.

Following public comments on its draft of the $7.8 billion restoration plan, the Corps released the Final Integrated Feasibility Report and Programmatic Environmental Impact Statement for the Comprehensive Restoration Plan. In response to criticisms from environmentalists, the schedule calls for completing forty-six of sixty-eight projects by 2010 so that water can flow in a broad sheet through state-owned marshes from southern Palm Beach to the Everglades National Park. Approximately 130,000 acres of reservoir will be built, and urban and agricultural runoff will be treated in twenty-eight thousand STAs. According to Rosenbaum (2005), the overall effort will require the collaboration of eleven federal agencies, the state of Florida, ten counties, and hundreds of regional and local governments for at least a thirty-year period. The federal government is expected to pay for half of the cost of implementing the plan. The scale of the Everglades restoration plan is unprecedented and represents an exercise in sustainable ecological management of historic proportions.

Congressional representatives have seriously questioned the level of commitment on the part of Florida to restore the Everglades. A report by the U.S. General Accounting Office, for example, found that interagency feuds had dramatically increased costs and led to significant delay of restoration projects. In addition, Republican Governor Jeb Bush has signed legislation, similar to the two bills Governor Chiles had vetoed, which will delay and probably prevent complete reclamation of the Everglades. The state legislature allowed a bill authorizing $100 million per year in state bond funds to die and has failed to allocate any money for restoration. In October 1999 Congress appropriated only $10 million for reviving the Everglades on the condition that all parties provide proof that actions taken will indeed restore the ecosystem. To the disappointment of Governor Bush, Congress gave ecosystem goals a higher funding priority than agricultural and urban needs. Because of the importance of Florida to his brother's 2000 presidential campaign, Governor Bush was forced to reverse his position and pushed through legislation to spend $2 billion in the next ten years to reclaim the Everglades.

Also prior to the presidential election, President Clinton signed the Water Resources Development Act of 2000. The bill approved the Comprehensive Everglades Restoration Plan and appropriated $1.4 billion for ten critical restoration projects. During the late 1990s both Congress and the executive branch made a serious attempt to fund efforts to abate pollution and revive the Everglades.

President Bush took three important steps to protect and improve the Everglades in 2002. First, he and Governor Bush signed an agreement to ensure that the water-deprived Everglades has first rights to water reclaimed through the Corps' $7.8 billion restoration program. After signing the agreement, President Bush hailed the Everglades as a "unique national treasure" and declared "restoration of this ecosystem is a priority for my administration" (Shogren 2002). Later in the year he blocked oil and gas drilling in three sensitive areas in the Everglades by spending $120 million to buy oil- and gas-drilling rights held by private individuals. (Congress still must approve the purchase.) The three areas are located in southwestern Florida and include the Big Cypress National Preserve, the Florida Panther National Wildlife Refuge, and the Ten Thousand Islands National Wildlife Refuge. Third, President Bush's 2002 budget allocated more than $219 million for restoring the Everglades, $58 million more than was allocated in 2001. Although efforts to protect and revive the Everglades have begun to have a positive impact, continued development and population growth in booming South Florida are likely to increase demands for urban water and threaten the long-term success of restoration projects (Layzer 2002).

Sugarcane growers have asked the state legislature and Governor Bush to rethink previously agreed-on pollution control standards and the timeframe for compliance. Under provisions of the 1994 Everglades Forever Act, by December 31, 2006, levels of phosphorous are not to exceed 10 ppb. Sugarcane growers argue that it will be too expensive for them to meet this deadline. In spring 2003 the Florida Sugar Cane League, an industry association, led a successful lobbying effort to persuade the state legislature and Governor Bush to postpone the legal ceiling for phosphorous until at least 2013 (Goodnough 2003). Florida Crystals Corporation and other sugar companies drafted the legislation, which also called for additional changes in the 1994 act favorable to agricultural interests (Dahlburg 2003). In order to lay the groundwork for passage of this legislation, the sugar industry spent more than $13 million in political contributions in Florida during 2002 alone. U.S. District Court Judge William M. Hoeveler, who issued the 1992 Consent Decree, criticized the new law as "defective" and argued that it reneges on a promise made by the state to reduce substantially phosphorous levels sooner rather than later (Goodnough 2003).[6] Congressional Republicans were equally dismayed by the state's action and threatened to postpone federal funding for the Everglades because of doubts that Florida remains committed to improving water quality as soon as possible (Dalhberg 2003; Goodnough 2003).

Three weeks before the 2004 presidential election Governor Bush announced the state will allocate $1.5 billion to jump start the nearly $8 billion effort to restore the Everglades (Grunwald 2004). The project has fallen about two years behind schedule in less than four years. The new initiative, called "Acceler8," marks a significant departure from the coequal federal-state partnership to improve the ecosystem. Thus far, little progress has been made, and a great deal more needs to be done before the Everglades are returned to their natural state as a "river of grass."

### The Changing Policy Landscape

Several political and economic variables help account for agenda building and corporate influence in the management of the Florida Everglades, a particularistic conflict. Perhaps most significantly, the ability of environmental groups and scientists to provide a countermobilization force against economic interests favoring the continued exploitation of the Everglades helps to explain changes in the government's agenda (both federal and state) and the adoption of new policies to protect and improve the wetland's ecosystem over time. By joining together, they sometimes were able to garner public support for their policy solutions. At other times, the sugar industry was able to obtain public support for its positions by conducting expensive public relations campaigns. The defeat of the state ballot initiative to place a one-cent tax on every pound of sugar sold, for example, was due to a successful political campaign by sugarcane growers against the measure. Although support for restoration plans tended to be bipartisan in Congress and the White House, such proposals divided the state legislature and the governor's office along party lines.[7] More often than not, Democratic state officeholders were more likely to support restoration efforts than Republican officeholders. The ability of business and agricultural interests, especially the sugar industry, to contribute large sums of money to state political campaigns helped mitigate the influence of public opinion and environmental groups on many occasions, allowing them to affect the government agenda and public policy. Changing political conditions have caused the state to vacillate in its commitment to restore the Everglades, thereby appearing schizophrenic to congressional leaders on this policy issue. Finally, Florida and particularly South Florida have experienced considerable economic growth and expansion. Agribusiness and development interests employ tens of thousands of workers, thus providing supporters of continued economic growth with considerable leverage. National economic conditions have had no bearing on policy change.

Theories of issue definition and framing processes provide additional insight into agenda building concerning the Florida Everglades. Although the actions of the SFWMD and especially the Army Corps of Engineers supported the economic development of the Everglades for a significant period of time, their perspective changed almost 180 degrees when they began to call for the adoption of restoration measures. The change of attitude on the part of these two agencies was probably brought on by the growing scientific knowledge regarding the need for effective ecosystem management in the Everglades and the realization that the federal government and, to a certain extent, the state government were moving in the direction of pollution control and restoration. They thus needed to change their orientation in order to maintain political support for their mission and continued funding for their activities. As Snow and his colleagues (1986) might explain, this was an instance where frame transformation took place; new values were planted and nurtured, old meanings or understandings were eliminated, and erroneous beliefs or "misframings" were altered as a way to increase support. The Corps' Comprehensive Everglades Restoration Plan was, using Riker's (1996) term, a heresthetical maneuver because it restructured the choice process.

As the analysis of the Florida Everglades case shows, the sugar industry and environmental groups tried to influence the government agenda by structuring how leaders and citizens viewed the issues associated with the Everglades. The sugar industry engaged in frame bridging by arguing that certain restoration efforts would have a severe negative impact on employment and the economy in South Florida. Relying on the work of their own scientists, agricultural interests also used belief amplification when they initially argued that the phosphorous in the Everglades was not the result of their farming practices and that it was not having an impact on the environment. Environmentalists and their allies in the scientific community, of course, rebutted these assertions. Proponents of restoration utilized frame extension when they appealed on economic grounds to owners of outdoor recreation businesses and fishermen for their support.

Certain theories of agenda building explain the early policy dominance of the sugar industry and the subsequent policy change that took place. The entire federal-state government apparatus that supported the exploitation of the Everglades was, in Baumgartner and Jones's (1993) words, a "policy monopoly." Agricultural interests expanded and profited a great deal as a result. Few questioned the economic expansion that took place in South Florida until the environmental movement began.

Previous governors of Florida attempted to act as "policy entrepreneurs" but with varying success (Kingdon 1995; Layzer 2002). Governors Kirk and Askew laid the groundwork for the passage of the Water Resources and the Environmental Land and Water Management Acts. Governor Graham's attempt to redefine the Everglades issue and place greater importance on ecology over urban water supply by introducing the "Save Our Everglades" initiative had only minor success. The replacement of SFWMD board members by him also did not lead to the implementation of dramatic new policies. In contrast, Governor Chiles was a successful "policy entrepreneur" when he willingly told a court that water flowing into the Everglades was polluted. This proved to be a major turning point in the debate over the need for pollution abatement and restoration.

As Layzer (2002) observes, Interior Secretary Babbitt was an effective "policy entrepreneur," too. He brought numerous stakeholders together and tried to persuade them to adopt a collaborative plan to revive the Everglades. In this sense, he was successful at coupling solutions to problems and at coupling both problems and solutions to politics (Kingdon 1995).

The sugar industry was highly successful in engaging in agenda denial (Cobb and Ross 1997b). They were able to convince Florida legislators on a number of occasions to allow restoration-funding measures to die. They also were able to thwart, or at least delay, federal attempts to reach pollution abatement and restoration agreements by filing numerous law suits in court. They generally employed medium- and high-cost strategies in their overall effort to block proposals from reaching the government agenda and being implemented. For a long time the sugar industry and other business interests were able to get their way in the policymaking process.

Finally, Sabatier's (1993) advocacy coalition framework helps explain agenda setting and policy change in the battle to reclaim the Everglades. Since the late 1960s, federal, state, and local officials, environmental leaders, representatives of the sugar industry and development interests, and other stakeholders met numerous times to forge collaborative agreements on restoring the Everglades. The ability of scientists on both sides of the issue to reach a consensus on desirable short- and long-term phosphorous levels in water and other issues led to the establishment of an epistemic community (Haas 1992) and provided the foundation for stakeholders to move forward generally. As Sabatier's (1993) framework would suggest, significant policy learning took place, and there has been noticeable change in belief systems among different stakeholder groups. Whether the present advocacy coalition will remain intact over time is uncertain at this point. A strong and enduring advocacy coalition, which includes the sugar industry, is necessary if the Florida Everglades is to revert to its natural state.

### The Northern Spotted Owl and Old-Growth Forests

The dispute over the northern spotted owl (*Strix occidentalis caurina*) and the protection of its habitat, old-growth forests in northern California, Oregon, and Washington, is one of the most difficult natural resource issues policymakers have had to address.[8] According to Noon and McKelvey (1996), numerous scientific studies show that the fate of the northern spotted owl is inextricably tied to the fate of large, old (at least 150 years) trees. By 1950 nearly all old-growth forests on private lands in the Pacific Northwest had been logged. The remaining 10–15 percent of old-growth forests was found almost exclusively on public lands managed by the Forest Service and BLM. Following World War Two, old forests on these lands began to be harvested at the rate of twenty-eight to forty thousand acres per year, making the listing of the spotted owl under the ESA of 1973 inevitable (Noon and McKelvey 1996). In fact, the vulnerability of the owl to continuing habitat loss was noted as early as 1975 when Oregon officially designated the bird as "threatened."

By the time questions about the future of old-growth forests were being raised, the logging industry had already become closely tied to the economy of the Pacific Northwest. Based on data Layzer (2002) cites, in 1988, the Forest Service reported that approximately 44 percent of Oregon's economy and 28 percent of Washington's were directly or indirectly based on logging in the national forest. Numerous small communities and several counties were almost entirely dependent on the industry for their economic survival by the mid-1980s.

More generally, the debate over protecting the northern spotted owl reflects the long-standing conflict between fundamentally different philosophies about the relationship between humans and nature. Those who favor preserving the nation's old-growth forests have been pitted against those who want to protect their way of life and the region's historical economic base (Layzer 2002). The discourse regarding the need to protect the northern spotted owl has been characterized by major disagreements over the amount and accuracy of available scientific information, the impact protecting the subspecies might have on employment and the economy in the region, and the normative values attached to forest conservation. In the battle to control the government's agenda, the timber industry and environmentalists have tried to convince leaders and the public that their positions are right. The resulting bitter political confrontation reflects how much is at stake for both sides as well as an absence of mutually agreed-on principles that could provide a basis for settling the controversy.

### Legal Actions to Protect Old-Growth Forests

The preservation of old-growth forests in the Northwest was not a significant policy issue until late 1987 (Yaffee 1994; Hoberg 2001). Up until then there was an active and fairly balanced forest policy subsystem in place, whose main concern was the designation of alpine wilderness areas. A dramatic change in policy focus took place when GreenWorld, an obscure environmental group in Massachusetts, requested that the FWS list the owl as either threatened or endangered (Layzer 2002). Following a preliminary review of the group's request, the FWS Region 1 (Pacific Northwest) director appointed three biologists to evaluate the bird's population size and prepare a report. Less than a year after the assessment was underway, the Region 1 director signed a report stating that, although declining in number, the bird was not facing extinction. The conclusion went against the findings of the agency's own scientists and was the result of pressure from officials in the Reagan administration (GAO 1989). GreenWorld and other environmental groups were angry and accused the FWS of basing its decision on political rather than scientific grounds.

In May 1988 the Sierra Club Legal Defense Fund (SCLDF), which had recently opened a new office in Seattle, sued the Department of Interior and the FWS under the ESA, arguing that the FWS had ignored scientific evidence showing that the owl was endangered in certain parts of the Pacific Northwest. In November 1988 Federal District Judge Thomas Zilly concluded that the FWS's decision was "arbitrary and capricious" and remanded the case to the agency for reconsideration. The FWS finally listed the spotted owl as "threatened" in June 1990. After reviewing the petition process and the role politics played in reaching a final decision, the U.S. Government Accounting Office (GAO) (1989) questioned whether the FWS maintained its scientific objectivity during its evaluation of the spotted owl's population and the bird's likelihood of survival.

This case was immediately followed by a series of legal challenges by SCLDF to the Forest Service's efforts to comply with the requirements of the National Environmental Policy Act (NEPA) of 1969 (which mandates federal agencies to prepare environmental impact statements for any proposed activity that will significantly affect the environment) and the National Forest Management Act (NFMA) of 1976 (which, among other things, directs the Forest Service to promulgate regulations establishing standards and guidelines for timber management and the protection of other resources). In December 1988, the Forest Service released its supplemental environmental impact statement on the spotted owl, which contained guidelines for its protection. The SCLDF, the Seattle chapter of the

National Audobon Society, the Oregon Natural Resources Defense Council, and other environmental groups sued and challenged the adequacy of
the Forest Service's plans to protect the owl (Layzer 2002). In March 1989,
Federal District Judge William Dwyer, an appointee of President Reagan,
found the plan to be inadequate and issued a temporary injunction on
timber sales in Washington and Oregon. In Hoberg's view:

> This injunction, as it turned out the first of many, was a pivotal event in
> the history of northwestern forest policy because it shifted who benefited
> from the status quo. Now, for affected timber sales to go forward, either
> the Forest Service had to comply with the judge's strict interpretation of
> the law or Congress had to take specific action to change the law as it
> applied in this case. (2001, 68)

Following the ruling, Oregon Republican Senator Mark Hatfield
and Washington Democratic Senator Brock Adams intervened by attach-
ing a rider to the Interior Appropriations Bill of 1990 in an effort to shield
the timber industry (Yaffee 1994; Noon and McKelvey 1996; Hoberg
2001). Section 318 required additional protection for the northern spotted owl, established a harvest-level acceptable to logging companies, and
exempted both the Forest Service and the BLM timber sales from ongoing litigation (Balmer 1990; Johnston and Krupin 1991). Section 318 also
created an Interagency Scientific Committee charged with the establishment of a long-term conservation strategy for the owl on public lands.
Jack Ward Thomas, a veteran Forest Service biologist, was chosen to head
the committee.

### Recommendations by the Thomas Committee

After six months of deliberation the Thomas Committee delivered
its report to four agency heads (the Forest Service, the BLM, the National
Park Service, and the FWS) and Congress. The report called for a system of
habitat conservation areas (HCAs) on federal lands and a prohibition on
logging in the HCAs. Land already logged in the HCAs would be returned
to old-growth status. The Thomas Committee recommended preserving
7.7 million acres of habitat, of which 3.1 million acres contained forests
designated for harvest. Other sections of land were already in national
parks or designated wilderness areas or otherwise too remote, steep, high,
or scenic for logging. The committee admitted that its plan represented

a minimum strategy to prevent the disappearance of the owl. If adopted, 40 to 50 percent of the owl population would still be lost over the next century due to logging. After a scientific review by the Bush administration found no serious flaws in the study, the Forest Service agreed not to take action inconsistent with the report's recommendations and halted tree sales in the region (Dietrich 1992; Yaffee 1994). Timber industry leaders, who were stunned by the amount of land the Thomas Committee recommended should be set aside, and environmentalists, who believed even more must be done to preserve the old-growth forests and save the spotted owl, severely criticized the report.

Given the authoritative scientific basis of the Thomas Committee's analysis, timber industry groups decided it was a better idea to focus their attack campaign on the high implementation costs of the recommendations. They directed their criticisms at the potential impact of the plan on timber-harvest levels and the loss of jobs in the Northwest. The American Forest Resource Alliance convened a panel of statisticians who argued that the plan would cost the region 102,757 jobs (Layzer 2002). In comparison, the Wilderness Society, the Forest Service, and the Scientific Panel on Late-Successional Forest Ecosystems projected the region would lose a total of between thirty and thirty-five thousand jobs by implementing technological change, federal forest plans, and recommendations by the Thomas Committee. The Bush administration cited a Forest Service projection of twenty-eight thousand jobs lost, while some members of Congress believed the figure was actually closer to thirteen thousand (Layzer 2002). Regardless whose figures were accurate, most news media reporters predicted an economic and social disaster for the region if the federal government adopted preservation measures.[9]

Environmentalists redirected their litigation to focus on the constitutionality of Section 318, arguing that by attempting to decide the outcome of particular court cases, Congress violated the separation of powers. In September 1990 the Ninth Circuit Court of Appeals sided with environmentalists and struck down key parts of Section 318 as unconstitutional. The Appeals Court justices ruled that Congress had intervened in pending litigation without amending the statutes used as the basis for litigation, thereby violating judicial review. Needless to say, the decision shook the timber industry and northwestern legislators.

### Expanding the Scope of Conflict

Following the passage of Section 318, environmentalists realized that so long as old-growth forests were considered a regional issue, they would continue to lose in Congress (Hoberg 2001). They knew that in order to win politically they would have to expand the scope of conflict and transform the old-growth issue from a regional concern to a national one (Schattschneider 1960; Cobb and Elder 1983). Surveys at the time revealed that those who lived in the Pacific Northwest tended to be much less supportive of environmental initiatives than most Americans (Hoberg 2001). As a consequence, environmentalists launched an aggressive nationwide campaign to convince the country of the need to protect old-growth forests and "save the owl." They referred to old-growth forests as "ancient" forests and a "national treasure." They argued that the remaining old growth was almost entirely in national forests owned by all U.S. citizens. The national news networks ran stories about protest activities against continued logging, and featured stories about the issue appeared in the *New Yorker* and *National Geographic*. As a clear indicator of the campaign's success, the northern spotted owl appeared on the cover of *Time* magazine on June 25, 1990. Environmental groups also mobilized to convince congressional representatives outside the Northwest that the issue had caught the attention of the broad public, and they should therefore take an interest in the issue. According to Sher and Hunting (1991), environmental groups effectively undermined the legitimacy of the practice of using appropriation riders to exempt Northwest forests from the application of federal environmental laws.

In March 1992 the U.S. Supreme Court reversed the ruling of the Ninth Circuit Court on Section 318. By the time the right of members of Congress to protect their own constituents was restored, however, the use of riders to change forest policy had become politically untenable. Representatives outside the Northwest began taking an interest in the plight of old-growth forests, and relevant committees, whose legislation was being quietly altered, began to reassert their jurisdictional claim on the issue. As a result of extensive national media coverage of the issue, the spotlight was now on the entire Congress, and pressure was growing from all sides to resolve the matter.

*Efforts to Comply with the Endangered Species Act*

In an effort to comply with the ESA, in April 1991 the FWS announced its intention to designate as critical habitat 11.6 million acres of forests in the Pacific Northwest to protect the spotted owl. Logging would therefore be banned in this region. Roughly 3 million of the 11.6 million acres were on private land and contained not only ancient forests but land where old growth might be planted in the future to connect habitat areas. The agency's plan did not include the nearly 4 million acres now preserved in national parks and wilderness areas. Under pressure from the timber industry and the BLM to exclude private, state, and Native American lands, the FWS later reduced the amount of land it desired to set aside to just under 7 million acres (Layzer 2002).

In May 1991 environmentalists won a major battle when Judge Dwyer blocked all new Forest Service timber sales in the old-growth forest until the agency could provide an acceptable plan to protect the spotted owl habitat. Also, in 1992, Portland Judge Helen Frye issued an injunction against the BLM until the agency presented an acceptable plan to protect the owl. In July 1992 Judge Dwyer made his injunction against the Forest Service permanent and ordered the agency to develop plans that would protect not only the owl but other species dependent on old-growth forest in the Northwest. The Bush administration was unable to formulate a strategy that would satisfy all participants in the policy debate.

While the executive and judicial branches were wrestling with the old-growth forest issue, congressional activity increased substantially. George Miller, a Democrat from California, chairman of the House Interior Committee, and a strong supporter of environmental causes, attempted to push through a bill that would adhere to the ESA guidelines and protect the habitat of the owl. House Speaker Thomas Foley, a Democrat from Washington and a leader of the Northwest congressional delegation attempting to restore logging rights in the region, intervened and blocked the committee's bill. Congress had thus reached a stalemate on the issue. Environmentalists had enough support to thwart appropriations riders, but not enough influence to enact their own laws (Hoberg 2001). Nonetheless, judicial injunctions against harvesting timber in old-growth forests remained in effect. By the early 1990s, the volume of timber harvested in the national forest in the Pacific Northwest had been reduced by about 50 percent (Farnham and Mohai 1995).

### Clinton's Election

The dispute over the spotted owl had become sufficiently salient to be a campaign issue in the 1992 presidential race. The election of President Bill Clinton and Vice President Al Gore gave hope to environmentalists who had been waging a fierce fight against logging interests to preserve old-growth forests. Pro-environmental officials replaced pro-growth and pro-timber ones (for example, Bruce Babbitt, previously president of the League of Conservation Voters, replaced Manuel Lujan as secretary of the interior). The logging orientation of members of the Forest Service had already begun to change prior to the election. For the first time in twelve years, the Forest Service and the FWS faced pressure from the White House to *expand* wildlife and habitat protection.

In April 1993 the Clinton administration fulfilled a campaign promise and convened a "forest summit" in Portland, Oregon. President Clinton, Vice President Gore, and several cabinet officials, along with scientists, environmentalists, timber workers, and industry leaders spent an entire day listening to brief speeches on the old-growth forest issue. At the end of the meeting the president promised to develop a plan that would be "scientifically sound, ecologically credible, and legally responsible" (Pryne and Matassa 1993, A1). Three working groups comprised of representatives from various relevant agencies were assigned to formulate the plan.[10]

President Clinton unveiled his Northwest Forest Plan on July 1, 1993. The plan called for an annual harvest of 1.2 billion board feed (later reduced to 1 billion board feet) from old-growth forests on federal land, down from the more than 5 billion board feet per year in 1987 and 1988, and less than the approximately 3 billion board feet per year in the early 1980s (Layzer 2002). Reflecting the latest scientific thinking, the plan provided for extensive reserves for spotted owl protection in which logging was limited to salvage of dead or dying trees and some thinning of new trees, but only if the harvesting did not harm the northern spotted owl. It created ten "adaptive management" areas of 78,000 to 380,000 acres for ecological research (Layzer 2002). Furthermore, the plan significantly expanded riparian reserves for the protection of fish habitat.

Government scientists evaluated the plan's impact on the condition of more than one thousand species.[11] Of the eighty-two vertebrate species studied, the plan provided an 80 percent chance that populations of all but three species of salamanders would remain viable (Hoberg 2001). Overall, 80 percent of the remaining old-growth forests would be set aside for habitat protection.

The Northwest Forest Plan also allocated $1.2 billion over five years for economic assistance for workers and families in Oregon, Washington, and northern California.[12] Although the White House projected that almost six thousand jobs would be immediately lost, it anticipated that employing displaced workers to repair streams and roads would create more than fifteen thousand new jobs in the next five years.[13] Most components of the plan did not require congressional approval and could be implemented administratively. Therefore, if Congress wanted to raise timber harvest levels above those included in the plan or make any other changes concerning the protection of species, it would have to revise existing environmental legislation (Layzer 2002).

The compromise offered by the Clinton administration was attacked from all sides. Industry and labor groups argued that it would devastate timber-dependent rural communities.[14] Environmentalists objected to the size of the cut and opposed, in particular, the salvage of dead or dying trees and the thinning of second-growth stands to promote old-growth characteristics (Hoberg 2001). In the meantime, new scientific evidence clearly showed that the spotted owl population was declining more rapidly than originally thought and the trend was accelerating (Layzer 2002). Thus, scientists declared that action must be taken immediately in order to protect the old-growth forests and prevent the extinction of the owl.

The Clinton administration presented the Northwest Forest Plan to Judge Dwyer, and he approved it in December 1994. His seventy-page opinion addressed substantive objections from all sides, thereby leaving little room for appeals. The plan took effect in early 1995.

### The Battle over National Forest Policy

The intense debate over protecting old-growth forests and the northern spotted owl spilled over into the controversy involving logging in the national forest more generally. Since timber companies were barred from the kind of indiscriminate logging that had taken place in old-growth forests before, they began seeking permission to increase logging in other areas of the national forest. Certain politicians responded by redefining the issue from a need to protect the spotted owl to a need to protect trees from diseases and local communities from wildfires. At the same time, environmentalists were attempting to expand habitat protection beyond old-growth forests by applying the ESA to threatened species of wildlife in other sectors of the national forest. As a consequence, the dispute over old-growth forests was extended into disagreements over how best to manage the nation's forests. A brief discussion of more recent conflicts over federal forest policy is therefore relevant to this analysis.

### Redefining the Forest Policy Issue

After taking control of Congress in 1996, Republicans attached a timber salvage rider to the Budget Recissions Act. The sponsors of the rider claimed that a forest "health crisis" existed and something must be done before conditions became worse. At congressional hearings concerning the rider, scientists disputed the notion that a health crisis existed and, if one did exist, questioned whether the proposed thinning and salvage operations would actually improve the well-being of the forests. Professional groups such as the Society for Conservation Biology, the Wildlife Society, and the Ecological Society of America criticized the large increase in thinning and salvage logging required by the rider. Allies of the timber industry in Congress used the threat of large wildfires to alarm constituents who lacked knowledge about forest ecology (Layzer 2002). President Clinton vetoed the legislation.

Following a series of meetings led by Senator Hatfield of Oregon, Clinton and congressional leaders reached an agreement on a budget-reduction bill that contained the timber salvage rider. Although Vice President Gore and other top advisers voiced their strong opposition to the rider, the president signed the bill. He promised environmental groups and others that federal officials would follow sound environmental practices in implementing the rider.

After Clinton signed the bill, a small group of congressional representatives sent a letter to Secretary of Agriculture Dan Glickman and

Secretary of Interior Bruce Babbitt reminding them that the rider applied to all timber sales not yet awarded in western Oregon and western Washington regardless of their designation as endangered species habitat (Layzer 2002). The Clinton administration disagreed and, as promised, attempted to implement the rider while also protecting the environment. The Forest Service was caught in the middle of the dispute and was publicly criticized by several members of Congress for not obeying a legislative mandate. U.S. District Judge Michael Hogan supported the interpretation of the law by congressional sponsors, dismissing challenges to timber sales as provided by the legislation. President Clinton later said he deeply regretted agreeing to the rider and called for its repeal. The timber salvage rider expired in January 1998, but not before the reputation of the Forest Service had been damaged.

Republicans were extremely angry about the new environmental focus of the Forest Service, and they threatened to cut the agency's budget and reduce its authority (Layzer 2002). They also introduced a variety of "fire salvage" and "forest health" bills. Democrats and moderate Republicans, however, suspected these bills were disguised efforts to increase logging in the national forests and voted against them.

In 1999 the Clinton administration took several major steps to protect the national forest. The president banned road building on forty-three million acres of remote national forest and approved a rule banning nearly all commercial logging from fifty-four million acres in the national forest. Environmental groups, of course, applauded these actions while legislators from western states criticized the president's policies.

Just after President Clinton left office, the research firm of Davis & Hibbitts, Incorporated, released the results of a survey of six hundred Oregon and Washington residents about their attitudes toward logging in old-growth forests (*Oregonian* 2001). Overall, 75 percent of those interviewed wanted an end to old-growth logging in the national forest. Republicans and Democrats equally shared this sentiment. Surprisingly, urban and rural citizens took similar stands on this issue; 79 percent of urban residents either strongly supported or somewhat supported old-growth protection, while 67 percent of rural residents expressed the same view. Support for old-growth protection declined an average of only 5 percent in urban and rural localities after arguments both in favor and against protection were presented.

### The Bush White House

A joint report by Earthjustice and Public Campaign indicates that the timber industry contributed generously to President George W. Bush and the RNC during the 2000 and 2002 election cycles (Weidner and Watzman 2002). The president and the RNC received a total $3.4 million during this short time. The largest contributors among timber companies included DR Johnson Lumber ($133,960), Weyerhauser ($40,500), and Louisiana-Pacific Corporation ($30,250). The American Forest and Paper Association, the national trade association for the timber, paper, and wood products industry, contributed $55,050. In Oregon alone, fourteen timber companies donated more than $670,000 to President Bush and the Republican party during the 2000, 2002, and 2004 election cycles (Commoncause 2004). The Democratic Party, in contrast, received little money from logging interests nationally and in Oregon.

Needless to say, the timber industry was pleased with the outcome of the 2000 and 2004 presidential elections, and logging interests believed they had a friend in the White House once again. In April 2002 President Bush announced that his administration intended to overhaul the Northwest Forest Plan adopted by the Clinton administration. Dale Bosworth, chief of the Forest Service, claimed the plan's cumbersome and costly procedures have held logging far short of projected levels and rendered the Forest Service ineffective (*Oregonian* 2002). Although the Clinton plan permitted the logging of one billion board feet (since downscaled to eight hundred million board feet) of federal timber each year, lawsuits and appeals by environmental groups, court orders, and procedural requirements kept logging at less than two hundred million board feet in 2001. Environmental groups disagreed with Bosworth and contended that the plan barely did enough to protect wildlife given the results of recent scientific research.[15]

Just as congressional Republicans and Democrats from the Northwest had argued during the Clinton administration, President Bush declared that the national forests were experiencing a serious "health crisis." A bad wildfire season in 2002 was used as a main reason why increased thinning and salvage logging were necessary to avoid future disasters. In August 2002 President Bush unveiled the "Healthy Forest Initiative," a legislative plan to reduce risks posed by wildfires. In announcing the initiative, he maintained that current forest policy is misguided and did not work. He cited endless litigation and "red tape" among the major problems with forest policy. Forest officials in the administration contended that the main culprit was a long-standing policy that called for protecting the forests at all costs, thereby preventing logging and the use of fires to burn off dry brush and create natural burn lines that might stop the spread of wildfires. As a result, there was too much underbrush and small trees on forest floors creating mounds of wildfire fuel. Environmentalists and scientists agreed that a problem existed, but they disagreed that increased thinning and logging was the solution. Critics of the initiative charged that it was a thinly veiled attempt to increase logging.

The 2003 wildfire season was as bad as the 2002 season. During 2003, approximately sixty thousand wildfires burned nearly four million acres, caused the deaths of about thirty firefighters, destroyed nearly sixty-eight hundred structures (about forty-eight hundred in California alone), and cost hundreds of millions of dollars to contain. As a shocked nation watched on television, smoke from wildfires was so thick throughout Southern California that airline flights had to be canceled and all the region's airports were closed. Twenty-two people died in the California fires. The devastation was enormous, and pressure quickly grew on Congress to act.

Using President Bush's Healthy Forest Initiative as a framework, Congress passed the Healthy Forests Restoration Act. Most Democrats in Congress opposed the measure, while most Republicans supported it. President Bush signed it into law on December 3, 2003. The bill is supposed to reduce the threat of destructive wildfires by encouraging thinning and directs courts to consider the long-term risks that could result if thinning projects are delayed. It hastens the environmental review process and places a time limit on litigation. The legislation facilitates the creation of forest health projects around the nation. Thus far, about ten projects of this kind have been initiated in various parts of the country. The timber industry was pleased with the final bill. Environmentalists, however, accused the Bush administration of trying to increase timber harvests by conveying the false impression that, because of their past legal challenges, the nation's forests are now "sick" and need repair. Forest-fire experts are more concerned about arson and the tendency of many homeowners to grow trees and brush too close to their homes. Scientists remain skeptical as to whether the bill will live up to its goal of significantly reducing forest fires and the damage they cause.

In summer 2004 U.S. District Court Judge Morrison C. England, a George W. Bush appointee, blocked a national forest logging project in a roadless tract of the Sierra Nevada (Boxall 2004). In a highly critical opinion, the judge found the Forest Service ignored several scientific studies as well as backcountry protections when it approved the timber cutting in the Tahoe National Forest. He concluded that the project may increase the chance of severe fire, not diminish it, and was therefore not in the public interest. Although the decision involved a relatively small logging effort, it touched on a much larger battle over Bush administration policies for the nearly two hundred million acres of national forest.

In July 2004 the Bush administration proposed new forest rules that can lead to logging, mining, and oil and gas development in remote areas that had been protected under a policy issued in the last days of the Clinton presidency. Finalized in May 2005, the new rules replace January 2001 rules that banned road building and timber cutting on tens of millions of acres of roadless terrain in national forests with a policy allowing state governors a significant say in the management of natural resources in remote areas of the country, primarily in twelve western states (Clinton 2004b). Under the new rules governors can petition the federal government to maintain road-building bans on all or part of the affected forestland. They also can request federal officials to open the land to road construction, whether for logging, mining, gas or oil development or off-road vehicle use. The secretary of agriculture will review all petitions and make a final decision. Providing individual state governors this much influence in the management of public lands owned by the entire country represents a major departure from past practice. Critics argue that future decisions on the use of public lands will be more likely to reflect the will of narrow state and local economic interests than the advice of forest conservation scientists and the views of the American public.[16]

### Why Forest Policy Change Occurred

Political and regional economic factors have influenced policy-making regarding the protection of the northern spotted owl and old-growth forests in the Pacific Northwest. Prior to the successful campaign by environmentalists to expand the scope of conflict of this issue from the regional to the national level, the timber industry and northwestern law-makers were able to maintain the status quo and protect logging interests. Regional and local politics were bipartisan in nature and dominated the policy arena until national political forces entered the debate. As the analysis showed, once the issue reached the national stage, Congress balked at increasing timber harvests and endangering the spotted owl. Media coverage undoubtedly influenced public opinion, which, in turn, put the breaks on cutting trees in the national forest where the owl resides. (This supports Mark Smith's [2000] findings about the importance of public opinion when business seeks to influence congressional agenda building.) At that point conservative Republicans were more likely than Democrats to support timber companies. The wealth of the timber industry allowed it to contribute heavily to the Republican Party in general, and the Bush presidential campaign in 2000 in particular. Leaders of the timber industry and environmental groups have taken turns mobilizing and countermobilizing political support. Unless Congress and the president are willing to overhaul (or at least grant major exceptions to) the ESA and other environmental laws involving the national forest, the judiciary will be obligated to protect the critical habitat of threatened and endangered species in old-growth areas. Finally, the high level of economic dependence of communities on the timber industry in the Pacific Northwest provided logging interests with a considerable advantage in the debate over harvesting old-growth forests prior to the late 1980s. Although national political leaders were sympathetic to the plight of timber workers, unemployment in the logging industry was less important to members of Congress outside the Northwest. Overall, the dispute over old-growth forests and the effort to protect the northern spotted owl can be considered a particularistic conflict.

Theories of issue definition and framing processes provide additional understanding of wildlife protection and forest policy change. Environmentalists, for example, used value amplification (Snow et al. 1986) in their efforts to convince the American public of the need to protect the spotted owl and preserve the national forest. Rather than viewing the issue in economic terms, most Americans were persuaded by the aesthetic and long-term value of the nation's natural resources and the need to conserve them. Using belief amplification (Snow et al. 1986), environmentalists and scientists convinced citizens across the country that the spotted owl was in jeopardy and only by preserving old-growth forests would they be able to survive. Environmentalists effectively expanded the focus of the conflict by extending the boundaries of their central framework to include a set of diverse interests and viewpoints relevant to the controversy. In this sense, Riker's (1996) Dominance Principle applies here.

President Bush also adeptly employed value and belief amplification (Snow et al. 1986) when he introduced his "healthy forest" initiative. By portraying one of the country's national treasures, the forest, as seriously "ill" and in need of immediate treatment, he was able to convince the public that more thinning and increased salvage operations were required to prevent further harm caused by forest fires. After a second straight year of record-setting wildfires, Congress adopted the president's approach and enacted the Healthy Forests Restoration Act. President Bush's clever strategy of redefining the issue from a need to preserve the spotted owl and the national forest to a need to protect communities from wildfires (frame transformation) resulted in agenda setting and new policy beneficial to the timber industry.

As Kamieniecki (2000) explains, timber companies in Europe, Canada, and the United States greatly benefited from a "policy monopoly" (Baumgartner and Jones 1993) for more than one hundred years. Professional foresters, following supposedly correct scientific management principles, were deliberately optimistic in believing that progressive clearcutting and aggressive harvesting could continue indefinitely. They behaved like an epistemic community (Haas 1992) and convinced sympathetic policymakers and the public that it was possible to cut trees at a high, sustainable rate. Year after year, however, more trees were cut than became available for harvesting, severely impacting forest ecosystems in the process. Timber companies and forest scientists used symbolic devices (for example, full employment, economic development, and society's growing need for more housing and wood products) to manipulate issue characteristics (Cobb and Elder 1983), making it appear as though they were simply describing scientific facts (Litfin 1994).

Although ecologists had challenged these assumptions since the 1960s, it was not until the late 1980s and early 1990s that forest scientists employed in government and industry started to question the dominant paradigm in which they had been trained and were now operating.

As Snow et al. (1986) might observe, a frame transformation took place within the forest profession. Environmentalists strategically exploited this change in orientation to convey new scientific thinking and persuade policymakers and citizens of the need to protect the spotted owl and old-growth forests. Drawing from Litfin's (1994) work, environmentalists framed political debates in new scientific terms to achieve legitimacy and make a case for immediate action. Perhaps society's association of the owl with wisdom engendered sympathy and also aided environmentalists in their appeals to preserve old-growth forests.

Both sides of the controversy engaged in agenda blocking and used medium- and high-cost strategies to protect their interests. The timber industry fought judicial decisions to cease the harvesting of old-growth forest on federal land by persuading its congressional allies to enact Section 318 in 1990 and the timber salvage rider during the Clinton administration. For the most part, however, environmentalists were able to use the federal courts to protect old-growth forests in the Pacific Northwest. After successfully transforming the spotted owl issue from a regional to a national concern, they were able to persuade Democrats and moderate Republicans representing constituencies outside the Northwest to oppose riders intended to relax restrictions and increase logging. Nevertheless, initiatives adopted during President Bush's administration after the turn of the century may result in the demise of the spotted owl (and other threatened species of wildlife) in the long run.

### Conclusion

This chapter examined the extent to which business gets its way in natural resource policy in the United States. The chapter analyzed corporate involvement in amending the General Mining Law of 1872, restoring the Florida Everglades, and protecting the northern spotted owl and old-growth forests in the Pacific Northwest. Various political and economic variables and theories of issue definition, framing processes, and agenda building were used to explain corporate influence in natural resource politics and policymaking. Table 7.1 summarizes the general importance of various theoretical explanations of business influence over natural resource policy.

Similar to the analysis of environmental regulatory cases presented in the last chapter, the table shows that theoretical explanations of

TABLE 7.1

*Summary of Theoretical Explanations for Business Influence*
*and Policy Outcomes in Three Natural Resource Conflicts*

| Natural Resource Conflicts | Theoretical Explanations / Importance |
|---|---|
| General Mining Law of 1872 (a particularistic issue) | Political and Economic Variables:<br>  partisanship / minor<br>  mobilization / major<br>Issue Definition and Framing Processes:<br>  frame amplification, values / major<br>  Dominance Principle / major<br>Agenda Building:<br>  agenda denial / major |
| Florida Everglades (a particularistic issue) | Political and Economic Variables:<br>  mobilization / major<br>  countermobilization / major<br>  partisanship / minor<br>  public opinion / minor<br>  state economic conditions / major<br>Issue Definition and Framing Processes:<br>  frame transformation / major<br>  frame bridging / major<br>  frame amplification, beliefs / minor<br>  frame extenstion / minor<br>  heresthetic / major<br>Agenda Building:<br>  policy monopoly / major<br>  policy entrepreneurs / minor<br>  streams of problems, proposed policies, politics / minor<br>  agenda denial / major<br>  advocacy coalition framework / minor<br>  epistemic community / major |
| Northern Spotted Owl and Old-Growth Forests (a particularistic issue) | Political and Economic Variables:<br>  regional and local economic conditions / major<br>  public opinion / major<br>  mobilization / major<br>  countermobilization / major<br>Issue Definition and Framing Processes:<br>  frame amplification, beliefs and values / major<br>  frame transformation / major<br>  Dominance Principle / minor<br>Agenda Building:<br>  policy monopoly / major<br>  epistemic community / major<br>  issue characteristics / minor<br>  language and symbols / major<br>  agenda denial / major |

business influence differ depending on the conflict. (Again, theoretical concepts and principles not included in the table failed to have a bearing on the level of success of business in the conflicts.) The table also implies that natural resource conflicts tend to involve particularistic policy issues. However, more cases need to be studied to verify this finding.[17]

Based on the analysis of the three case studies, it appears that business interests exert a great deal of influence over natural resource policy; however, they do not always get their way. Mining interests have been able to thwart efforts to amend the 1872 law for decades. Indeed, their level of success at blocking and defeating reform measures in Congress is striking and unparalleled within the interest group community. For a long time agricultural and development companies were effective in their attempts to exploit the Everglades. Yet, now they are being forced to change their practices significantly and help clean up and protect the ecosystem. Similarly, the timber industry greatly benefited from logging old-growth forests, but their activities have been severely limited for the most part by the ESA and other environmental laws.

The previous chapter explored the influence of business in different areas of environmental regulation. Yet, one must be cautious in making comparisons between how much influence business has in environmental regulation versus natural resource policy. In places where a particular natural resource is closely tied to the regional or state economy, regional and state-oriented businesses have a political advantage. They are likely to have considerable influence in the states and localities in which they operate and within the congressional delegation that represents their particular area's constituency. Yet, the same level of influence does not normally extend more broadly to the national level. Most major polluting industries, in contrast, are scattered throughout the country. In environmental regulation, with some exceptions, businesses have therefore tended to concentrate their lobbying at the federal rather than the state level. Whether companies choose to engage primarily in regional politics or national politics plays a role in issue framing, agenda setting, and policymaking. It also impacts the nature and dynamics of intergovernmental relations. For this and other reasons, environmental regulation and natural resource policy are distinct and must be treated as such when examining the influence of business in policymaking.

# 8    Conclusion

This book provided a comprehensive investigation of how much corporate America has influenced agenda building and environmental policymaking since 1970. The study began by charting the development of business interests since the founding of the nation and by raising important issues about democratic theory and the role of business in American politics. A review of the literature on interest groups addressed collective-action issues and the emergence of citizen groups in the agenda-setting process. Research by the neopluralists (for example, Baumgartner and Leech 1998; Berry 1999; M. Smith 2000) suggests that public opinion and citizen groups have tempered the influence of business interests in social policymaking. Based on their findings, one would expect this to be the case in environmental and natural resource policy. Theories addressing certain political and economic variables, issue definition, framing processes, and agenda building were introduced and applied in the analysis of the role of business in Congress, at the EPA and natural resource agencies, in federal court, and in environmental and natural resource disputes.

This last chapter discusses the study's major findings and the nature and extent of corporate influence over environmental policy. The chapter begins with an assessment of the strengths and weaknesses of the investigation. The implications of the study's findings for research on interest groups, democratic theory, and environmental policymaking are then examined. Possible directions for future research are outlined at the end of the analysis.

The book began with a summary of the major corporate scandals that took place at the turn of the twentieth century. It was noted how formerly well-respected companies and corporate leaders committed serious crimes in their quest to remain profitable. Never before had the nation seen so many business executives, financial managers, and accountants arrested and put on trial. A number of large firms were found to have engaged in serious illegal accounting practices and fraudulent stock trading. Some companies went out of business, leaving tens of thousands of workers unemployed and without a pension. These business scandals shook the corporate world and, no doubt, caused many citizens to reassess their trust and confidence in corporate America.

For many, these incidents raise doubts about the sincerity and commitment of business interests to improving environmental quality and natural resource conservation. Many of the policy approaches advocated by business today, such as voluntary self-regulation and cap-and-trade market mechanisms, require honesty, forthrightness, and ethical behavior on the part of corporate leaders in order for them to work. This is an appropriate time, therefore, to analyze corporate influence in environmental policymaking.

This book has sought to determine how often business gets it way on environmental issues. A number of scholars believe that business gets its way quite often (see, for example, Milbrath 1989; Cahn 1995; Korten 1995; Ehrlich and Ehrlich 1996; Dryzek 1997; Brown 2001; Gonzalez 2001; Devra Davis 2002; Press and Mazmanian 2003). In order to examine this claim, this study has addressed the following research questions: How much do certain sectors of industry (for example, agriculture, chemical, mining, logging, energy production, and so on) and business as a whole affect environmental policy? Related to this, what determines business success or failure in the environmental policy arena? The results of the analysis concerning the first two questions are used to answer a third question: Is the amount of influence business has proportionate to other interests in society and appropriate in view of the competitive needs and well-being of a large, complex, and democratic society?

### Strengths and Weaknesses of the Study

Like all social science studies, this research has certain strengths and weaknesses. In terms of the analysis of agenda building on environmental and natural resource policy issues in Congress, one might think of additional variables to include in the investigation. For example, the empirical analysis lacks measures of lobbying capacity and activities for business interests and environmental groups. Although partisan composition of Congress is considered, no attempt is made to gauge and analyze ideological composition of Congress over time.[1] The role of third-party organizations, such as "think tanks," is not considered either. Moreover, the number of years covered by the empirical analysis as well as the number of legislative proposals on which business alignments are based is somewhat small, thereby introducing some error in the multivariate analyses. This should be taken into account when reviewing the findings of this portion of the investigation.

Some readers might quibble with the selection of rules examined in the chapter on business influence in federal agencies and with the fact that public comments on only two rules proposed by natural resource agencies were studied. An effort was made to select rules that differed along various important dimensions (for example, possible theoretical explanations, profile level, and issue area). The breadth of the rules provides meaningful insights into the influence of business and other interests in the rulemaking process. Although the EPA was the main focus of the analysis, much additional information was gained from examining salient rules proposed by the National Park Service and the FWS, two principal natural resource agencies. This investigation could have explored the success rate of business in federal district trial courts over time. Yet, it is the federal court of appeals and not the trial courts that make judicial policy.

In addition, this study examined three case studies of environmental regulatory disputes and three case studies of natural resource controversies. Case study analysis is always vulnerable to criticism that results reflect the particular cases chosen for inquiry and that the findings cannot be broadly generalized. The six case studies were carefully selected according to important criteria such as democratic theory, geography, political culture, saliency, and possible theoretical explanations. Importantly, the environmental and natural resource controversies explored in this research provide the most rigorous investigation of explanations underlying political and economic factors, issue definition, framing processes, and agenda building (including agenda blocking). As a consequence, the overall findings offer a full and in-depth understanding of the strategies and tactics business interests use and the extent to which they are successful in shaping agenda setting and policy outcomes.

The major strength of this study is that it employs both quantitative and qualitative approaches to determine how much corporations affect environmental and natural resource policymaking. The aggregate analysis provides vital information about the influence of business in Congress, the bureaucracy, and the courts. At the same time the results of the analysis demonstrate the need to delve deeper into particular contexts. Accordingly, case studies of environmental and natural resource protection were included in this research. The broad methodological approach taken here along with the wide range of data analyzed in this investigation lead to greater knowledge about the role of business in shaping—and often times thwarting—efforts to protect the nation's environment and natural resources. No other study examines so many competing theoretical perspectives and sources of data. Although more work certainly remains to be done, this research has taken a significant first step toward unraveling the complex and misunderstood nature of business influence in environmental and natural resource policymaking at the federal level. Consequently, the study makes a valuable contribution to the literature on environmental politics and policy.

### Major Findings

This book reports a number of major findings. In sharp contrast to the conventional wisdom that business interests actively oppose environmental and natural resource protection on a continuous basis, the data presented in Chapter 4 clearly show that corporations do not take a position on proposed legislation in Congress about four-fifths of the time. The widely held belief that business frequently opposes environmental regulation and natural resource conservation is also not true. Regardless of how companies align (that is, unified or particularized), they tend to support environmental legislation more often than not. In addition, firms rarely take opposite sides on congressional bills despite recent claims that they frequently do. Furthermore, results generated by factor analyses indicate that there are different patterns of agenda building across different business alignments (that is, unified for and against and particularized for and against). A regression analysis of certain political and economic variables and agenda building in Congress demonstrates that the public mood of the country impacts agenda setting only when business is unified in its endorsement of environmental legislation. In such instances the public tends to be more liberal than conservative, which is the opposite of what Mark Smith (2000) finds in his analysis of a wide range of legislative issues. Public attitudes toward corporations, thought to be a key independent variable in this research, is solely relevant when particular business interests reject environmental and natural resource policy proposals. Despite the rhetoric regarding the debate over jobs versus environmental protection, percent employed is not a significant predictor of agenda building on environmental and natural resource policy in Congress for nearly all identified positions of business interests.

The study also reports several important findings concerning the influence of business over federal agencies and the courts. As the data indicate, the number of public comments on proposed environmental and natural resource rules and which segments of the population participate in the rulemaking process varies depending on the saliency and nature of the policy issue involved. As Golden (1998) discovers, a large percentage of those who submit comments are located outside Washington DC. The exceptionally large number of comments submitted by citizen groups on the natural resource rules examined in this research supports the position by the neopluralists that the dramatic rise in the number and size of such groups is effectively competing against the lobbying activities of business interests. Comments by corporations were generally hostile toward the EPA's efforts to promulgate new environmental regulations. Overall, public comments on proposed rules by EPA, the Forest Service, and the FWS have no or very little effect on the composition of final rules. Comments that contain new facts and information normally receive the closest attention by agency officials. Thus, as Golden (1998) finds, business does not exercise an undue influence over rulemaking involving environmental and natural resource issues. Instead, what kinds of rules are proposed to begin with is most important. This is determined by who occupies the

White House and who the president appoints to senior positions in the environmental protection and natural resource agencies.

An analysis of the influence of business in the federal court of appeals was pursued as well. Specifically, the study examined the outcome of cases involving the EPA and corporate interests in the District of Columbia Circuit between 1995 and 2002. The rate of success of business in this court tends to differ somewhat across policy issues. Corporate interests won as many cases as they lost on appeal, thereby revealing that they get their way a fair amount of time in the judicial system.

The findings from the analyses of business influence in government institutions provide compelling reasons for investigating the influence of corporate interests within specific contexts involving disputes over environmental regulation and the use of natural resources. As this study indicated, in the end GE did not get its way in its fight to block the EPA's order that it clean up the PCBs it had dumped in the Hudson River. Likewise, the coal companies and utilities were unable to persuade Congress to exclude controls on sulfur dioxide emissions to reduce acid rain from the Clean Air Act Amendments of 1990. In both cases, the scientific evidence concerning the negative impact of PCBs and $SO_2$ emissions on the environment and public health was overwhelming and undercut opposing political and economic forces in the debate over policy. Public concern was also high, prompting the EPA and Congress, respectively, to take action against the wishes of powerful economic interests.

The battle over controlling GHG emissions and climate change, however, presents a very different story. Extremely influential energy producers and consumers have teamed up to prevent the U.S. government from ratifying the Kyoto agreement and from taking a leadership role at the international level to address the climate change issue. The ratification of the Kyoto treaty by Russia represents a significant step forward to resolving the global climate change problem. Nonetheless, the global effort is considerably weakened without the participation of large $CO_2$ emitters such as the United States and Australia. It is unlikely that U.S. policy on climate change will reverse course during President Bush's second term.

In addition, the study explored the influence of business in three controversies concerning natural resource issues. Despite calls for reform, mining interests have successfully beaten back attempts to revise the General Mining Law of 1872. Sugarcane growers and development forces were able to thwart efforts to restore the Florida Everglades until scientists and environmentalists banded together and persuaded the federal government, particularly the U.S. Army Corps of Engineers and Congress, to take action. The state government, which has been continuously pressured from all sides, has waffled in its intentions to improve the wetlands ecosystem in South Florida. Environmentalists have been successful in attracting media attention, expanding the scope of conflict beyond the region and the state, and using the courts to protect the northern spotted owl and old-growth forests in the Pacific Northwest. The ESA continues to provide a strong pillar in the debate over logging old-growth trees on public lands. Revision of the ESA by the Republican-controlled White House and Congress in the coming years could place economic interests ahead of habitat protection and eventually spell the demise of the northern spotted owl and other endangered species across the country.[2]

### Application of Theories

The theoretical perspectives identified in the framework in Figure 3.1 and discussed in Chapter 3 were applied throughout this study. Theories of internal management dynamics and corporate strategies offer some insight into GE's failed attempt to avoid abating the PCB contamination of the Hudson River. To a large extent, rational choice theory explains why the company fought long and hard against calls by state officials and environmentalists to remove PCB-contaminated sediment from the river. Certain aspects of organization theory and corporate culture theory also are applicable to this dispute. GE's traditional hierarchical and centralized management structure effectively limited debate inside the company over the best course of action it should take. The strong desire to shield financial assets outweighed the firm's concern for protecting the environment and public health. Ironically, a company that had built its reputation and success on the application of science and technology purposely engaged in an expensive and lengthy campaign to distort science in order to protect its profits.

Political and economic variables account for the ability of business interests to influence agenda building and environmental and natural resource policy. In certain instances public mood, public attitudes toward corporations, partisan composition of Congress, employment, and GDP explain agenda building on environmental and natural resource issues in Congress. These and other political and economic variables, however, do not add to knowledge about the influence of corporations in the rule-making process. Countermobilization efforts by environmentalists were successful in countering claims by GE that a pollution problem did not exist in the Hudson River. This also occurred in the acid rain controversy, the attempt to restore the Florida Everglades, and the battle to protect the northern spotted owl and old-growth forests in the Pacific Northwest. Public pressure on Congress to act lessened partisan conflict and facili-tated the adoption of acid rain regulations. Likewise, extensive media coverage influenced public opinion on the need to protect the spotted owl and, as a result, curtailed congressional attempts to permit logging in the old-growth forests. These results support Mark Smith's (2000) finding re-garding the importance of public opinion in congressional decision mak-ing. In contrast, the intensity of public opinion necessary to reform min-ing practices and control climate change is absent at this point in time. Except when highly charged regional issues are being considered (for ex-ample, in the case of conserving old-growth forests), Democrats are more likely than Republicans to support environmental and natural resource measures (for example, in the climate change debate). Overall, industry has successfully leveraged regional political and economic forces to op-pose legislative proposals to conserve natural resources in Congress (for example, in attempts to reform the General Mining Law of 1872).

Theories of issue definition and framing processes are important in explaining how business influences policy outcomes. Companies have al-most no influence over final agency rules concerning environmental and natural resource issues. More generally, however, they are effective in defining issues and framing debates to their advantage. For example, they employed belief amplification (Snow et al. 1986) when they argued that new regulations were too expensive and not supported by science, and were unnecessary in efforts to clean up the Hudson River, adopt acid rain controls, implement climate change policy, restore the Florida Ever-glades, and protect old-growth forests. In an effort to aid the timber in-dustry, President Bush cleverly utilized value and belief amplification (Snow et al. 1986) when he introduced his "healthy forest" initiative and when Congress enacted legislation along the same lines. In so doing, he and certain members of Congress reframed the issue from a need to protect the spotted owl and the national forest to a need to control the causes of disease and destructive wildfires. The fossil-fuel industry has employed frame bridging (Snow et al. 1986) in their appeals to other industrial sectors to join them in their fight against $SO_2$ and GHG emissions controls. The sugar industry relied on frame bridging to broaden its base of support in its attempt to continue decades-old agricultural practices as well. Environmental interests were able to dominate the volume of rhetorical appeals on the need to protect the environment and public health in the battle to clean up the Hudson River and in the controversy regarding the logging of old-growth forests (Riker's [1996] Dominance Principle). In contrast, industry has dominated rhetorical appeals on climate change. Frame transformation (Snow et al. 1986) took place when the SFWMD and the U.S. Army Corps of Engineers reversed their position and began to call for the adoption of restoration measures in the dispute over the Everglades. Similarly, this happened when forest scientists became concerned about ecosystem management and the need to cease clear-cutting. In both cases, new values were planted and nurtured, old meanings or understandings were eliminated, and erroneous beliefs or "misframings" were altered to increase support.

Finally, theories of agenda building significantly furthered understanding of business influence in environmental and natural resource policymaking. In instances where business interests strongly object to the adoption of new laws and regulations, for example, they tend to engage in agenda denial (Cobb and Ross 1997b). Although unsuccessful, this was evident in the debate over the roadless area rule analyzed in this study. Efforts to reform the General Mining Law of 1872 have failed primarily because of the hardrock mining industry's ability to block access to the government agenda (Cobb and Ross 1997b). To different degrees, this was true in cases involving GE and the Hudson River, energy companies and climate change, sugarcane growers and the restoration of the Everglades, and the timber industry and the protection of old-growth forests. Hirschman's (1991) perversity, futility, and jeopardy theses explain the nature of business appeals in these controversies to varying degrees. In addition, the EPA, the Forest Service, and the FWS tend to propose rules when scientific consensus about a problem exists and an "epistemic community" (Haas 1992) supports taking action (for example, the dispute over increasing the standard for arsenic in drinking water). The presence of "epistemic communities" in controversies over measures to control acid rain and the revival of the Everglades played a central role in the respective policy debates. In the case of the abatement of the Hudson River, "knowledge brokers" (Litfin 1994) in federal and state agencies transformed scientific findings into a call for government to require GE to remove PCBs from the river. Kingdon's (1995) theory of how streams of problems, proposed policies, and politics shape the government agenda accounts for the evolution of the acid rain controversy. In this policy area entrepreneurs gained the attention of critical members of Congress, coupled solutions to problems, and connected both problems and solutions to politics. The establishment of an advocacy coalition (Sabatier 1993) made it possible to reach final agreement on reductions of $SO_2$ emissions. Cobb and Elder's (1983) set of issue characteristics sheds light on why the scope of conflict concerning climate change has barely expanded in the United States. The ability of opponents to shape the discourse through the use of language (for example, the disagreement over scientific evidence) and symbols (for example, unemployment on a mass scale) (Litfin 1994) explains how business interests have been able to define the climate change issue and prevent it from being elevated to the formal government agenda. Similar to the dominant paradigm in forest science and policy that perpetuated unlimited logging for many years, the federal-state government coalition that early supported the exploitation of the Everglades was, in Baumgartner and Jones's (1993) terms, a "policy monopoly." Agricultural and development interests profited as a result. Previous governors of Florida, such as Lawton Chiles, and former interior secretary Babbitt were effective policy entrepreneurs in the Everglades dispute. In this case policy learning has led to the creation of an advocacy coalition (Sabatier 1993) consisting of a variety of stakeholders. A cohesive and enduring advocacy coalition, which includes the sugar industry and development interests, is necessary if the Florida Everglades is to ever revert back to its natural state.

### Implications of the Study's Findings

This study's findings have a number of implications for the way analysts view the role of business in environmental and natural resource policymaking. At the aggregate level it is clear that business interests selectively choose which bills to oppose or support in Congress, and they do not, as environmentalists, media commentators, and some scholars assume, continuously and unrelentingly pressure legislators for favorable treatment. They are most likely to become active in critical and salient policy debates. Although their participation in the legislative process is far less than expected, the controversies in which they decide to become involved tend to be ones where there is much at stake for them *and* the environment. In this sense, the lobbying activities of business can have an enormous impact on the nation's effort to protect the environment and natural resources.

When business does choose to lobby Congress on environmental legislation, it more often supports rather than opposes such legislation. This result probably indicates that the views of business interests are often conveyed and considered during the initial writing of bills. The multiple indicators approach used by Mark Smith (2000) and employed in this research unfortunately does not include this somewhat hidden but critical facet of the agenda-building process in Congress. Of course, business interests will actively oppose legislation when their views are not reflected in legislative proposals and when there is much at stake. Such legislation is adopted when pressure from environmental groups and public opinion requires congressional representatives to take immediate action to address urgent pollution or natural resource problems. Congress is unable to always act according to the desires of the business community because of the existence of previous, and oftentimes landmark, law. In such cases corporations seldom get their way.

Although companies may express different attitudes toward environmental protection (or none at all), they rarely oppose one another in the legislative process. Recent literature tends to exaggerate the extent to which companies disagree with one another over environmental and natural resource policy. Of course, this could change in the future as the United States is forced to make increasingly difficult decisions on how best to control pollution and conserve natural resources. This is most likely to take place in deliberations over clean air and water policy, climate change, and the use of the public lands.

The factor analyses of the multiple indicators of agenda building in Congress across various business alignments show that, at least on environmental and natural resource issues salient to corporations, legislative agenda setting is far more complex than the literature implies. The discovery of few significant predictors of agenda setting irrespective of corporate alignments further underscores the intricacy of legislative policymaking. For the most part, the political and economic dynamics in Congress are constantly changing and differ from one legislative item to the next. This underscores the multitude of factors that come into play for legislators when they consider and vote on bills addressing environmental and natural resource issues. While institutional rules and procedures virtually remain the same, each policy issue raises a very different and often conflicting set of concerns for legislators. What might be good for the country might also place a heavy burden on a particular constituency and vice versa. Business and other interest groups, including environmental organizations, also tend to approach legislative proposals in a wide variety of ways, and they rarely line up for or against proposals in the exact same manner. Over time the partisan and ideological composition of Congress and the executive branches change, and support for many legislative initiatives rises and falls accordingly. External forces, individually and relative to one another, vary substantially over time as well. Agenda building in Congress concerning environmental legislation, therefore, is in a constant state of flux, with policy stability and equilibrium being achieved for only brief moments. Agenda setting is a multifaceted and dynamic process, and no one theory can account for legislative outcomes from one period of time to the next.

The analyses of the environmental regulatory and natural resource case studies demonstrate the ever-changing nature of agenda building, too. Each controversy has its own distinctive and separate set of issue characteristics that define the nature of the case, how stakeholders position themselves, and the outcome. This is why a certain theory of agenda building can explain the policy evolution of one dispute rather well but is less relevant in another conflict at the same time.

The neopluralists believe that citizen groups and public opinion play an important role in checking the influence of business in the agenda-building and policymaking process. This was found to be true only to a limited extent in this study's aggregate analysis of Congress. As the data on campaign contributions show, environmental groups are not a consistent force in the agenda-setting process regardless how business interests align themselves on environmental and natural resource bills. Public mood does impact agenda building when business is unified in support of environmental legislation, but it plays no role in shaping legislative outcomes when business is positioned differently. Similarly, public attitudes toward corporations only affect agenda setting when particular business interests oppose environmental policy proposals. Although environmental organizations participate at a high level in rulemaking regarding natural resource issues, they are much less active in rulemaking regarding environmental regulatory issues. Thus, this research on environmental policymaking in Congress and federal agencies demonstrates that environmental groups participate less often and less effectively than neopluralists might suggest. Also, public opinion is not a major factor in the agenda-building process in both Congress and the bureaucracy.

Analysis of the six case studies, however, offers more support for the position of the neopluralists. Generally, when much is at stake, environmental groups tend to mobilize and provide an effective check on the influence of business interests. This is evident in the conflicts involving GE and the dumping of PCBs in the Hudson River, the promulgation of acid rain regulations, the restoration of the Everglades, and protection of the northern spotted owl and old-growth forests. Public opinion was a factor in all these controversies, though to varying degrees. Therefore, when conflicts are salient, environmental groups and public opinion tend to present an important, countervailing force to business interests. Mancur Olson (1965) would not have predicted this finding.

Finally, the overall results of the investigation have important implications for the influence of business in environmental and natural resource policymaking in particular, and democratic theory in general. Corporations strategically select which legislative debates to enter, and they take positions on environmental and natural resource legislation only a small percentage of the time. Furthermore, business interests do not exert an undue influence in the rulemaking process. Yet, they tend to win as many cases as they lose in the federal court of appeals. Overall, however, business does not get what it wants from government institutions a majority of the time, as some argue. This study's findings suggest that the influence of business in environmental and natural resource policymaking is modest at best.

The examination of the case studies presents a similar picture. Although business interests experienced early success in conflicts over the contamination of the Hudson River, $SO_2$ emissions, the pollution of the Everglades, and the logging of old-growth forests, they eventually were forced to bow to the demands of federal officials. This is not the situation, of course, in disputes over hardrock mining and climate change. In these instances, corporations have thus far been able to defeat efforts to reform the General Mining Act of 1872 and reduce GHG emissions. Based on the overall analysis of the environmental regulatory and the natural resource case studies, however, business interests do not often get their way. As this study shows, they tend to have a mixed rate of success in influencing the outcomes of salient policy controversies.

In addition to environmental groups and public opinion, other factors also mitigate the influence of business in agenda building and policymaking. Competing elites in the media and scientific community, for example, can point out differences between what corporations are claiming and the actual evidence. As this study revealed, the media played a central role in the controversy over the northern spotted owl and old-growth forests. What started out as a regional (Pacific Northwest) issue quickly expanded to the national level as a result of extensive media coverage of the plight of the owl and its habitat. The timber industry was thus forced to reduce logging on public land considerably. Likewise, scientists brought to light the negative impacts of PCB contamination of the Hudson River, $SO_2$ emissions on aquatic bodies and forests, and agricultural runoff in the Everglades.[3] In each case business groups were forced to moderate significantly their stands. Federal district trial court judges, too, placed controls on pollution of the Everglades and logging in old-growth forests. This was only possible because of the existence of groundbreaking federal laws governing environmental and natural resource protection (for example, the Clean Water Act and the ESA). As James Madison suggested would generally happen in *Federalist Paper Number 10*, the environmental policy arena is characterized by a healthy balance between competing interests and stakeholders. The system of checks and balances between the three branches of government and the protection of individual rights allow business interests to pursue aggressively their aims but at the same time prevent them from completely destroying the environment and severely harming public health.[4]

Still, one has to wonder why the United States has been unable to achieve more progress in improving its environmental quality and managing its natural resources. Government has not enforced existing pollution control laws and regulations as aggressively as possible. Thus, many states and localities are still in violation of clean air and water standards, and hazardous-waste contamination of inland waterways and coastal ocean regions continues to be a problem. The federal government has done almost nothing to control GHG emissions and climate change. Public lands in the West are increasingly being opened up to mining, drilling for natural gas and oil, and logging. Clearly, industry leaders have succeeded in convincing government that current levels of pollution are tolerable, the nation possesses an overabundance of natural resources, and employment and economic growth must be sustained. Their wealth and collective action advantages (M. Olson 1965) translate into access to policymakers and the governmental process, providing them with many opportunities to present their arguments. In comparison, environmental groups have been less effective in shaping the discourse over environmental protection and natural resource conservation, and they have not convincingly made their case as to why immediate action is necessary. The public, too, has been unwilling to take stronger stands on environmental issues and vote for politicians who will improve pollution control and conserve the nation's natural resources. Until environmental groups and citizens produce a groundswell of broad public support, business interests will continue to get their way a fair amount of the time without significantly violating basic principles of democracy.

### Theoretical Implications

The application of different theories throughout the study leads to several implications regarding competing explanations of agenda building and policymaking. The political and economic variables explored in this analysis vary in their importance in accounting for environmental and natural resource policy. For instance, while decisions to regulate pollution tend to be shaped by national-level political and economic factors, natural resource issues tend to succumb to the influence of regional political and economic forces. In addition, certain theories of internal company management dynamics explain the decision by GE executives to fight unrelentingly against cleaning up PCB-laden sediment in the Hudson River. The hierarchical and closed nature of the company's leadership and decision making made it more difficult for the firm to negotiate with federal and state officials and reach a settlement. Preserving present and future profit margins was the main goal of the company.

Theories of issue definition and framing are extremely valuable in accounting for the tactics and strategies business interests use to influence leader and citizen opinion and environmental policy. The ability of industry leaders to define the nature of issues by amplifying critical beliefs and values (Snow et al. 1986) allow them to postpone, and often defeat, important policy proposals. For a long time, this was the case in the conflict over the restoration of the Everglades. Business interests, as this study shows, are particularly successful when they are able to control the discourse and dominate the rhetoric of the debate (Riker 1996). This appears to happen most frequently when scientific uncertainty exists. This is the situation in the areas of hardrock mining and climate change (though scientific knowledge about the latter is rapidly increasing). Indeed, the more scientific uncertainty exists, the more easily business groups can define (and often misframe) the issues and control the discourse of the debate.

Cobb and Ross's (1997b) analysis of agenda denial was useful in explaining two policy debates in this study. Specifically, their theory helps account for the highly successful efforts of the mining industry to thwart attempts to reform the General Mining Act of 1872. Similarly, their theory explains how fossil-fuel producers and consumers have been effective at blocking legislative proposals to control GHG emissions.

More generally, different theories of agenda setting tend to be more or less applicable in different contexts. Thus, while Baumgartner and Jones's (1993) notion of a "policy monopoly" explains the early stages of Everglades and forest politics, Kingdon's (1995) discussion of streams of problems, proposed policies, and politics better accounts for the early history of the acid rain issue. At the same time, while Hirschman's (1991) perversity, futility, and jeopardy theses explain GE's fight against cleaning up the Hudson River, Sabatier's (1993) advocacy coalition framework expands understanding of why acid rain controls were eventually included in the Clean Air Act Amendments of 1990. The fact that different theories of agenda building are applicable in different issue domains further underscores the enormous complexity and multidimensional nature of agenda setting and policymaking involving environmental and natural resource conflicts.

### Future Directions for Research

The findings generated in this investigation point to a number of possible avenues for future research. This study focused almost exclusively on issues at the federal level, and future researchers might want to adopt the theoretical and analytic approach employed here to explore the influence of business over environmental policy at the state and local level. More specifically, it would be fruitful to examine how much business impacts agenda setting and policymaking in the executive, legislative, and judicial branches of state and local governments. One would expect to find that corporations have substantial influence in the American states since competition from environmental groups is absent in many areas of the country. At the same time, certain companies and industries are quite dominant in particular localities. Almost no research has been pursued in this area, and an exploration of business influence over government institutions below the national level could further understanding of interest group politics and public policymaking.

Given the limited results yielded by the aggregate analysis of agenda building in Congress involving environmental and natural resource policy issues, it makes sense to investigate the evolution of individual bills through the different stages of legislative enactment. Rather than beginning at the committee- or subcommittee-hearing stage, researchers should closely study how ideas for bills are formulated from the outset and the manner in which bills are written prior to submission. This represents a critical phase in the agenda-setting process, one that is generally ignored in the literature. Collecting data on which groups and individuals participate in and shape the initial writing of legislation may be difficult given the somewhat hidden nature of the procedure.

This study analyzed three cases of environmental regulatory conflicts and three cases of natural resource disputes. Future policy research should examine additional cases studies of environmental and natural resource protection. This will permit confirmation or rejection of the findings reported in this investigation and will likely increase knowledge of agenda building and policymaking more generally.

The finding that business and other interests have very little influence over rulemaking regarding environmental regulation and natural resource management suggests the need to examine how approaches to rulemaking differ across presidential administrations. There is ample evidence to suggest that the political and ideological orientation of the president and his agency appointees, along with other factors, dictate the content of rules initially proposed. More data must therefore be collected on the nature and contents of rules that have been proposed by various administrations. Clearly, which interest groups and individuals participate in the initial selection and formulation of rules prior to regulatory negotiations taking place is likely to affect rulemaking greatly. Other factors such as types of legislative mandates, input from the scientific community, and media involvement may also play a part in an administration's decision to promulgate particular new rules and change existing rules.

Additional research can be conducted on how successful business interests are in the adjudication of disputes over environmental and natural resource issues. Future analysts might wish to study the participation of corporations in the federal district trial courts as well as in the U.S. Supreme Court. Furthermore, almost no research has been done on out-of-court, negotiated settlements by the EPA and polluters. How the EPA approaches this process and what types of outcomes are produced should be addressed. Of course, obtaining data on these deliberations might be difficult.

Little research exists on the lobbying activities and level of influence of foreign corporations involving environmental and natural resource legislation.[5] Nearly all the work that has been done has focused almost exclusively on lobbying activities concerning domestic issues in Congress. This is true for research that specifically addresses lobbying efforts by business groups (for example, Baumgartner and Leech 1998; M. Smith 2000). In recent years, however, many companies have increasingly pressured Congress and the president's foreign-policy advisors to open up new markets abroad (for example, in Asia and Central and South America) and to endorse multinational and international free-trade initiatives. At the same time, American industry has placed considerable pressure on the federal government not to sign international agreements that will undercut their profits and compromise their interests both here and abroad (for example, the transfer of technology). Such lobbying activities have been largely ignored by American politics specialists in their research on the role of interest groups in policymaking. No doubt, only certain kinds of businesses, principally large companies and multinational corporations, attempt to persuade government to join or not to join international regimes. The frequency and success with which domestic-based citizen groups (for example, consumer, social service, and environmental groups) affect American policy at the international level is also unknown.

We do know that American companies have been heavily involved in shaping U.S. policy on the depletion of the ozone layer and climate change, but with opposite results. Despite pressure from a certain sector of the chemical industry, the government played a leadership role in forging a series of successful international agreements to reduce chlorofluorocarbons (CFC) emissions and to protect the ozone layer. In contrast, the government, especially during the George W. Bush administration, has been roundly criticized by environmental groups and nearly all advanced industrialized and developing nations for doing too little to reduce "greenhouse gas" emissions, principally carbon dioxide ($CO_2$) emissions, which is necessary to halt the continued warming of the earth's atmosphere. The United States is the largest emitter of $CO_2$ in the world. Nevertheless, American energy companies, led by the fossil-fuel industry, have been quite successful in blocking government action on this issue. As a consequence, the federal government has not signed the Kyoto climate change treaty, nor has it formulated and implemented a comprehensive plan of its own. Of course, the economic impact of reducing "greenhouse gases" will be broader and deeper on industry, consumers, and the nation than the economic impact of reducing CFC emissions has been. This book discussed the role of energy companies in shaping U.S. policy on climate change. More generally, however, empirical research needs to be conducted on the ability of domestic-based companies and citizen groups to influence U.S. involvement in international regimes, including those that address environmental and natural resource concerns.

Specifically, future studies should at least address the following questions: Do the tactics and strategies of foreign companies differ from those of their American counterparts and, if so, in what way? How often do they get their way in the legislative process? Do they lobby various units of government for favorable treatment or just Congress? Do foreign companies tend to form coalitions amongst themselves, or do they form coalitions with U.S. companies within the same industrial sector (for example, automobile manufacturing)? Answers to these questions will add to our understanding of legislative outcomes involving environmental and natural resource policy.

In recent years "think tanks" have played an increasingly important role in policymaking. Mark Smith (2000) analyzes the role of think tanks in his study of business influence over agenda building in Congress. Polluting industries, in particular, have established and funded such organizations in an effort to influence media coverage and public opinion on salient issues. Such organizations often present themselves as neutral, third parties conducting balanced research and offering objective views. Exactly how effective they are in shaping the government's agenda concerning environmental protection and natural resource use is unknown and should be studied.

In Chapter 3 there was a discussion of the kind of training business students receive in the nation's top MBA degree programs. The author had analyzed whether and, if so, to what extent business graduate students take courses on topics related to environmental policy and natural resource management. Of the thirty highest-ranked business programs in the United States, very few degree programs included any exposure to issues concerning environmental protection. Future investigators might want to examine why this is the case and exactly what the consequences have been. This finding should encourage research on the environmental beliefs and attitudes of business leaders, perhaps especially those working in environmental audit and compliance offices inside companies.

More work also needs to be done on theory development, particularly in the areas of issues definition, framing, and agenda building. Political scientists can contribute a great deal to the literature in sociology and communications on issue definition and framing processes. Moreover, the existing literature on agenda denial is quite thin, which is surprising given the frequency with which it occurs and its importance in policymaking. A clearer picture must be developed on interest group tactics and strategies and on the political dynamics underlying agenda blocking if researchers are to ever develop a full understanding of agenda formation and policymaking.

Also, researchers should strive for greater clarity in their analyses of business interests. Business is not a single entity; rather, it is comprised of many different people, individual companies, industries, and associations having different missions, priorities, and goals. At the same time, as the findings of this study suggest, there needs to be further investigation into the particular conditions under which business groups become politically active and succeed or fail in influencing public policy. This will no doubt require new theories of interest group access and influence related to business. Given the important role business plays in American politics, it is surprising that so few researchers have closely examined its activities and level of influence.

Finally, this study exclusively focused on the influence of business interests over environmental and natural resource policy, a fairly broad yet unique issue domain. Future researchers are encouraged to adopt the theoretical framework and research design employed in this investigation to determine whether similar findings hold in other policy areas such as transportation, health care, and national defense. This will require a substantial data-gathering effort. The Policy Agendas Project data sets developed by Baumgartner, Jones, and Wilkerson (2002) represent a good first step toward expanding the study of agenda building and policymaking. Additional data on agenda setting and agenda blocking in different policy areas will provide analysts with a better idea of how much American (and possibly foreign) corporations influence government policy in particular, and whether such influence undermines central principles of democratic theory in general.

*Reference Matter*

# Notes

## Chapter 1

1. In an effort to stem the tide of business scandals, Republican President George W. Bush signed a sweeping corporate-fraud bill (the Sarbanes-Oxley Act) on July 30, 2002 (Bumiller 2002). The bill represents the most far-reaching reform of American business practices since the Franklin Delano Roosevelt era. The new law creates a regulatory panel, the Public Company Accounting Oversight Board, with investigative and enforcement powers to monitor the accounting industry and punish corrupt auditors. William McDonough, a former head of the Federal Reserve Bank of New York, became the first chairman of the Oversight Board in 2003. The legislation also establishes standards for prosecuting fraud and provides corporate whistleblowers with broad new protections. Corporate executives who deliberately defraud investors will receive long prison sentences under the new law. HealthSouth founder and former chief executive Richard Scrushy faced an eighty-five-count indictment in November 2003, the first time the government brought charges under the Sarbanes-Oxley Act, for systematically inflating the earnings of the health care giant by $2.7 billion during a seven-year period and for placing pressure on company managers not to confess their fraudulent actions to authorities. The Scrushy case stands out because of the huge amount of money involved and the government's portrayal of his brazen self-enrichment at shareholders' expense. He was tried and cleared of all charges, however, at the end of June 2005.

2. Of course, what exactly is "appropriate and necessary" is open to debate. In this study, "appropriate and necessary" refers to cases where the health and quality of life of individuals are at stake.

3. Parts of this section are drawn from Hahn and Kamieniecki (1987) with assistance from Janie Steckenrider.

4. Mancur Olson (1965) examines this collective action dilemma in his work. His research is discussed in the next chapter.

### Chapter 2

1. Mancur Olson's (1965) study of collective action has spawned numerous analyses of various aspects of his theory (for example, Salisbury 1969; Moe 1980, 1981; Hardin 1982; Rothenberg 1988, 1992; Gamson 1990; Ostrom 1990; Walker 1991; Lichbach 1995, 1996; Hansen, Mitchell, and Drope 2004), nearly all of which are cited in Baumgartner and Leech's (1998) insightful and exhaustive analysis of the interest group literature.

2. Lowery and Gray (2004) employ the term "neopluralist" in their analysis of the literature on interest groups. My application of the concept in this study is different from their application of it.

3. Hansen and Mitchell (2000) find that the degree of government regulation of a firm or its industry is an important factor in determining business PAC formation and campaign contributions. In other words, the more companies or industries are regulated by government, the more likely they will belong to a PAC, contribute money to election campaigns, and resist future regulation. Also see Hansen, Mitchell, and Drope (2004). Grier, Munger, and Roberts (1994) show that companies that can act as an industry are much more effective at deflecting or diluting unfavorable regulation.

4. In addition to influencing rulemaking, Lehne lists several techniques used by business lobbyists to affect administrative decision making: influence agency decisions through political channels, participate in the appointment process for top agency officials, mobilize public support, shape the context of agency decisions through bureaucratic reorganization, serve on agency advisory committees, and maintain contacts with key individuals and staff at the agency (2001, 157–58). Previous research on the influence of business over public policy has paid almost no attention to these lobbying opportunities, including at the EPA. Such an investigation is beyond the scope of this study.

5. Kettl (2002) discusses the problems associated with the new partnerships between business and the EPA and the attempt by the EPA to reinvent itself. He believes citizens are being excluded from environmental policymaking and must be brought into the decision-making process. A complete list of partnerships between industry and EPA can be found at www.epa.gov/epahome/industry.

6. Miller defines "greenwashing" as "new industry posturing to pursue the same old profit motive, a transparent attempt to pose as a friend of the environment

without changing practices or procedures that would actually improve it" (2002, 124).

## Chapter 3

1. It is doubtful that such an approach can lead to the long-term development of sustainable societies without a significant transformation in values.

2. Readers should also see Prakash (2000) and Robbins (2001).

3. Prakash (2002) refers to the kinds of decisions firms make regarding the environment as "environmental policies." This study refers to them as "environmental strategies" since policy normally implies government action rather than private action.

4. For an explanation of the new institutionalism from the perspective of political science, see March and Olsen (1984), Hall and Taylor (1996), and Immergut (1998).

5. Robbins (2001) also examines a broad set of theoretical principles associated with "green economics and business." His discussion of these principles, however, is not relevant to the present study.

6. Also see Gamson (1992).

7. Parts of this section are drawn from Kamieniecki (2000).

8. In addition, see Rochefort and Cobb (1994); Cobb and Ross (1997a); Leech et al.(2002); and Jones and Baumgartner (2004).

9. Petracca (1992) also underscores the importance of language in agenda building and public policymaking. In addition, see Kamieniecki (2000).

10. In contrast to Litfin's (1994) findings and in line with Haas's (1992) theoretical perspective, Benedick (1998) argues that the accumulation of scientific evidence led to a consensus among scientists for the need to take international action to reduce CFC emissions in order to protect the ozone layer.

11. Although not applied in this study, Stone's (1989) notion of "causal ideas" and the role they play in the transformation of difficulties into political problems offers additional insights into agenda building. Scheberle (1994) uses Stone's (1989) theoretical framework in her analysis of agenda building in radon and asbestos policymaking.

12. A notable exception in the environmental policy field is Crenson (1971).

13. Later work by McCarthy and Zald (1977) and others underscores the critical role organization and resources play in determining the success of social movements and interest groups over time. In addition, see McAdam, Tarrow, and Tilley (1997).

### Chapter 4

1. In addition, the data set contains all environmental legislation listed in Mayhew's (1991) analysis of important enactments by Congress between 1970 and 1990.

2. This study's identification of unifying issues concerning environmental bills matches Mark Smith's (2000) designation of unifying issues concerning environmental legislation in nearly every case during the period under study.

3. Also see Su, Neustadtl, and Clawson (1995).

4. As in Smith (2000), voice votes are considered as passing with complete unanimity, but voice votes that simply ratify amendments added by the other house are excluded. In cases where there are multiple floor votes in the House or Senate on the same item, the score for the individual item is calculated by averaging across these votes.

5. Adopting Mark Smith's (2000) guideline, resolutions requiring a vote in only one congressional chamber, and no signature by the president, are not included in the "enactment scorecard," but they are counted with the other measures.

6. His dimension explains 85 percent of the variance.

7. See http://www.unc.edu/jstimson/time.html. Best (1999) argues that Stimson's measure of public mood primarily addresses economic, government-spending, and size-of-government issues. Changes in public attitudes on social and racial issues, however, exhibit different patterns. His concerns are not thought to be relevant to the present study.

8. Smith (2000) altered Stimson's measure of public mood so that higher values represent increasing conservatism.

9. One would assume that the widely publicized scandals involving corporate leaders at the turn of the century have reduced public confidence in business.

10. As Smith (2000) does, any seat changing parties during a congressional term is counted for the party holding it for the longest period of time.

11. Data on party control of Congress and presidential leadership opening are derived from Orenstein, Mann, and Malbin (2002).

12. Smith (2000) centers each economic indicator by subtracting the mean from each observation, thereby stipulating that the value zero is included in each measure. The same approach is taken here.

13. Smith (2000) suggests that public mood is a more important indicator of public opinion in his study of a broad range of legislative policies.

14. Admittedly, the small number of cases in both equations introduce statistical error that may affect the results. Also, the dependent variable is based on a somewhat small number of proposed bills, thereby introducing additional error. Readers should keep these points in mind when reviewing the results of the multivariate analysis.

15. The size of the Durbin-Watson statistics in the regression models indicate that autocorrelation is not a major problem. In addition, Smith (2000) reports that endogeneity is not a problem in his analysis, and it does not appear to be a problem in this research. See King, Keohane, and Verba (1994).

### Chapter 5

1. Some of the discussion in this section is derived from Cohen, Kamieniecki, and Cahn (2006).

2. Due to congressional impatience with the length of time some government agencies take to promulgate rules, Congress has inserted "hammer" provisions in certain types of legislation (Cohen and Kamieniecki 1991; Cohen, Kamieniecki, and Cahn 2006). These regulations are required to go into effect by a specified date unless the agency adopts its own regulations. These "regulations by statute" normally include regulatory requirements that no one, including Congress, truly prefers. They are used to place pressure on agency officials to accelerate the rule-making process. Hammer provisions, along with deadlines, have become a widely used popular accountability tool of Congress.

3. Kerwin (2003) also questions his results on methodological grounds.

4. Langbein and Freeman (2000) contend that negotiated rulemaking also has a "legitimacy benefit." According to them, participants tend to possess a deeper appreciation for the intricacies of government policymaking and a deep understanding of views by people with different interests.

5. Businesses also employ this strategy at the state level. In California the automobile industry has used delay tactics in order to avoid having to produce, market, and sell zero-emission vehicles (ZEVs), specifically electric-powered vehicles. The industry has accomplished this by intensely lobbying the public and the California Air Resources Board (CARB), arguing that the battery technology is not well developed and that the vehicles are too costly to produce and sell. Deadlines for the major automobile manufacturers to make available a certain percentage of ZEVs for sale have been postponed more than once. The threat of setting deadlines, however, has spawned the development of new technologies to lower automobile emissions, including advanced hybrid vehicles (O'Dell 2003).

6. For example, the EPA initially experienced serious delays in the rulemaking process involving RCRA.

7. See McGarity (1991b). Not everyone, however, agrees with this perspective. For example, see Bryner (1987).

8. These actions are not considered "regulatory actions."

9. For example, the U.S. Department of Agriculture's recommended national organic standard received more than 250,000 responses (Shulman 2003).

10. She randomly selects these rules from the *Federal Register*; however, she does not explain her methodology.

11. There is minimal business participation and considerable participation by government agencies, public interest organizations, and citizen advocacy groups.

12. This should have no bearing on the findings. As the reader will soon see, the rule concerning the emissions of hazardous air pollutants from mobile sources was not changed between the time it was proposed and the time it was adopted. However, President Bush reconsidered the arsenic standard and, following intense pressure from both the political and scientific community, agreed to follow the arsenic standard included in the final rule.

13. This was done because government officials tend to analyze public comments based on the contents of the input rather than the number of people who sign e-mail messages, letters, and other forms of communication.

14. Although the rule employs the term "conservation," nearly all participants use the term "protection" in expressing their views on the proposal.

15. Such scientific consensus existed when President Bush unsuccessfully tried to block the arsenic standard recommended by EPA.

16. The survey of the agency's scientific staff of fourteen hundred had a 30 percent response rate. It is likely that additional scientists also have experienced the same pressure to change findings but were afraid to indicate this in writing.

17. Business has also used the courts to blunt actions by environmental groups. Cobb and Ross note how "Developers have used Strategic Lawsuits Against Public Participation (SLAPPs) against environmentalists to keep them from placing political obstacles in the way of their desired projects" (1997b, 39). Pring and Canan (1996) report that the Sierra Club has been the nation's most frequent SLAPP target. SLAPPs are intended to prohibit environmentalists from testifying in public hearings, lobbying zoning boards, and advertising against development projects by charging that they have defamed or libeled the developer in opposing the projects (McSpadden 2000). Most SLAPP suits are thrown out of court (normally state trial courts) because judges believe they interfere with the right of citizens to petition their government for redress of grievance. Nevertheless, this tactic seeks delay, costs environmental defendants valuable time and money, and causes emotional distress. Moreover, the threat of such suits may dissuade environmentalists from becoming involved in future issues in their communities (McSpadden 2000).

18. Some research also has been done on the possible effect amicus curiae, or "friend of the court," briefs may have on decisions by the U.S. Supreme Court (for example, Caldeira and Wright 1988, 1990).

19. Both the Fourth Circuit Court of Appeals (comprising four states adjacent to Washington DC) and the Ninth Circuit Court of Appeals (representing several

western states) hear only a very small number of cases involving business interests and the EPA. They are therefore not included in the analysis.

20. Cases where both business interests and the EPA are successful are classified as split in Table 5.6.

21. Only two or three companies appeared twice (that is, were repeat players) with the EPA in the District of Columbia Circuit Court between 1995 and 2002.

### Chapter 6

1. Those interested in the history of the Hudson River as well as the contamination of the river by GE should view the film documentary, *America's First River, The Fight to Save the River: Bill Moyers on the Hudson* (Moyers 2004).

2. Superfund is examined in O'Brien, Clarke, and Kamieniecki (1984); Mazmanian and Morell (1992); Hird (1994); Rahm (1998); and Probst and Konisky (2001).

3. For an excellent analysis of early acid rain issues, see Regens and Rycroft (1988).

4. For a good discussion of the development of clean air policy over time, see Bryner (1995); R. Cohen (1995); and Rosenbaum (2005).

5. Kamieniecki, Shafie, and Silvers (1999) compare the national sulfur dioxide cap-and-trade program with the Regional Clean Air Incentives Market (RECLAIM) program in Southern California. Also, see Mazmanian (1999). Wang et al. (2004) consider whether a sulfur dioxide cap-and-trade program can work in China.

6. Most of the academic literature and popular press use the term "global warming" as a synonym for "climate change." This study primarily uses the term "climate change" because it indicates that a number of critical geophysical and ecosystem effects (for example, changes in weather patterns, more violent tropical storms, a rise in sea levels, shifts in ocean currents that could cause major regional climate changes, shifts in ecological zones, alterations in the areas suitable for agriculture, and the melting of glaciers and polar ice caps) may be taking place as a result of the warming of the earth's atmosphere. Increasing temperatures alone, which global warming implies, are only one potential consequence of global climate change (Kempton 1997).

7. Readers should also consult the International Bank for Reconstruction and Development / The World Bank (2003).

8. Many of these changes are reported in Mayell (2001); *Los Angeles Times* (2002b); and Revkin (2004). Also, see Chang (2002).

9. Bernstein (2001) questions, however, whether science is a principal informer of policy direction on international environmental concerns including

climate change. He argues that scientists have not played, and do not want to play, a major role in climate change policymaking.

10. In addition, Economides and Oligney (2000) contend that the oil industry has always been the heart and soul of the American economy. Climate change policy, however, could dramatically change this and significantly weaken the United States. They believe that policymakers should do everything they can to defeat proposals to reduce GHG emissions. Engler (1977) paints an entirely different picture of the petroleum industry.

11. For a more detailed discussion of international climate change meetings and agreements, consult Molitor (1999); Layzer (2002); Organization for Economic Co-Operation and Development (2004); Soroos (2004); Betsill (2005); and Hempel (2006).

12. Dolsak (2001) analyzes a number of variables that might explain why some countries are more committed to reducing GHG emissions than others. She finds that national commitment is substantially affected by government incentives and the ability of governments to reduce GHG emissions. Aggregate levels of economic benefits are not related to level of commitment.

13. Sebenius (1995) argues that there is strong economic motivation for opposing climate change regulations in the United States. Benefits, however, are uncertain, diffuse, and will mainly accrue to future generations.

14. Engler (1977) provides persuasive evidence concerning the power, wealth, and influence of the American oil industry.

15. Romm's (1999) work suggests that a growing number of large companies are looking beyond the political debate on global warming and are increasing profits and productivity by reducing their GHG emissions.

16. Some senators also expressed fear that the United States would lose a portion of its sovereignty if it entered into an international agreement on climate change.

17. In a dramatic shift in the way the Bush administration has portrayed the science of climate change, an August 2004 report to Congress focused on federal research indicating that emissions of carbon dioxide and other GHGs by humans are the only likely explanation for global warming during the last three decades. The study was conducted jointly by the Climate Change Science Program and the Subcommittee on Global Change Research (2004). Whether this new position will lead to new public policy is unknown.

18. Similarly, Dryzek (1992) calls for the development of political institutions at a decentralized level as a way to deal with climate change. The mayor of Seattle, Greg Nickels, is leading a national campaign to persuade the mayors of other cities to adopt the terms of the Kyoto Protocol (Tizon 2005).

19. In addition to exploring the nature and effectiveness of programs at the state and local level, Rabe (2004) examines the broader implications of the clash

between the federal government and the states over the authority to implement climate change policy.

20. Economides and Oligney (2000) forcefully make this point in their work.

21. Romm (1999) provides a number of detailed examples where companies have changed their views on climate change and now support the reduction of GHGs in the atmosphere. Thus far, in terms of its actions, industry has clearly been unified against required reductions of GHGs.

22. Hempel (2006) also reaches this conclusion in his research. Kempton (1997) believes that the information available to the public about climate change has been distorted by strong economic interests promoting the views of "skeptic scientists." He argues that schools, museums, the science news media, and the government must do a much better job of educating the public about climate change. In addition, see Kempton, Boster, and Hartley (1995); Holdren (2002); and Rennie (2002).

### Chapter 7

1. Warrick (2004) reveals how the Bush administration has changed rules concerning environmental practices in order to make mountaintop removal for coal and mining for minerals a lot easier and cheaper. One rule change, described by administration officials as a "clarification" of the Clean Water Act, voids a ban on mining within one hundred feet of a stream. Other rule changes that negatively impact environmental quality concern allowable levels of mercury emissions, a reclassification of objectionable "waste" to legally acceptable "fill" (the "fill rule"), and a reclassification of certain "high-level" radioactive waste as "incidental" waste.

2. This is more fully explained in C. Davis (2001).

3. This process is described in Dahlburg (2003).

4. According to Switzer (2004), the Corps has also interfered with the work of the FWS in the Everglades region.

5. Supported by environmentalists, the Miccosukee Indian tribe has been engaged in a long battle with the SFWMD to cease pumping polluted water from agricultural runoff on land the tribe leases from the state. Water discharged on their land has contained phosphorous levels averaging 20 ppb. The small five-hundred-member tribe filed suit in court under the Clean Water Act to halt the discharge. The suit went all the way to the U.S. Supreme Court, which, in 2004, sent the case back to a Florida court to resolve (Barringer 2004).

6. His remarks subsequently led to his removal from other cases involving Everglades restoration.

7. Kamieniecki (1995) analyzes partisan divisions in Congress and in many state legislatures, including Florida, over environmental legislation.

8. The habitat of the northern spotted owl also extends into British Columbia, Canada. The province has made an effort to restrict logging and protect the owl.

9. Gup (1990) predicted enormous economic hardship for Oregon. Based on a joint Forest Service–BLM study, he speculated that there might be increased rates of domestic disputes, divorce, acts of violence, vandalism, suicide, and alcoholism.

10. One working group addressed ecosystem management assessment, another group analyzed labor and community assistance, and a third group studied agency coordination.

11. This study was conducted by the working group on ecosystem management assessment.

12. According to a study by Forest Community Research, a nonprofit California think tank, most of the $1.2 billion promised to help beleaguered timber communities was not new funds, and the effort was not as effective as intended. See Milstein (2003b).

13. An analysis by ECONorthwest, an economic consulting firm, and economists at Oregon State University and the Oregon State Employment Department found that more than half the sixty thousand workers who held jobs in the wood-products industry at the beginning of the 1990s had left the industry by 1998. About half who left disappeared from work rolls altogether; perhaps they moved to another state, retired, or became unemployed. Approximately eighteen thousand of the workers who left the industry found a job in Oregon. See Milstein (2003a).

14. Bill Freudenburg, a sociologist at the University of Wisconsin, analyzes job losses due to placing the northern spotted owl on the "threatened" list and denying timber companies access to millions of acres of federal forest (Foster 1997). He examines employment data from the U.S. Bureau of Labor Statistics and data on log exports from the Forest Service. He also reviews dozens of studies on logging and environmental regulation. He finds that the listing of the spotted owl did not cause the predicted loss of thousands of jobs in Washington and Oregon. His investigation shows, instead, that heavy cutting between 1947 and 1964 and technological advances explain the greatest decline in employment in the timber industry.

15. In February 2004 U.S. District Judge Owen M. Panner rejected a lawsuit by six environmental groups claiming the government was not sufficiently protecting the spotted owl on federal lands in southwestern Oregon. In August 2005 Federal District Judge Marsha J. Pechman in Seattle ruled, however, that the Bush administration broke environmental laws in 2004 when it cleared the way for more commercial logging of old-growth forests in the Pacific Northwest and Northern California (Boxall 2005).

16. The problems related to state involvement in national forest policy are discussed in Koontz (2002).

17. A review of the data provided on Congress in Chapter 4 shows that about half the particularistic legislative proposals involve natural resource issues.

### Chapter 8

1. To a certain extent, partisanship is a proxy for ideology. However, there exist unique components of ideology that are directly relevant to environmental policy, which partisanship measures fail to tap.

2. The gains the Republicans made in the Senate and House of Representatives as a result of the 2004 election—along with holding on to the White House—increase the possibility of this happening.

3. Layzer (2002) argues that science plays a critical role in nearly all policy conflicts over environmental and natural resource issues.

4. With the reelection of President Bush in 2004, the EPA plans to promote a pro-industry agenda during the coming years. According to Mike Leavitt, former administrator of the EPA, "The election was a validation of the philosophy and the agenda. Environmental protections must be done in a way that maintains the economic competitiveness of the country" (Shogren and Weiss 2004). Environmental groups fear that the federal government will attempt to weaken, in particular, the ESA, the Clean Water Act, and NEPA.

5. Hansen and Mitchell (2000) and Hansen, Mitchell, and Drope (2004) examine the lobbying activities of foreign firms, but their research does not focus on environmental policy issues.

# References

Abramson, Paul R., John H. Aldrich, and David W. Rohde. 2003. *Change and continuity in the 2000 and 2002 elections*. Washington DC: CQ Press.

Ainsworth, Scott H. 2002. *Analyzing interest groups: Group influence on people and policies*. New York: W. W. Norton and Company.

Alperovitz, Gar. 2005. *America beyond capitalism: Reclaiming our wealth, our liberty, and our democracy*. Hoboken, NJ: John Wiley and Sons.

Anderson, Terry L., and Donald R. Leal. 2001. *Free market environmentalism*. Rev. ed. New York: Palgrave.

Andrews, Edmund L. 2001a. Bush angers Europe by eroding pact on warming. *New York Times*, April 1, A3.

——— 2001b. Frustrated Europeans set out to battle U.S. on climate. *New York Times*, July 16, A3.

Arctic Council. 2004. *Impacts of a warming Arctic: Arctic climate impact assessment*. International Arctic Research Center, University of Alaska, Fairbanks, www.acia.uaf.edu/.

Bachrach, Peter, and Morton S. Baratz. 1962. Two faces of power. *American Political Science Review* 56:947–52.

——— 1963. Decisions and non-decisions: An analytical framework. *American Political Science Review* 57:632–42.

Balling, Robert C. 1992. *The heated debate: Greenhouse predictions versus climate reality*. San Francisco: Pacific Research Institute for Public Policy.

——— 1994. Global warming—the Gore vision versus climate reality. In *Environmental Gore: A constructive response to earth in the balance*, edited by John A. Baden. San Francisco: Pacific Research Institute for Public Policy.

Balmer, Donald G. 1990. United States federal policy on old-growth forests in its institutional setting. *Northwest Environmental Journal* 6:331–60.

Barke, Richard P. 1984. Regulatory delay as political strategy. In *Federal administrative agencies: Essays on power and politics*, edited by Howard Ball. Englewood Cliffs, NJ: Prentice-Hall.

Barringer, Felicity. 2004. Water pump case tests federal law. *New York Times*, January 14, A11.

Barrow, Clyde W. 1993. *Critical theories of the state*. Madison: University of Wisconsin Press.

Bauer, Raymond A., Ithiel de Sola Pool, and Lewis Anthony Dexter. 1963. *American business and public policy: The politics of foreign trade*. New York: Atherton Press.

Baumgartner, Frank R., and Bryan D. Jones. 1993. *Agendas and instability in American politics*. Chicago: University of Chicago Press.

——— 2002. Positive and negative feedback in politics. In *Policy Dynamics*, edited by Frank R. Baumgartner and Bryan D. Jones. Chicago: University of Chicago Press.

Baumgartner, Frank R., Bryan D. Jones, and John D. Wilkerson. 2002. Studying policy dynamics. In *Policy Dynamics*, edited by Frank R. Baumgartner and Bryan D. Jones. Chicago: University of Chicago Press.

Baumgartner, Frank R., and Beth L. Leech. 1998. *Basic interests: The importance of groups in politics and in political science*. Princeton, NJ: Princeton University Press.

Beardsley, Dan, Terry Davies, and Robert Hersh. 1997. Improving environmental management: What works what doesn't. *Environment* (September):6–9, 28–35.

Benedick, Richard Elliot. 1998. *Ozone diplomacy: New directions in safeguarding the planet*. Enlarged ed. Cambridge, MA: Harvard University Press.

Bentley, Arthur F. 1949. *The process of government*. Evanston, IL: Principia Press.

Bernstein, Steven. 2001. *The compromise of liberal environmentalism*. New York: Columbia University Press.

Berry, Jeffrey M. 1999. *The new liberalism: The rising power of citizen groups*. Washington DC: Brookings Institution Press.

Best, Samuel J. 1999. The sampling problem in measuring public mood: An alternative solution. *Journal of Politics* 61:721–40.

Betsill, Michele M. 2005. Global climate change policy: Making progress or spinning wheels? In *The global environment: Institutions, law, and policy*, 2d ed., edited by Regina S. Axelrod, David Leonard Downie, and Norman J. Vig. Washington DC: CQ Press.

Blake, Nelson M. 1980. *Land into water—water into land*. Tallahassee: University Presses of Florida.

Bolch, Ben, and Harold Lyons. 1993. *Apocalypse not: Science, economics, and environmentalism*. Washington DC: Cato Institute.

Bosso, Christopher J. 2005. *Environment, inc.: From grassroots to beltway*. Lawrence: University Press of Kansas.

Bosso, Christopher J., and Michael Thomas Collins. 2002. Just another tool? How environmental groups use the Internet. In *Interest group politics*, 6th ed., edited by Allan J. Cigler and Burdett A. Loomis. Washington DC: CQ Press.

Bowers, James. 1993. Looking at OMB's regulatory review through a shared powers perspective. *Presidential Quarterly* 23:331–45.

Boxall, Bettina. 2004. Judge bans logging in Tahoe site. *Los Angeles Times*, August 24, B4.

———— 2005. Judge says Bush's easing of forest plan is illegal. *Los Angeles Times*, August 3, A12.

Boyte, Harry C. 1980. *The backyard revolution*. Philadelphia, PA: Temple University Press.

Brown, Lester R. 2001. *Eco-economy: Building an economy for the earth*. New York: W. W. Norton and Company.

Browne, John. 2004. Beyond Kyoto. *Foreign Affairs* 83:20–32.

Browne, William. 1988. *Private interest, public policy in American agriculture*. Lawrence: University of Kansas Press.

Bruff, Harold H. 1989. Presidential management of agency rulemaking. *George Washington Law Review* 57:533–95.

Bryner, Gary C. 1987. *Bureaucratic discretion: Law and policy in federal regulatory agencies*. Elmsford, NY: Pergamon Press.

———— 1992. The challenge of global warming. In *Global warming and the challenge of international cooperation: An interdisciplinary assessment*, edited by Gary C. Bryner. Provo, UT: Kennedy Center Publications, Brigham Young University.

———— 1995. *Blue skies, green politics: The Clean Air Act of 1990 and its implementation*. 2d ed. Washington DC: CQ Press.

Buff, Harold H. 1989. The Reagan era in retrospect: Presidential management of agency rulemaking. *George Washington Law Review* 57:533–95.

Bumiller, Elisabeth. 2002. Bush signs bill aimed at fraud in corporations. *New York Times*, July 31, A1.

Burnett, H. Sterling. 2004. Climate science or science fiction? *The Washington Times*, February 23, A18.

Burnham, Walter Dean. 1987. The turnout problem. In *Elections American style*, edited by James A. Reichley. Washington DC: Brookings Institution Press.

Bustillo, Miguel. 2004a. Greenhouse gases are targeted. *Los Angeles Times*, June 10, B1.

——— 2004b. Stakes high as state targets greenhouse gas from cars. *Los Angeles Times*, September 23, A1.

——— 2004c. Tough car emissions rules ok'd. *Los Angeles Times*, September 25, B1.

Cahn, Matthew A. 1995. *Environmental deceptions: The tension between liberalism and environmental policymaking in the United States*. Albany: State University of New York Press.

Caldeira, Gregory A., and John R. Wright. 1988. Organized interests and agenda setting in the U.S. Supreme Court. *American Political Science Review* 82:1109–28.

——— 1990. Amici curiae before the Supreme Court: Who participates, when, and how much? *Journal of Politics* 52:782–806.

Campbell, Angus, Philip E. Converse, Warren E. Miller, and Donald E. Stokes. 1960. *The American voter*. New York: John Wiley and Sons.

Carey, John. 2004. Global warming: Consensus growing among scientists, governments and businesses that they must act fast to combat climate change. *Business Week*, August 16, 60–68.

Carlson, Darren K. 2001. Scientists deliver serious warning about effects of global warming. *Gallup Poll Releases* (January 23).

Carmin, Jo Ann, Nicole Darnall, and Joao Mil-Homens. 2003. Stakeholder involvement in the design of U.S. voluntary environmental programs: Does sponsorship matter? *Policy Studies Journal* 31:527–43.

Carmines, Edward G., and James A. Stimson. 1989. *Issue evolution: Race and the transformation of American politics*. Princeton, NJ: Princeton University Press.

Cart, Julie. 2005. U.S. scientists say they are told to alter findings. *Los Angeles Times*, February 10, A13.

Cater, Douglass. 1964. *Power in Washington*. New York: Random House.

Chang, Kenneth. 2002. Arctic ice is melting at record level, scientists say. *Los Angeles Times*, December 8, 40A.

Christoff, Peter. 1996. Ecological modernization, ecological modernities. *Environmental Politics* 5:476–500.

Clarkson, M. B. E. 1995. A stakeholder framework for analyzing and evaluating corporate social performance. *Academy of Management Review* 20:92–117.

Clawson, Dan, Alan Neustadtl, and Mark Weller. 1998. *Dollars and votes: How business campaign contributions subvert democracy*. Philadelphia, PA: Temple University Press.

Clean Air Council. 1995. Public comment on EPA's proposal to establish a national LEV program, December 1.

Climate Change Science Program and the Subcommittee on Global Change Research. 2004. Our changing planet: The U.S. climate change science program for fiscal years 2004 and 2005. Washington DC. www. climatescience.gov. Accessed August 27, 2004.

Cline, William R. 1992. *Global warming: The economic stakes*. Washington DC: Institute for International Economics.

Clinton, Bill. 2004a. *My life*. New York: Alfred A. Knopf.

———— 2004b. Our forests may be on a road to ruin. *Los Angeles Times*, August 4, B15.

Cobb, Roger W., and Charles D. Elder. 1983. *Participation in American politics: The dynamics of agenda-building*. 2d ed. Baltimore, MD: Johns Hopkins University Press.

Cobb, Roger W., and Marc Howard Ross. 1997a. Agenda setting and the denial of agenda access: Key concepts. In *Cultural strategies of agenda denial: Avoidance, attack, and redefinition*, edited by Roger W. Cobb and Marc Howard Ross. Lawrence: University Press of Kansas.

———— 1997b. Denying agenda access: Strategic considerations. In *Cultural strategies of agenda denial: Avoidance, attack, and redefinition*, edited by Roger W. Cobb and Marc Howard Ross. Lawrence: University Press of Kansas.

———— 1997c. Conclusion: Agenda denial—The power of competing cultural definitions. In *Cultural strategies of agenda denial: Avoidance, attack, and redefinition*, edited by Roger W. Cobb and Marc Howard Ross. Lawrence: University Press of Kansas.

Coglianese, Cary. 1997. Assessing consensus: The promise and performance of negotiated rulemaking. *Duke Law Journal* 46:1255–1349.

———— 1998. Legal change at the margins: Revisiting the political disadvantage theory. Presented at the annual meeting of the Law and Society Association.

———— 1999. The limits of consensus. *Environment* (March/April):28–33.

Coglianese, Cary, and Laurie K. Allen. 2004. Does consensus make common sense? An analysis of EPA's common sense initiative. *Environment* (January/February):10–25.

Cohen, Richard E. 1995. *Washington at work: Back rooms and clean air*. 2d ed. New York: Allyn and Bacon.

Cohen, Steven, and Sheldon Kamieniecki. 1991. *Environmental regulation through strategic planning*. Boulder, CO: Westview Press.

Cohen, Steven, Sheldon Kamieniecki, and Matthew A. Cahn. 2006. *Strategic planning in environmental regulation: A policy approach that works*. Cambridge, MA: MIT Press.

Commoncause. 2004. Campaign finance reform: Big donations come from companies that stand to benefit from Bush administration's pro-logging policies. July 27 news release. www.commoncause.org/news

Commons, John R. 1950. *The economics of collective action*. New York: Macmillan.

———— 1959. *Institutional economics*. Madison: University of Wisconsin Press.

Content Analysis Enterprise Team (CAET). 2000. *Summary of public comment: Roadless area conservation proposed rule and DEIS*. Washington DC: United States Forest Service, United States Department of Agriculture.

———— 2001. *Summary of public comment for the United States Fish and Wildlife proposal to amend the classification of gray wolves in the conterminous Unites States*. Washington DC: United States Forest Service, United States Department of Agriculture.

Cortner, Robert C. 1968. Strategies and tactics of litigants in constitutional cases. *Journal of Public Law* 17:287–307.

Crenson, Matthew A. 1971. *The unpolitics of air pollution*. Baltimore, MD: Johns Hopkins University Press.

Crine, Jean-Pierre. 1988. *Hazards, decontamination, and replacement of PCB: A comprehensive guide*. New York: Plenum Press.

Cushman, John H. 1996. Clinton backing vast effort to restore Florida swamps. *New York Times*, February 18, A1.

———— 1998. U.S. unveils plan to revamp South Florida's water supply and save the Everglades. *New York Times*, October 14, A12.

Dahlburg, John-Thor. 2003. The sway of cattails and politics. *Los Angeles Times*, August 23, A1.

Daly, Emma. 2003. Europeans lagging in greenhouse gas cuts. *New York Times*, May 7, A8.

Dao, James. 1998. G.E. wins delay of study on cleaning up Hudson. *New York Times*, February 25, B1.

Davis, Charles. 1998. Gold or green? Efforts to reform the Mining Law of 1872. *Natural Resources and Environmental Administration* (February):2–4.

———— 2001. Introduction: The context of public lands policy change. In *Western public lands and environmental politics*, 2d ed., edited by Charles Davis. Boulder, CO: Westview Press.

Davis, David Howard. 1998. *American environmental politics*. Chicago: Nelson-Hall Publishers.

Davis, Devra. 2002. *When smoke ran like water: Tales of environmental deception and the battle against pollution*. New York: Basic Books.

Davis, Sandra K. 2001. Fighting over public lands: Interest groups, states, and the federal government. In *Western public lands and environmental politics*, 2d ed., edited by Charles Davis. Boulder, CO: Westview Press.

De-Shalit, Avner. 2000. *The environment: Between theory and practice*. Oxford: Oxford University Press.

Dietrich, William. 1992. *The final forest*. New York: Simon and Schuster.

Dolsak, Nives. 2001. Mitigating global climate change: Why are some countries more committed than others? *Policy Studies Journal* 29:414–36.

Donaldson, T., and L. E. Preston. 1995. The stakeholder theory of the corporation: Concepts, evidence, and implications. *Academy of Management Review* 20:65–91.

Douglas, Marjory Stoneman. 1988 [1947]. *The Everglades: River of grass*. Rev. ed. Sarasota, FL: Pineapple Press.

Dowie, Mark. 1995. *Losing ground: American environmentalism at the close of the twentieth century*. Cambridge, MA: MIT Press.

Druckman, James N. 2004. Political preference formation: Competition, deliberation, and the (ir)relevance of framing effects. *American Political Science Review* 98:671–86.

Dryzek, John S. 1990. *Discursive democracy*. Cambridge: Cambridge University Press.

——— 1992. Political institutions and climate change. In *Global warming and the challenge of international cooperation: An interdisciplinary assessment*, edited by Gary C. Bryner. Provo, UT: Kennedy Center Publications, Brigham Young University.

——— 1997. *The politics of the earth: Environmental discourses*. Oxford: Oxford University Press.

Dryzek, John S., David Downs, Hans-Kristian Hernes, and David Schlosberg. 2003. *Green states and social movements: Environmentalism in the United States, United Kingdom, Germany, and Norway*. New York: Oxford University Press.

Duffy, Robert J. 2003. *The green agenda in American politics: New strategies for the twenty-first century*. Lawrence: University Press of Kansas.

Durant, Robert F. 1984. EPA, TVA, and pollution control: Implications for a theory of regulatory policy implementation. *Public Administration Review* 44:305–15.

Easterbrook, Gregg. 1995. *A moment on the earth: The coming age of environmental optimism*. New York: Viking.

Economides, Michael, and Ronald Oligney. 2000. *The color of oil: The history, the money, and the politics of the world's biggest business*. Katy, TX: Round Oak Publishing Company.

Edelman, M. 1964. *The symbolic use of politics*. Champaign and Urbana: University of Illinois Press.

Ehrlich, Paul R., and Anne H. Ehrlich. 1996. *Betrayal of science and reason: How anti-environmental rhetoric threatens our future*. Washington DC: Island Press.

Eilperin, Juliet. 2004a. Standoff in Congress blocks action on environmental bills. *Washington Post*, October 18, A02.

——— 2004b. U.S. wants no warming proposal. *Washington Post*, November 4, A13.

——— 2004c. Arctic council urges action on warming. *Washington Post*, November 25, A01.

Eilperin, Juliet, and Rick Weiss. 2004. Report sounds alarm on pace of Arctic climate change. *Washington Post*, October 31, A08.

Ellison, Katherine. 2002. On warming, Bush is out of step. *Los Angeles Times*, February 24, M3.

Engler, Robert. 1977. *The brotherhood of oil: Energy policy and the public interest*. Chicago: University of Chicago Press.

Entman, Robert M. 1993. Framing: Toward clarification of a fractured paradigm. *Journal of Communication* 43:51–58.

——— 1996. Reporting environmental policy debate: The real media biases. *Press/Politics* 1:77–92.

Epstein, Lee. 1985. *Conservatives in court*. Knoxville: University of Tennessee Press.

Epstein, Lee, and C. K. Rowland. 1991. Debunking the myth of interest group invincibility in the courts. *American Political Science Review* 85:205–17.

Epstein, Richard. 1985. *Takings—Private property and the power of eminent domain*. Cambridge, MA: Harvard University Press.

Erickson, Mitchell D. 1993. *Remediation of PCB spills*. Boca Raton, FL: Lewis Publishers.

Farnham, Timothy J., and Paul Mohai. 1995. National forest timber management over the past decade: A change in emphasis for the Forest Service? *Policy Studies Journal* 23:268–80.

Feder, Barnaby J. 2003. Report faults big companies on climate. *New York Times*, July 10, C5.

Fellowes, Matthew C., and Patrick J. Wolf. 2004. Funding mechanisms and policy instruments: How business campaign contributions influence congressional votes. *Political Research Quarterly* 57:315–24.

Fiorina, Morris P. 1982. Legislative choice of regulatory forms: Legal process or administrative process? *Public Choice* 39:33–66.

Fiorino, Daniel J. 1995. *Making environmental policy.* Berkeley: University of California Press.

Fleming, James Rodger. 1998. *Historical perspectives on climate change.* New York: Oxford University Press.

Footer, Joshua, and J. T. VonLunen. 1999. A legacy of conflict: Mining and wilderness. In *Contested landscape: The politics of wilderness in Utah and the West,* edited by Doug Goodman and Daniel McCool. Salt Lake City: University of Utah Press.

Foreman, Christopher. 1998. *The promise and peril of environmental justice.* Washington DC: Brookings Institution Press.

Foster, Heath. 1997. Job losses blamed on past logging—not owls. *Seattle Post-Intelligencer.* February 15, A3.

Freeman, A. Myrick. 2006. Economics, incentives, and environmental policy. In *Environmental policy: New directions for the twenty-first century,* 6th ed., edited by Norman J. Vig and Michael E. Kraft. Washington DC: CQ Press.

Furlong, Scott R. 1995. The 1992 regulatory moratorium: Did it make a difference? *Public Administration Review* 55:254–62.

———— 1997. Interest group influence on rulemaking. *Administration and Society* 29:325–47.

Gainor, Dan, Peter Roybal, and Derek Willis. 1998. *Congressional Quarterly's federal PACs directory, 1998–1999.* Washington DC: Congressional Quarterly Incorporated.

Gamson, William. 1990. *The strategy of social protest.* 2d ed. Belmont, CA: Wadsworth.

———— 1992. *Talking politics.* New York: Cambridge University Press.

Garcia-Johnson, Ronie. 2000. *Exporting environmentalism: U.S. multinational chemical corporations in Brazil and Mexico.* Cambridge, MA: MIT Press.

Gardiner, David, and Lisa Jacobson. 2002. Will voluntary programs be sufficient to reduce U.S. greenhouse gas emissions?: An analysis of the Bush administration's global climate change initiative. *Environment* (October):24–33.

Gelbspan, Ross. 1998. *The heat is on: The climate crisis, the cover-up, the prescription.* Updated ed. Cambridge, MA: Perseus Books.

General Accounting Office (GAO). 1989. *Endangered species: Spotted owl petition beset by problems.* (GAO/RCED-89-79). Washington DC: General Accounting Office.

General Electric Company. 2004. www.GE.com. Accessed January 6, 2004.

George, Alexander L., and Andrew Bennett. 2005. *Case studies and theory development in the social sciences.* Cambridge, MA: MIT Press.

Gerring, John. 2004. What is a case study and what is it good for? *American Political Science Review* 98:341–54.

Glanz, James. 2004. Scientists accuse White House of distorting facts. *New York Times*, February 19, A18.

Glazer, Amihai, and Lawrence S. Rothenberg. 2001. *Why government succeeds and why it fails.* Cambridge, MA: Harvard University Press.

Glionna, John M. 2001. Dredging up ill will on the Hudson. *Los Angeles Times*, October 1, A17.

Godwin, R. Kenneth, and Barry J. Seldon. 2002. What corporations really want from government: The public provision of private goods. In *Interest group politics*, 6th ed., edited by Allan J. Cigler and Burdett A. Loomis. Washington DC: CQ Press.

Goffman, Erving. 1974. *Frame analysis: An essay on the organization of experience.* Cambridge, MA: Harvard University Press.

Goklany, Indur M. 2001. *The precautionary principle: A critical appraisal of environmental risk assessment.* Washington DC: Cato Institute.

Golden, Marissa Martino. 1998. Interest groups in the rule-making process: Who participates? Whose voices get heard? *Journal of Public Administration Research and Theory* 2:245–70.

Goodnough, Abby. 2003. Letter from the Everglades: In the Everglades, environmental war endures. *New York Times* November 4, A14.

Gonzalez, George A. 1997. Conclusion: Obstacles to achieving sustainability. In *Flashpoints in environmental policymaking: Controversies in achieving sustainability*, edited by Sheldon Kamieniecki, George A. Gonzalez, and Robert O. Vos. Albany: State University of New York Press.

——— 2001. *Corporate power and the environment: The political economy of U.S. environmental policy.* Lanham, MD: Rowman and Littlefield.

Gore, Al. 1993. *Creating a government that works better and costs less: Report of the national performance review.* Washington DC: U.S. Government Printing Office.

Gormley, William. 1989. *Taming the bureaucracy: Muscles, prayers and other strategies.* Princeton, NJ: Princeton University Press.

Grier, Kevin B., Michael C. Munger, and Brian E. Roberts. 1994. The determinants of industry political activity, 1978–1986. *American Political Science Review* 88:911–26.

Grunwald, Michael. 2004. Florida steps in to speed up state-federal Everglades cleanup. *Washington Post*, October 14, A3.

Gup, Ted. 1990. Owl vs. man. *Time*, June 25, 57–60.

Haas, Peter M. 1992. Introduction: Epistemic communities and international policy coordination. *International Organization* 46:1–35.

Hadwiger, Don F. 1982. *Political agricultural research*. Lincoln: University of Nebraska Press.

Hahn, Harlan, and Sheldon Kamieniecki. 1987. *Referendum voting: Social status and policy preferences*. Westport, CT: Greenwood Press.

Haider-Markel, Donald P. 1999. Redistributing values in Congress: Interest group influence under sub-optimal conditions. *Political Research Quarterly* 52:113–44.

Hajer, Maarten A. 1995. *The politics of environmental discourse: Ecological modernization and the policy process*. Oxford: Oxford University Press.

Hall, Peter A., and Rosemary C. R. Taylor. 1996. Political science and the three new institutionalisms. *Political Studies* 44:936–57.

Hamburger, Tom, and Alan C. Miller. 2004. Groups appeal rule on plant emissions. *Los Angeles Times*, September 29, A14.

Hansen, Wendy L., and Neil J. Mitchell. 2000. Disaggregating and explaining corporate political activity. *American Political Science Review* 94:891–903.

Hansen, Wendy L., Neil J. Mitchell, and Jeffrey M. Drope. 2004. Collective action, pluralism, and the legitimacy tariff: Corporate activity or inactivity in politics. *Political Research Quarterly* 57:421–29.

Hardin, Russell. 1982. *Collective action*. Baltimore, MD: Johns Hopkins University Press.

Harter, Philip J. 1982. Negotiating regulations: A cure for malaise. *The Georgetown Law Journal* 71:1–118.

——— 1997. Fear of commitment: An affliction of adolescents. *Duke Law Journal* 46:1389–1429.

Haver Analytics. 2003. www.haver.com.

Hawken, Paul, Amory Lovins, and L. Hunter Lovins. 1999. *Natural capitalism: Creating the next industrial revolution*. Boston: Little, Brown.

Heinz, John P., Edward O. Laumann, Robert L. Nelson, and Robert H. Salisbury. 1993. *The hollow core: Private interests in national policymaking*. Cambridge, MA: Harvard University Press.

Hempel, Lamont C. 2006. Climate policy on the installment plan. In *Environmental policy: New directions for the twenty-first century*, 6th ed., edited by Norman J. Vig and Michael E. Kraft. Washington DC: CQ Press.

Hird, John A. 1994. *Superfund: The political economy of risk*. Baltimore, MD: Johns Hopkins University Press.

Hirschman, A. O. 1991. *The rhetoric of reaction*. Cambridge, MA: Belknap Press of Harvard University Press.

Hirshleifer, J. 1988. *Price, theory and its applications.* 4th ed. Englewood Cliffs, NJ: Prentice Hall.

Hoberg, George. 2001. The emerging triumph of ecosystem management: The transformation of federal forest policy. In *Western public lands and environmental politics*, 2d ed., edited by Charles Davis. Boulder, CO: Westview Press.

Hoffman, Andrew J. 1997. *From heresy to dogma.* San Francisco: New Lexington Press.

———— 2000. Integrating environmental and social issues into corporate practice. *Environment* (June):22–33.

Holdren, John P. 2001. The energy-climate challenge: Issues for the new U.S. administration. *Environment* (June):8–21.

———— 2002. Energy: Asking the wrong question. *Scientific American* (January):65–67.

Huber, Joseph. 1982. *Die verlorene unschuld der okologie.* Frankfurt: Fischer Verlag.

Immergut, Ellen M. 1998. The theoretical core of the new institutionalism. *Politics and Society* 26:5–34.

Inglehart, Ronald. 1977. *The silent revolution.* Princeton, NJ: Princeton University Press.

Intergovernmental Panel on Climate Change (IPCC). 2001. *Climate change 2001: The scientific basis.* Cambridge: Cambridge University Press.

International Bank for Reconstruction and Development/The World Bank. 2003. *Sustainable development in a dynamic world: Transforming institutions, growth, and quality of life.* New York: Oxford University Press.

Iyengar, Shanto. 1991. *Is anyone responsible?* Chicago: University of Chicago Press.

Janicke, Martin. 1985. *Preventive environmental policy as ecological modernization and structural policy.* Berlin: Wissenschaftszentrum.

*Japan Times.* 2004. Japan struggles to cut emissions as levels increase. June 17, 1.

Johnson, Geoffrey. 2004. "Greenwashing" leaves a stain of distortion. *Los Angeles Times*, August 22, M2.

Johnston, Bryan, and Paul Krupin. 1991. The 1989 Pacific Northwest timber compromise: An environmental dispute resolution case study of a successful battle that may have lost the war. *Willamette Law Review* 27:613–43.

Jones, Bryan D., and Frank R. Baumgartner. 2004. Representation and agenda setting. *Policy Studies Journal* 32:1–24.

Kahneman, Daniel, and Amos Tversky. 1984. Choice, values, and frames. *American Psychologist* 39:341–50.

Kamieniecki, Sheldon. 1991. Political mobilization, agenda building, and international environmental policy. *Journal of International Affairs* 44:339–58.

————— 1995. Political parties and environmental policy. In *Environmental politics and policy: Theory and evidence*, 2d ed., edited by James P. Lester. Durham, NC: Duke University Press.

————— 2000. Testing alternative theories of agenda setting: Forest policy change in British Columbia, Canada. *Policy Studies Journal* 28:176–89.

Kamieniecki, Sheldon, David Shafie, and Julie Silvers. 1999. Forming partnerships in environmental policy. *American Behavioral Scientist* 43:107–23.

Kamieniecki, Sheldon, and Janie Steckenrider. 1997. Two faces of equity in Superfund implementation. In *Flashpoints in environmental policymaking: Controversies in achieving sustainability*, edited by Sheldon Kamieniecki, George A. Gonzalez, and Robert O. Vos. Albany: State University of New York Press.

Kates, Robert W., and Thomas J. Wilbanks. 2003. Making the global local: Responding to climate change concerns from the ground. *Environment* (April):12–23.

Kelly, David. 2004. In west, old mines haunted by pollution. *Los Angeles Times*, September 13, A10.

Kempton, Willett. 1997. How the public views climate change. *Environment* (November):12–21.

Kempton, Willet, James S. Boster, and Jennifer A. Hartley. 1995. *Environmental values in American culture*. Cambridge, MA: MIT Press.

Kerwin, Cornelius M. 2003. *Rulemaking: How government agencies write law and make policy*. 3d ed. Washington DC: CQ Press.

Kerwin, Cornelius M., and Scott R. Furlong. 1992. Time and rulemaking: An empirical test of theory. *Journal of Public Administration Research and Theory* 2:113–38.

Kettl, Donald F., ed. 2002. *Environmental governance: A report on the next generation of environmental policy*. Washington DC: Brookings Institution Press.

Key, V. O., Jr. 1958. *Politics, parties, and pressure groups*. 4th ed. New York: Crowell.

King, Gary, Robert O. Keohane, and Sidney Verba. 1994. *Designing social inquiry: Scientific inference in qualitative research*. Princeton, NJ: Princeton University Press.

King, Robert. 1998. Business group rips Everglades restoration plan's costs. *Palm Beach Post*, November 10, B1.

Kingdon, John W. 1984. *Agendas, alternatives, and public policies*. Boston: Little, Brown.

———— 1995. *Agendas, alternatives, and public policies.* 2d ed. New York: Harper-Collins.

Klyza, Christopher McGrory. 1996. *Who controls public lands: Mining, forestry, and grazing policies, 1879–1990.* Chapel Hill: University of North Carolina Press.

———— 2001. Reform at a geological pace: Mining policy on federal lands. In *Western public lands and environmental politics,* 2d ed., edited by Charles Davis. Boulder, CO: Westview Press.

Koontz, Tomas M. 2002. *Federalism in the forest: National versus state natural resource policy.* Washington DC: Georgetown University Press.

Korten, David C. 1995. *When corporations rule the world.* West Hartford, CT: Kumarian Press.

Kovacs, William L. 2001. Public comment on EPA's proposed new standards for arsenic in drinking water, U.S. Chamber of Commerce, September 20.

Kraft, Michael E. 2004. *Environmental policy and politics.* 3d ed. New York: Pearson Longman.

Kraft, Michael E., and Norman J. Vig. 2006. Environmental policy from the 1970s to the twenty-first century. In *Environmental policy: New directions for the twenty-first century,* 6th ed., edited by Norman J. Vig and Michael E. Kraft. Washington DC: CQ Press.

Kraft, Michael E., and Diana Wuertz. 1996. Environmental advocacy in the corridors of government. In *The symbolic earth,* edited by James G. Cantrill and Christine L. Oravec. Lexington: University of Kentucky Press.

Kruger, Joseph A., and William A. Pizer. 2004. Greenhouse gas trading in Europe: The new grand policy experiment. *Environment* (October): 8–23.

Landy, Marc K., Marc J. Roberts, and Stephen R. Thomas. 1994. *The Environmental Protection Agency: Asking the wrong questions.* 2d ed. New York: Oxford University Press.

Langbein, Laura, and Jody Freeman. 2000. Regulatory negotiation and the legitimacy benefit. *New York University Environmental Law Journal* 9:60–151.

Langbein, Laura, and Cornelius M. Kerwin. 2000. Regulatory negotiation: Claims, counter-claims and empirical evidence. *Journal of Public Administration Research and Theory* 10:599–632.

Latham, Earl. 1952. *The group basis of politics.* Ithaca, NY: Cornell University Press.

Layzer, Judith A. 2002. *The environmental case: Translating values into policy.* Washington DC: CQ Press.

Lee, Jennifer 8. 2003a. EPA drafts new rules for emissions from power plants. *New York Times,* December 4, A24.

——— 2003b. EPA says it lacks power to regulate some gases. *New York Times*, August 28, A17.

——— 2003c. The warming is global but the legislating, in the U.S., is all local. *New York Times*, October 29, A20.

Leech, Beth L., Frank R. Baumgartner, Jeffrey M. Berry, Marie Hojnacki, and David C. Kimball. 2002. Organized interests and issue definition in policy debates. In *Interest group politics*, 6th ed., edited by Allan J. Cigler and Burdett A. Loomis. Washington DC: CQ Press.

Lehne, Richard. 2001. *Government and business: American political economy in comparative perspective*. New York: Chatham House.

Leiserowitz, Anthony A. 2004. Before and after *The Day After Tomorrow*: A U.S. study of climate change perception. *Environment* (November): 22–37.

Leshy, John. 1987. *The mining law: A study in perpetual motion*. Baltimore, MD: Johns Hopkins University Press.

Libby, Ronald T. 1998. *Eco-wars: Political campaigns and social movements*. New York: Columbia University Press.

Lichbach, Mark Irving. 1995. *The rebel's dilemma*. Ann Arbor: University of Michigan Press.

——— 1996. *The cooperator's dilemma*. Ann Arbor: University of Michigan Press.

Lindblom, Charles E. 1977. *Politics and markets: The world's political-economic systems*. New York: Basic Books.

Lipset, Seymour Martin. 1981. *Political man: The social bases of politics*. Exp. ed. Baltimore, MD: Johns Hopkins University Press.

Litfin, Karen T. 1994. *Ozone discourses: Science and politics in global environmental cooperation*. New York: Columbia University Press.

Lodge, Thomas E. 1998. *The Everglades handbook: Understanding the ecosystem*. Boca Raton, FL: CRC Press.

Lomborg, Bjorn. 2001. *The skeptical environmentalist: Measuring the real state of the world*. Cambridge: Cambridge University Press.

*Los Angeles Times*. 2001. EU ministers bash Bush, agree to pursue global warming pact. April 1, A8.

——— 2002a. Alaskan glaciers melting faster than once thought. July 19, A19.

——— 2002b. One in six CFOs tells of pressure to "cook" books. August 2, A27.

——— 2004. Carbon dioxide levels rising faster; buildup sets record. March 21, A26.

Lovins, Amory B., L. Hunter Lovins, and Paul Hawken. 1999. A road map for natural capitalism. *Harvard Business Review* (May–June): 145–58.

Lowery, David, and Virginia Gray. 2004. A neopluralist perspective on research on organized interests. *Political Research Quarterly* 57:163–75.

Lowi, Theodore J. 1969. *The end of liberalism*. New York: W. W. Norton.

——— 1979. *The end of liberalism*. 2d ed. New York: W. W. Norton.

——— 1987. Two roads to serfdom: Liberalism, conservatism and administrative power. *The American University Law Review* 36:295–322.

Lowry, William R. 2000. Natural resource policies in the twenty-first century. In *Environmental policy*, 4th ed., edited by Norman J. Vig and Michael E. Kraft. Washington DC: CQ Press.

——— 2006. A return to traditional priorities in natural resource policies. In *Environmental policy: New directions for the twenty-first century*, 6th ed., edited by Norman J. Vig and Michael E. Kraft. Washington DC: CQ Press.

Luke, Timothy W. 1989. *Screens of power: Ideology, domination and resistance in an information society*. Urbana: University of Illinois Press.

Magat, Wesley A., Alan J. Krupnick, and Winston Harrington. 1986. *Rules in the making: A statistical analysis of regulatory agency behavior*. Washington DC: Resources for the Future.

Mahoney, James. 2000. Strategies of causal inference in small-n analysis. *Sociological Methods and Research* 28:387–424.

Majone, Giandomenico. 1989. *Evidence, argument and persuasion in the policy process*. New Haven, CT: Yale University Press.

March, J., and H. Simon. 1958. *Organizations*. New York: John Wiley and Sons.

March, James G., and Johan P. Olsen. 1984. The new institutionalism: Organizational factors in political life. *American Political Science Review* 78:734–49.

Marcus, Alfred A., Donald A. Geffen, and Ken Sexton. 2002. *Reinventing environmental regulation: Lessons from project XL*. Washington DC: Resources for the Future.

Mayell, Hillary. 2001. Is warming causing Alaska meltdown? www.news.nationalgeographic.com/news/2001 Accessed, June 6, 2004.

Mayhew, David R. 1991. *Divided we govern: Party control, lawmaking, and investigations, 1946–1990*. New Haven, CT: Yale University Press.

Mazmanian, Daniel A. 1999. Los Angeles' transition from command-and-control to market-based clean air policy strategies and implementation. In *Toward sustainable communities*, edited by Daniel A. Mazmanian and Michael E. Kraft. Cambridge, MA: MIT Press.

Mazmanian, Daniel A., and David Morell. 1992. *Beyond superfailure: America's toxics policy for the 1990s*. Boulder, CO: Westview Press.

McAdam, Doug, Sidney Tarrow, and Charles Tilley. 1997. Toward an integrated perspective on social movements and revolution. In *Comparative politics:*

*Rationality, culture, and structure*, edited by Mark Irving Lichbach and Alan S. Zuckerman. Cambridge: Cambridge University Press.

McCally, David. 1999. *The Everglades: An environmental history.* Gainesville: University Press of Florida.

McCarthy, John D., and Mayer N. Zald. 1977. Resource mobilization and social movements: A partial theory. *American Journal of Sociology* 82:1212–41.

McClure, Robert, and Andrew Schneider. 2001a. A 129–year-old federal mining law has left a legacy of riches and ruin. *Seattle-Post Intelligencer*, June 11, A1.

——— 2001b. More than a century of mining has left the West deeply scarred. *Seattle-Post Intelligencer*, June 12, A1.

——— 2001c. A good deal for miners often isn't for Uncle Sam. *Seattle-Post Intelligencer*, June 13, A1.

McClure, Robert, Lise Olsen, and Andrew Schneider. 2001. Powerful friends in Congress. *Seattle-Post Intelligencer*, June 14, A1.

McConnell, Grant. 1966. *Private power and American democracy.* New York: Alfred A. Knopf.

McFarland, Andrew S. 1991. Interest groups and theories of power in America. *British Journal of Political Science* 21:257–84.

——— 1998. Social movements and theories of American politics. In *Social movements and American political institutions: People, passions, and power*, edited by Anne N. Costain and Andrew S. McFarland. Lanham, MD: Rowman and Littlefield.

McGarity, Thomas O. 1991a. *Reinventing rationality: The role of regulatory analysis in the federal bureaucracy.* New York: Cambridge University Press.

——— 1991b. The internal structure of EPA rulemaking. *Law and Contemporary Problems* 54:57–111.

——— 1992. Some thoughts on "deossifying" the rulemaking process. *Duke Law Journal* 41:1385–1462.

McKeown, Timothy J. 2004. Case studies and the limits of the quantitative worldview. In *Rethinking social inquiry: Diverse tools, shared standards*, edited by Henry E. Brady and David Collier. Lanham, MD: Rowman and Littlefield.

McKinley, James C. 1999a. Sugar industry's pivotal role in Everglades effort. *New York Times*, April 16, A19.

——— 1999b. U.S. unveils plan to aid 68 species in Everglades. *New York Times*, May 19, A18.

McSpadden, Lettie. 1995. The courts and environmental policy. In *Environmental politics and policy: Theories and evidence*, 2d ed., edited by James P. Lester. Durham, NC: Duke University Press.

———— 2000. Environmental policy in the courts. In *Environmental policy*, 4th ed., edited by Norman J. Vig and Michael E. Kraft. Washington DC: CQ Press.

Michaels, Patrick J., and Robert C. Balling. 2000. *The satanic gases: Clearing the air about global warming.* Washington DC: Cato Institute.

Milbrath, Lester W. 1963. *The Washington lobbyists.* Chicago: Rand McNally.

———— 1989. *Envisioning a sustainable society: Learning our way out.* Albany: State University of New York Press.

Milbrath, Lester W., and M. Lal Goel. 1977. *Political participation: How and why do people get involved in politics?* 2d ed. Chicago: Rand McNally.

Miller, Alan C., and Tom Hamburger. 2004. EPA relied on industry for plywood plant pollution rule. *Los Angeles Times*, May 2, A1.

———— 2005. EPA faults findings on mercury. *Los Angeles Times*, February 4, A15.

Miller, Norman. 2002. *Environmental politics: Interest groups, the media, and the making of policy.* Boca Raton, FL: Lewis Publishers.

Milstein, Michael. 2003a. Loggers displaced in 1990s left behind, study finds. *Oregonian*, January 7, online.

———— 2003b. Study says federal aid was little boon to loggers. *Oregonian*, January 23, online.

Moe, Terry M. 1980. A calculus of group membership. *American Journal of Political Science* 24:593–632.

———— 1981. Toward a broader view of interest groups. *Journal of Politics* 43:531–43.

Mohai, Paul, and Bunyan Bryant. 1992. Environmental racism: Reviewing the evidence. In *Race and the incidence of environmental hazards*, edited by Bunyan Bryant and Paul Mohai. Boulder, CO: Westview Press.

Mol, Arthur P. J. 2001. *Globalization and environmental reform: The ecological modernization of the global economy.* Cambridge, MA: MIT Press.

Molitor, Michael R. 1999. The United Nations climate change agreements. In *The global environment: Institutions, law, and policy*, edited by Norman J. Vig and Regina S. Axelrod. Washington DC: CQ Press.

Monastersky, Richard. 2005. Researchers present what they call conclusive evidence of global warming from greenhouse gases. *The Chronicle of Higher Education*, February 18, www.chronicle.com.

Moore, Curtis. 2002. Rethinking the think tanks: How industry-funded "experts" twist the environmental debate. *Sierra* 87:56–59, 73.

Moore, Patrick. 2002. Greens don't see forest for the trees. *Los Angeles Times*, March 26, B13.

Moore, Thomas Gale. 1995. Why global warming would be good for you. *Public Interest* (winter): 83–99.

—— 1998. *Climate of fear: Why we shouldn't worry about global warming.* Washington DC: Cato Institute.

Morriss, Andrew. 1988. Supporting structures for resolving environmental disputes among friendly neighbors. In *Acid rain and friendly neighbors,* rev. ed., edited by Jurgen Schmandt, Judith Clarkson, and Hilliard Roderick. Durham, NC: Duke University Press.

Moyers, Bill. 2004. *America's first river, the fight to save the river: Bill Moyers on the Hudson.* Princeton, NJ: Films for the Humanities and Sciences.

National Academy of Sciences (NAS). 1992. *Policy implications of greenhouse warming: Mitigation, adaptation, and the science base.* Washington DC: The National Academy Press.

—— 1999. *Hardrock mining on federal lands.* Washington DC: The National Academy Press.

—— 2004. Emissions pathways, climate change, and impacts on California. www.pnas.org/cgi/doi Accessed September 15, 2004.

Nature Conservancy. 2003. Financials. *Nature Conservancy Magazine* 53:74.

Neustadtl, Alan. 1990. Interest-group PACsmanship: An analysis of campaign contributions, issue visibility, and legislative impact. *Social Forces* 69:549–64.

New York State Department of Environmental Conservation. 2004. www.dec.state.ny.us

New York State Department of Health. 2004. 2003–2004 health advisories: Chemicals in sportfish and game. www.health.state.ny.us/nysdoh/fish

Noon, Barry R., and Kevin S. McKelvey. 1996. Management of the spotted owl: A case history in conservation biology. *Annual Review of Ecological Systems* 27:135–62.

Nounes, Anthony J. 2002. *Pressure and power: Organized interests in American politics.* Boston: Houghton Mifflin Company.

Nuclear Energy Institute. 2004. Nuclear energy can avoid global warming, ecologist says. *Nuclear Energy Insight* July, 1.

O'Brien, Robert, Michael Clarke, and Sheldon Kamieniecki. 1984. Open and closed systems of decision making: The case of toxic waste management. *Public Administration Review* 44:334–40.

O'Dell, John. 2003. Rewrite of emissions rule may roll out more hybrids. *Los Angeles Times,* April 7, C2.

Office of Solid Waste and Emergency Response. 1990. *The nation's hazardous waste management program at a crossroads.* Washington DC: U.S. Environmental Protection Agency.

O'Leary, Rosemary. 1989. The impact of federal court decisions on the policies and administration of the U.S. environmental protection agency. *Administrative Law Review* 41:549–74.

——— 1993. *Environmental change: Federal courts and the EPA*. Philadelphia, PA: Temple University Press.

——— 2006. Environmental policy in the courts. In *Environmental policy: New directions for the twenty-first century*, 6th ed., edited by Norman J. Vig and Michael E. Kraft. Washington DC: CQ Press.

Oliver, C. 1991. Strategic responses to institutional processes. *Academy of Management Review* 16:145–79.

Olson, Mancur. 1965. *The logic of collective action: Public goods and the theory of groups*. Cambridge, MA: Harvard University Press.

Olson, Susan. 1990. Interest group litigation in federal district court: Beyond political disadvantage theory. *Journal of Politics* 52:854–82.

*Oregonian.* 2001. Survey finds backing for old-growth forests. June 28, online.

——— 2002. Bush will overhaul Northwest Forest Plan. April 8, online.

Orenstein, Norman J., Thomas E. Mann, and Michael Malbin. 2002. *Vital statistics on Congress*. Washington DC: American Enterprise Institute.

Organization for Economic Co-Operation and Development (OECD). 2003. *Voluntary approaches for environmental policy: Effectiveness, efficiency and usage in policy mixes*. Paris: OECD Publications.

——— 2004. *Oil crisis and climate challenges: 30 years of energy use in International Energy Agency (IEA) countries*. Paris: OECD Publications.

Ostrom, Elinor. 1990. *Governing the commons: The evolution of institutions for collective action*. New York: Cambridge University Press.

Pateman, Carole. 1970. *Participation and democratic theory*. New York: Cambridge University Press.

Perez-Pena, Richard. 1999. State sues G.E. over pollution in the Hudson. *New York Times*, November 16, B1.

Petracca, Mark P. 1992. Issue definitions, agenda building, and policymaking. *Policy Currents* 2(3):1, 4.

Pew Center on Global Climate Change. 2004. Business Environmental Leadership Council. www.pewclimate.org. Accessed January 5, 2004.

Pittock, A. Barrie. 2002. What next for IPCC? *Environment* (December):20–36.

Pizer, William A. 2004. A tale of two policies: Clear skies and climate change. In *Painting the White House green: Rationalizing environmental policy inside the executive office of the president*, edited by Randall Lutter and Jason F. Shogren. Washington DC: Resources for the Future.

Portney, Kent, and Jeffrey Berry. 1995. Centralizing regulatory control and interest group access: The Quayle Council on competitiveness. In *Interest Group Politics*, 4th ed. Washington DC: CQ Press.

Prakash, Aseem. 2000. *Greening the firm: The politics of corporate environmentalism*. Cambridge: Cambridge University Press.

Press, Daniel, and Daniel A. Mazmanian. 2003. Understanding the transition to a sustainable economy. In *Environmental policy: New directions for the twenty-first century*, 5th ed., edited by Norman J. Vig and Michael E. Kraft. Washington DC: CQ Press.

Pring, George. W., and Penelope Canan. 1996. *SLAPPs: Getting sued for speaking out*. Philadelphia, PA: Temple University Press.

Probst, Katherine N., and David M. Konisky (with Robert Hersh, Michael B. Batz, and Katherine D. Walker). 2001. *Superfund's future: What will it cost?* Washington DC: Resources for the Future Press.

Program on International Policy Attitudes (PIPA). 2004. Eight in ten support McCain-Lieberman climate change legislation. School of Public Affairs, University of Maryland. June 25.

Pruitt, James C. 1995. Public comment on EPA's proposed rule to establish a nation LEV program, Federal Government Affairs, Texaco Incorporated, December 1.

Pryne, Eric, and Mark Matassa. 1993. Clinton not in favor of changing environment laws or halting suits. *Seattle Times*, April 3, A1.

Pulakovic, Gary, and Miguel Bustillo. 2002. Davis signs bill to cut greenhouse gases. *Los Angeles Times*, July 23, A1.

Putnam, Robert D. 2000. *Bowling alone: The collapse and revival of American community*. New York: Simon and Schuster.

Rabe, Barry G. 2004. *Statehouse and greenhouse: The emerging politics of American climate change policy*. Washington DC: Brookings Institution Press.

Ragin, Charles C. 2004. Turning the tables: How case-oriented research challenges variable-oriented research. In *Rethinking social inquiry: Diverse tools, shared standards*, edited by Henry E. Brady and David Collier. Lanham, MD: Rowman and Littlefield.

Rahm, Dianne. 1998. Controversial cleanup: Superfund and the implementation of U.S. hazardous waste policy. *Policy Studies Journal* 26:719–34.

Reeves, Hope. 2002. New York: Harm from acid rain persists. *New York Times*, May 2, 5B.

Regens, James L., and Robert W. Rycroft. 1988. *The acid rain controversy*. Pittsburgh, PA: University of Pittsburgh Press.

Rennie, John. 2002. Misleading math about the earth. *Scientific American* (January):61.

Renshaw, Gabrielle. 2004. Communication in a letter to the author. Content Analysis Enterprise Team.

Revkin, Andrew C. 1997a. New studies show PCB's persist in Hudson, and are entering air. *New York Times*, February 22, A1.

——— 1997b. Babbitt assails G.E. over delay in ridding Hudson of chemicals. *New York Times*, September 26, A1.

——— 1998. U.S. environmental chief attacks G.E. pollution ads. *New York Times*, July 10, B4.

——— 2000. Invisible stain—a special report. In war over PCB's in Hudson, the E.P.A. nears its Rubicon. *New York Times*, June 5, A1.

——— 2003a. New view of data supports human link to global warming. *New York Times*, November 18, F2.

——— 2003b. U.S. is pressuring industries to cut greenhouse gases. *New York Times*, January 20, A1.

——— 2004. An icy riddle as big as Greenland. *New York Times*, June 8, F1.

Revkin, Andrew C., and Jennifer 8. Lee. 2003. White House attacked for letting states lean on climate. *New York Times*, December 11, A32.

Revkin, Andrew C., and Katharine Q. Seelye. 2003. Report by the EPA leaves out data on climate change. *New York Times*, June 19, A1.

Riker, William H. 1996. *The strategy of rhetoric: Campaigning for the American constitution*. New Haven, CT: Yale University Press.

Ringquist, Evan. 1997. Equity and the distribution of environmental risk. *Social Science Quarterly* 78:811–29.

——— 2003. Environmental justice: Normative concerns, empirical evidence, and government action. In *Environmental policy: New directions for the twenty-first century*, 5th ed., edited by Norman J. Vig and Michael E. Kraft. Washington DC: CQ Press.

Robbins, Peter Thayer. 2001. *Greening the corporation: Management strategy and the environmental challenge*. London: Earthscan Publications Ltd.

Rochefort, David A., and Roger W. Cobb, ed. 1994. *The politics of problem definition: Shaping the policy agenda*. Lawrence: University Press of Kansas.

Romm, Joseph J. 1999. *Cool companies: How the best businesses boost profits and productivity by cutting greenhouse gas emissions*. Washington DC: Island Press.

Rosenbaum, Walter A. 2005. *Environmental politics and policy*. 6th ed. Washington DC: CQ Press.

Rothenberg, Lawrence S. 1988. Organizational maintenance and the retention decision in groups. *American Political Science Review* 82:1129–52.

——— 1992. *Linking citizens to government: Interest group politics at Common Cause*. New York: Cambridge University Press.

——— 2002. *Environmental choices: Policy responses to green demands*. Washington DC: CQ Press.

Rowlands, Ian. 1995. *The politics of global atmospheric change*. New York: Manchester University Press.

Rozell, Mark J., and Clyde Wilcox. 1999. *Interest groups in American campaigns: The new face of electioneering*. Washington DC: CQ Press.

Sabatier, Paul A. 1993. Policy change over a decade or more. In *Policy change and learning: An advocacy coalition approach*, edited by Paul A. Sabatier and Hank C. Jenkins-Smith. Boulder, CO: Westview Press.

Sahagun, Louis. 2005. Gov. turns up heat in global warming fight. *Los Angeles Times*, July 5, A10.

Salisbury, Robert H. 1969. An exchange theory of interest groups. *Midwest Journal of Political Science* 13:1–32.

——— 1994. Interest structures and policy domains: A focus for research. In *Representing interests and interest group representation*, edited by William Crotty, Mildred A. Schwartz, and John C. Green. Washington DC: University Press of America.

Schattschneider, E. E. 1960. *The semi-sovereign people: A realist's view of democracy in America*. New York: Holt, Rinehart, and Winston.

Scheberle, Denise. 1994. Radon and asbestos: A study of agenda setting and causal stories. *Policy Studies Journal* 22:74–86.

Schlesinger, James. 2004. Cold facts on global warming. *Los Angeles Times*, January 22, B17.

Schlosberg, David. 1999. *Environmental justice and the new pluralism: The challenge of difference for environmentalism*. Oxford: Oxford University Press.

Schlozman, Kay Lehman, and John T. Tierney. 1986. *Organized interests and American democracy*. New York: Harper and Row.

Schneider, Anne, and Helen Ingram. 1993. Social construction of target populations: Implications for politics and policy. *American Political Science Review* 87:334–47.

Schneider, Stephen. 2002. Global warming: Neglecting the complexities. *Scientific American* (January):62–65.

Scott, Andrew M., and Margaret A. Hunt. 1965. *Congress and lobbies: Image and reality*. Chapel Hill: University of North Carolina Press.

Scott, W. R. 1987. The adolescence of institutional theory. *Administrative Science Quarterly* 32:493–511.

Sebenius, James K. 1995. *Overcoming obstacles to a successful climate convention: Shaping national responses to climate change*, edited by Henry Lee. Washington DC: Island Press.

Seelye, Katharine Q. 2001a. G.E. is accused of trying to undercut order to dredge Hudson River. *New York Times*, October 1, F1.

——— 2001b. Environmentalists oppose shift on Hudson dredging. *New York Times*, October 3, D4.

——— 2002a. Study sees 6,000 deaths from power plants. *New York Times*, April 18, A21.

——— 2002b. 2 western cities join suit to fight global warming. *New York Times*, December 24, A20.

Sekhon, Jasjeet S. 2004. Quality meets quantity: Case studies, conditional probability, and counterfactuals. *Perspectives on Politics* 2:281–93.

Sher, Victor, and Carol Sue Hunting. 1991. Eroding the landscape, eroding the laws: Congressional exemptions from judicial review of environmental laws. *Harvard Environmental Law Review* 15:435–91.

Shogren, Elizabeth. 2003. Bill on greenhouse gases gets a warmer reception. *Los Angeles Times*, October 31, A32.

——— 2004. White House accused of science bias. *Los Angeles Times*, February 19, A10.

Shogren, Elizabeth, and Gary Polakovic. 2003. U.S. Senate preempts California's curbs on small-engine smog. *Los Angeles Times*, November 13, A1.

Shogren, Elizabeth, and Kenneth R. Weiss. 2004. Environment officials see a chance to shape regulations. *Los Angeles Times*, November 10, A12.

Shogren, Jason F., and Michael A. Toman. 2000. Climate change policy. In *Public policies for environmental protection*, 2d ed., edited by Paul R. Portney and Robert N. Stavins. Washington DC: Resources for the Future.

——— 2001. How much climate change is too much? An economics perspective. In *Climate change economics and policy*, edited by Michael A. Toman. Washington DC: Resources for the Future.

Shulman, Stuart W. 2003. An experiment in digital government at the United States National Organic Program. *Agriculture and Human Values* 20: 253–65.

Siegler, Ellen. 1997. Regulating negotiations and other rulemaking processes: Strengths and weaknesses from an industry viewpoint. *Duke Law Journal* 46:1429–43.

Sierra Club. 1995. Public comment on EPA's proposed rule governing non-municipal facilities that receive hazardous waste. August 11.

Simon, Julian. 1981. *The ultimate resource*. Princeton, NJ: Princeton University Press.

——— 1999. *Hoodwinking the nation*. New Brunswick, NJ: Transaction Publishers.

Simon, Richard, Edmund Sanders, and Elizabeth Shogren. 2002. Industry's a key player in energy data. *Los Angeles Times*, March 26, A10.

Simon, Richard, and Elizabeth Shogren. 2002. GOP donors lobbied hard on energy. *Los Angeles Times*, March 27, B14.

Smith, Mark A. 2000. *American business and political power: Public opinion, elections, and democracy.* Chicago: University of Chicago Press.

Smith, Richard A. 1995. Interest group influence in the U.S. Congress. *Legislative Studies Quarterly* 20:89–139.

Snow, David A., and Robert D. Benford. 1988. Ideology, frame resonance, and participant mobilization. In *From structure to action: Comparing social movement research across cultures*, edited by Bert Klandermans, Hanspeter Kriesi, and Sidney Tarrow. Greenwich, CT: JAI Press.

Snow, David A., E. Burke Rochford, Jr., Steven K. Worden, and Robert D. Benford. 1986. Frame alignment processes, micromobilization, and movement participation. *American Sociological Review* 51:464–81.

Soroos, Marvin S. 2004. Science and international climate change policy. In *Science and politics in the international environment*, edited by Neil E. Harrison and Gary C. Bryner. Lanham, MD: Rowman and Littlefield.

Stevens, William K. 1996. At hot center of the debate on global warming. *New York Times*, August 6, C1.

——— 1998. Science academy disputes attacks on global warming. *New York Times*, April 22, A20.

Stimson, James A. 1999. *Public opinion in America: Moods, cycles, and swings.* 2d ed. Boulder, CO: Westview Press.

Stone, Deborah A. 1989. Causal stories and the formation of policy agendas. *Political Science Quarterly* 104:281–300.

Su, Tie-ting, Alan Neustadtl, and Dan Clawson. 1995. Business and the conservative shift: Corporate PAC contributions, 1976–1986. *Social Science Quarterly* 76:20–40.

Susskind, Laurence E., Ravi K. Jain, and Andrew O. Martyniuk. 2001. *Better environmental policy studies: How to design and conduct more effective analyses.* Washington DC: Island Press.

Suzuki, David, with Amanda McConnell. 1997. *The sacred balance: Rediscovering our place in nature.* Vancouver, BC: Greystone Books.

Switzer, Jacqueline Vaughn. 2004. *Environmental politics: Domestic and global dimensions.* 4th ed. Belmont, CA: Wadsworth.

Tarrow, Sidney. 2004. Bridging the quantitative-qualitative divide. In *Rethinking social inquiry: Diverse tools, shared standards*, edited by Henry E. Brady and David Collier. Lanham, MD: Rowman and Littlefield.

Teixeira, Ruy A. 1992. *The disappearing American voter.* Washington DC: Brookings Institution Press.

Thompson, Frank J. 1982. Deregulation by the bureaucracy: OSHA and the Augean quest for error correction. *Public Administration Review* 42:202–12.

Tilton, John E. 2003. *On borrowed time? Assessing the threat of mineral depletion*. Washington DC: Resources for the Future.

Tizon, Tomas Alex. 2005. Mayor is on a mission to warm U.S. cities to the Kyoto Protocol. *Los Angeles Times*, February 22, A15.

Toman, Michael A. 2001. Climate change economics and policies: An overview. In *Climate Change Economics and Policy*, edited by Michael A. Toman. Washington DC: Resources for the Future.

———— 2004. Economic analysis and the formulation of U.S. climate policy. In *Painting the Whitehouse green: Rationalizing environmental policy inside the executive office of the president*, edited by Randall Lutter and Jason F. Shogren. Washington DC: Resources for the Future.

Trenberth, Kevin. 2001. Stronger evidence of human influences on climate: The 2001 IPCC assessment. *Environment* (May):13.

Truman, David B. 1958. *The governmental process*. New York: Alfred A. Knopf.

United Nations Conference on Trade and Development Programme on Transnational Corporations. 1993. *Environmental management in transnational corporations: Report on the benchmark corporate environmental survey*. New York: United Nations.

United States Council of Economic Advisors. 1990. *Economic report of the president*. Washington DC: U.S. Government Printing Office.

United States Environmental Protection Agency (U.S. EPA). 1984. *Acid rain and transported air pollutants: Implications for public policy*. Washington DC: Government Printing Office.

———— 1998. Partners for the environment: A catalogue of the agency's partnership programs. Spring. EPA 100–B–97–003.

———— 2002. Clearing the air: The facts about capping and trading emissions. Office of Air and Radiation. Clean Air Markets Division. www.epa.gov/airmarkets.

———— 2003a. E.P.A. proposes quality of life standards to minimize impacts of the Hudson River cleanup on local communities. Region 2 News Release, December 19.

———— 2003b. Acid rain program: 2002 progress report. Office of Air and Radiation. Clean Air Market Division. www.epa.gov/airmarkets.

———— 2004a. Hudson River pcbs, www.epa.gov/hudson/pcb.

———— 2004b. Global Warming-Climate. www.epa.gov/globalwarming/climate. Accessed January 6, 2004.

———— 2004c. Global Warming-Climate Uncertainties. www.epa.gov/globalwarming/climate/uncertainties. Accessed January 6, 2004.

Uslaner, Eric M. 1998. Lobbying the President and the bureaucracy. In *The interest group connection: Electioneering, lobbying, and policymaking in Washington*, edited by Paul S. Herrnson, Ronald G. Shaiko, and Clyde Wilcox. Chatham, NJ: Chatham House.

Van Natta, Don, and Neela Banerjee. 2002. Documents show energy official met only with industry leaders. *New York Times*, March 27, A1.

Vedantam, Shankar. 2005. EPA distorted mercury analysis, GAO says. *Washington Post*, March 8, A09.

Verba, Sidney, and Norman H. Nie. 1972. *Participation in America: Political democracy and social equality*. New York: Harper and Row.

Victor, David. 2001. *The collapse of the Kyoto protocol and the struggle to slow global warming*. Princeton, NJ: Princeton University Press.

——— 2004. *Climate change: Debating America's policy options*. New York: Council on Foreign Relations.

Vig, Norman J. 2006. Presidential leadership and the environment. In *Environmental policy: New directions for the twenty-first century*, 6th ed., edited by Norman J. Vig and Michael E. Kraft. Washington DC: CQ Press.

Vig, Norman J., and Michael E. Kraft, eds. 2003. *Environmental policy: New directions for the twenty-first century*. 5th ed. Washington DC: CQ Press.

Vogel, David. 1978. *Lobbying the corporation: Citizen challenges to business authority*. New York: Basic Books.

——— 1989. *Fluctuating fortunes: The political power of business in America*. New York: Basic Books.

——— 1996. *Kindred strangers: The uneasy relationship between politics and business in America*. Princeton, NJ: Princeton University Press.

Vos, Robert O. 1997. Introduction: Competing approaches to sustainability: Dimensions of controversy. In *Flashpoints in environmental policymaking: Controversies in achieving sustainability*, edited by Sheldon Kamieniecki, George A. Gonzalez, and Robert O. Vos. Albany: State University of New York Press.

Wald, Patricia M. 1992. The role of the judiciary in environmental protection. *Boston College Environmental Affairs Law Review* 19:519–46.

——— 1997. ADR and the courts: An update. *Duke Law Journal* 46: 1445–73.

Walker, Jack L., Jr. 1983. The origins and maintenance of interest groups in America. *American Political Science Review* 77:390–406.

——— 1991. *Mobilizing interest groups in America*. Ann Arbor: University of Michigan.

Wang, Jinnan, Jintian Yang, Chazhong Ge, Dong Cao, and Jeremy Schreifels. 2004. Controlling sulfur dioxide in China: Will emission trading work? *Environment* (June):28–39.

Warren, Barbara. 2000. Public comment on U.S. EPA's proposed rule to control air toxics emissions from mobile sources. Consumer Policy Institute of Consumers' Union, September 18.

Warrick, Jody. 2004. Appalachia is paying the price for White House rule change. *Washington Post*, August 17, A01.

Wattenberg, Martin P. 1998. *The decline of American political parties, 1952–1996*. Cambridge, MA: Harvard University Press.

Weart, Spencer. 2003. *The discovery of global warming: New histories of science, technology, and medicine*. Cambridge, MA: Harvard University Press.

Weber, Max. 1947. *Theory of social and economic organization*. Translation by Talcott Parsons and A. M. Henderson. New York: Oxford University Press.

Weidner, Maria, and Nancy Watzman. 2002. *Paybacks: Policy, patrons, and personnel—How the Bush administration is giving away our environment to corporate contributors*. Washington DC: Earthjustice and Public Campaign.

Weisskoff, Richard. 2004. *The economics of Everglades restoration*. Northhampton, MA: Edward Elgar Publishing.

Wenner, Lettie McSpadden. 1982. *The environmental decade in court*. Bloomington: Indiana University Press.

West, William F. 1982. The politics of administrative rulemaking. *Public Administration Review* 42:420–26.

——— 1985. *Administrative rulemaking: Politics and processes*. Westport, CT: Greenwood Press.

Wilcher, Marshall E. 1986. The acid rain debate in North America: "Where you stand depends on where you sit." *The Environmentalist* 6:289–98.

Wildavsky, Aaron. 1995. *But is it true? A citizen's guide to environmental health and safety issues*. Cambridge, MA: Harvard University Press.

Williams, Carol J. 2001. Anger erupts over U.S. move to ease controls on emissions. *Los Angeles Times*, March 31, A1.

Wilson, Graham K. 1990. *Business and politics: A comparative introduction*. 2d ed. Chatham, NJ: Chatham House.

Winter, Greg. 2002. Timber company reduces cutting of old-growth trees. *New York Times*, March 27, A14.

Wolfinger, Raymond E., and Steven J. Rosenstone. 1980. *Who votes?* New Haven, CT: Yale University Press.

Wolfson, Richard, and Stephen H. Schneider. 2002. Understanding climate science. In *Climate change policy: A survey*, edited by Stephen H. Schneider, Armin Rosencranz, and John O. Niles. Washington DC: Island Press.

World Commission on Environment and Development. 1987. *Our common future*. Oxford: Oxford University Press.

World Meteorological Organization, United Nations. 2001. WMO statement on the status of the global climate in 2001. WMO Press Release #670, December 18.

www.planevada.org/cash. 2004. Resources and mining. Accessed August 13, 2004.

www.usnews.com. 2003. *U.S. News and World Report*. America's best graduate schools, 2002. Accessed November 1, 2003.

Yaffee, Steven L. 1994. *The wisdom of the spotted owl*. Washington DC: Island Press.

York, Richard, and Eugene A. Rosa. 2003. Key challenges to ecological modernization theory. *Organization and Environment* 16:273–88.

Zaller, John R. 1992. *The nature and origins of mass opinion*. New York: Cambridge University Press.

Zeller, Richard A., and Edward G. Carmines. 1980. *Measurement in the social sciences: The link between theory and data*. New York: Cambridge University Press.

Zuckerman, Edward. 2002. *The almanac of federal PACs: 2002–2003*. Hedgesville, WV: Amward Publications Incorporated.

# Index